Key Debates in Sustainable Investment

Many leading investment institutions, including asset managers, pension funds and insurance companies, have made commitments to sustainable investment or to the delivery of sustainability goals alongside their investment objectives.

This mainstreaming of sustainable investment raises many important questions, such as:

- Do sustainable finance strategies lead to meaningful real-world change? Are fears about greenwashing justified?
- Does sustainable investment deliver better financial outcomes? And is it consistent with investors' fiduciary duties?
- Can the sustainability data and ratings used in finance be trusted? Does sustainability information drive improved sustainability performance?
- How should sustainable investment be governed? What are the roles and responsibilities of public and private actors?

This book unpacks the key terms, concepts and debates – both theoretical and applied – that underpin sustainable investment. Through evidence-based analysis, it cuts through the hype to critically explore sustainable finance's transformative potential as well as its limitations. In doing so, the book enables public policymakers, financial institutions, companies, civil society organisations and academics to engage in a more informed discussion about the contribution that sustainable investment can make to sustainability goals.

Rory Sullivan is CEO of Chronos Sustainability and Visiting Professor in Practice in the Department of Geography and Environment at the London School of Economics and Political Science (LSE). Rory has advised government agencies and regulators around the world, including in Australia, the UK, Peru, Colombia, South Africa, Malaysia and Thailand, on the development and implementation of sustainable finance policy. He has also advised many asset owners and asset managers on the development and implementation of their responsible investment and net zero strategies.

Richard Perkins is Associate Professor in the Department of Geography and Environment at the London School of Economics and Political Science (LSE) where he is Programme Director of the MSc in Environmental Policy and Regulation. He is also Associate of the Centre for Economic Transition Expertise (CETEx) at the LSE. Richard's research examines the growing role of financial and corporate actors in governing sustainability.

RESPONSIBLE INVESTMENT
SERIES EDITOR: RORY SULLIVAN

The ground-breaking *Responsible Investment* series provides a forum for outstanding empirical and theoretical work on all aspects of responsible investment, allowing the tensions and practical realities of responsible investment to be addressed in a readable, robust and conceptually and empirically rigorous format. The subject areas covered include:

- The financial, environmental, social and governance outcomes from responsible investment.
- Responsible investment in different asset classes.
- Responsible investment in different geographies.
- The implementation of responsible investment by different actors (e.g. pension funds, asset managers, sovereign wealth funds, private equity funds, insurance companies), and in different geographic regions.
- The role that has been played by collaborative initiatives such as the Principles for Responsible Investment, UNEP FI and the investor networks on climate change.
- Public policy and responsible investment.

Dilemmas in Responsible Investment
Céline Louche and Steve Lydenberg

Valuing Corporate Responsibility
How Do Investors Really Use Corporate Responsibility Information?
Rory Sullivan

Responsible Investment
Edited by Rory Sullivan and Craig Mackenzie

Climate Change and the Governance of Corporations
Lessons from the Retail Sector
Rory Sullivan and Andy Gouldson

Responsible Investment in Fixed Income Markets
Edited by Joshua Kendall and Rory Sullivan

The Responsible Investor
An Introductory Guide to Responsible Investment
Anna Hyrske, Magdalena Lönnroth, Antti Savilaakso and Riikka Sievänen

Key Debates in Sustainable Investment
Edited by Rory Sullivan and Richard Perkins

For more information about this series, please visit: www.routledge.com/The-Responsible-Investment-Series/book-series/SERI1

Key Debates in Sustainable Investment

Edited by
Rory Sullivan and
Richard Perkins

Routledge
Taylor & Francis Group
LONDON AND NEW YORK

Designed cover image: Getty Images

First published 2026
by Routledge
4 Park Square, Milton Park, Abingdon, Oxon OX14 4RN

and by Routledge
605 Third Avenue, New York, NY 10158

Routledge is an imprint of the Taylor & Francis Group, an informa business

British Library Cataloguing-in-Publication Data
A catalogue record for this book is available from the British Library

ISBN: 978-1-032-74096-6 (hbk)
ISBN: 978-1-032-73023-3 (pbk)
ISBN: 978-1-003-46763-2 (ebk)

DOI: 10.4324/9781003467632

Typeset in Adobe Garamond
by Newgen Publishing UK

To Melinda, Claire and Laura
R.S.

To Molly
R.P.

Contents

Figures

Tables

Contributors

Robert Black is Manager, Responsible Investment at Chronos Sustainability. His recent projects include advising asset owners and asset managers on their net zero and climate change strategies, developing a stewardship and responsible investment reporting framework for UK Asset Owners, benchmarking Peruvian, Colombian and South African pension fund on their approaches to stewardship and responsible investment, and assessing corporate sustainability reporting practices in Colombia, Thailand and South Africa. Prior to joining Chronos, he was ESG Analyst at FTSE Russell. In this role, he was responsible for analysis and quality assurance on the corporate governance and social issues-related data used in FTSE Russell's indices and other investment products. He holds an MSc with Distinction in Sustainable Development from the University of Exeter.

Sumira Bothé recently completed an MSc in Environmental Policy and Regulation at the LSE, after completing a BSc in Environmental Sciences at Wageningen University and Research. Her work has centred around climate governance in Europe. Her MSc dissertation analysed the European Union's approach to sustainable finance regulations, and her BSc dissertation focused on climate citizens' assemblies, and their contribution to democratic directionality. She now works at the European Commission.

Cora Buentjen is Research Analyst at Chronos Sustainability, where she focuses on projects relating to sustainable finance policy and regulation. Her recent projects include supporting investors with developing their climate strategies, evaluating sustainable finance and disclosure regulations in South Africa and South-East Asia and producing guidance for companies on sustainability-related reporting. She holds a BA in Geography and an MSc in Environmental Policy and Regulation from the LSE.

Claudio Cichi recently completed an MSc in Environmental Policy at the LSE, with a dissertation focusing on the impacts of the just transition on Indigenous and non-Indigenous communities in remote Canada. Claudio works as Junior

Analyst in the Investor Relations team of a vertically integrated asset management firm specialising in solar energy and battery storage assets in OECD markets. She previously worked in the ESG division of one of Canada's largest banks, developing ESG memos and systematic reviews of ESG methodologies.

James Corah is Head of Sustainability at CCLA and a member of the CCLA Executive Committee. He is responsible for CCLA's approach to sustainable investing. This includes CCLA's work to deliver real and lasting change through active stewardship, through integrating environmental, social and governance factors into its investment processes and through ensuring that CCLA's portfolios are aligned with the values and mission of its clients.

Rachel Crossley is Head of Stewardship for Europe for BNP Paribas Asset Management, one of Europe's largest asset managers. She has more than 30 years of wide-ranging experience at the intersection of sustainability, international development and responsible investment. In her current role she engages with European companies to drive better policy, practice and disclosure on many sustainability issues, and she votes at these companies' annual meetings. She also participates in initiatives designed to encourage policymakers to adopt laws, regulations and standards to transition towards sustainable and equitable economies.

Emma De Fino is Analyst at The European House Ambrosetti, Italy's first think tank and a leading consultancy based in Milan. In this role, she focuses on reporting, strategic planning, stakeholder engagement and scenario analysis. She has recently completed an MSc in Environmental Policy and Regulation at the LSE, concluding with a dissertation on the role of fiscal, budgetary and monetary policy in the UK transition to net zero, which aimed at mapping institutional capacity to decarbonise. Prior to her studies at LSE, she completed an undergraduate programme in Politics and International Relations at SOAS, finishing with a first-class dissertation on the compatibility between sustainable development and economic growth in China.

Johan Florén has worked at the Swedish pension fund AP7 since 2009 as Chief Communication Officer and also as Head of ESG. He is a member of the Taskforce on Nature-related Financial Disclosures (TNFD) and has previously been Chairman of the Swedish Forum for Sustainable Investments (SWESIF) and Chairman of the Amnesty Business Group in Sweden. Johan holds Bachelor of Philosophy and Bachelor of Business Administration from Uppsala and Stockholm Universities and is currently a doctoral student at the Department of Communication, Lund University.

Tristan Gilet is the Sustainability Manager at the Rail Delivery Group. He advises the UK rail industry on decarbonisation and on adaptation to climate change, positioning the rail industry as a key actor in the UK's 'net zero' strategy.

He holds an MSc in Environmental Policy and Regulation from LSE, specialising in climate policy, decarbonisation strategy and economic evaluation of climate efforts. He worked with the Grantham Research Institute on Climate Change and the Environment at LSE for his dissertation, where he evaluated the institutional performance of British public bodies in the energy transition. Prior to his MSc, he completed a BA in Politics and International Relations.

Dido Gompertz is Policy Advisor at the climate change think tank E3G, where she focuses on global clean energy diplomacy. Her work involves analysis and government engagement to improve the financial and policy environment for power sector transitions across different regional contexts, particularly from coal to renewables. She holds an MSc in Environmental Policy and Regulation from the LSE, where she contributed research on adaptation and extreme heat to a project at the Grantham Institute for her dissertation, as well as an MA in History from the University of Edinburgh.

Fatima Husain is Research Analyst at Chronos Sustainability where she supports institutional investors, corporates and regulators on climate and nature strategy. She has also supported projects advising regulators in South Africa and Malaysia on climate-related policy frameworks. Her work analysing dominant narratives underpinning carbon forestry projects has been published in *Society & Natural Resources*. She holds an MSc in Environment and Development from the LSE, an MAM in Sustainability Management, and a BA (Hons) in Economics.

Krishnapriya J has recently completed her MSc in Environment and Development at the LSE where her dissertation focused on the socio-politics of water infrastructure in Bangalore. She also holds a BA in Economics and Environmental Science. She has been recognised for her work with street animals, street dogs in particular, and their welfare in South India.

Valentin Jahn is Deputy Director for Research and Operations at the Transition Pathway Initiative Centre at the LSE. Since joining the Centre in 2018, he has helped develop key methodologies to assess the decarbonisation progress of corporates and banks, supported high-profile investor initiatives and contributed to the Centre's institutional growth. He now plays a central role in shaping the Centre's research agenda, overseeing strategic project delivery and managing cross-functional teams. His academic training in climate finance, philosophy and economics underpins his focus on complex methodological and policy questions.

Hilary Lai is Research Analyst in Hong Kong, working on a wide range of projects such as nature-related finance, biodiversity conservation and environmental crime. She recently completed her MSc in Environmental Policy and Regulation at the LSE, where her dissertation focused on how environmental imaginaries of outer-space shape Earth's communities and landscapes. Hilary also holds a first-class BA Geography degree from University College London, where her dissertation on migrant networks and social infrastructure was awarded the UCL Claire Dwyer Dissertation Prize 2023 for the best social or cultural geography dissertation.

Kester Low is Kester Low is a Senior Associate, Trade Finance at Bank of China Singapore. He has previously undertaken internships at Shift4Good, Hera Capital, KPMG Singapore and SaladStop Group. His passion for sustainable finance grew during his under-graduate studies and experiences at Shift4Good, where he conducted commercial due diligence, financial valuations and impact scoring for early-stage sustainability start-ups. He completed a BSc in Geography with Economics at the LSE.

Ferth Vandensteen Manaysay is a Senior Programme Coordinator at Climate Catalyst, where he works on programmes and partnerships focused on accelerating steel and heavy industry decarbonisation in Asia. He holds an MSc in Environmental Policy and Regulation from the LSE as a Chevening Scholar, and an MA in International Relations from Waseda University under the *Monbukagakusho* Scholarship. His professional experience spans government, academic, and civil society organisations, including *Yayasan Peta Bencana* (Disaster Map Foundation), The Climate Reality Project, The Asia Foundation, the Philippine Office of Civil Defense, Hong Kong Baptist University, and the Ateneo School of Government.

Cecilia Meinardi is a trainee in the Climate Action Research and Tracking Service Unit at the European Parliament. She has recently completed her MSc in Environmental Policy and Regulation at the LSE where her dissertation focused on asset managers' proxy voting patterns on environmental proposals. She also holds a BSc in International Relations and Organisation from Leiden University.

Noga Natanson is currently working as Corporate Programme Officer at the Institutional Investors Group on Climate Change (IIGCC) in London. She previously worked as Research Assistant at the Grantham Research Institute on Climate Change and the Environment, where she contributed to a project examining the UK's institutional capacity to achieve net zero. She holds an MSc with Distinction in Environmental Policy and Regulation from the LSE, where her dissertation focused on how institutional investors approach biodiversity loss. She also holds a BSc in International Relations and Organisations from Leiden University.

Áine O'Dea has recently completed her MSc in Environmental Policy and Regulation at the London School of Economics. Her dissertation focused on the changing attitudes towards environmental reporting in Chinese firms, specifically looking at firms with high deforestation exposure. Prior to this she completed an undergraduate degree in International Relations at Dublin City University, where she researched public perceptions of Ireland's Carbon Tax, and was awarded a Dean's Honours List admission. Aine has previously worked as press secretary with Amnesty International Ireland's student division.

Padraig Oliver is Programme Officer in the climate finance team at the UNFCCC Secretariat. He supports climate finance negotiations and technical work assessing climate finance flows, financial system transition and progress on climate finance goals. He previously worked as a Manager and Senior Analyst for Climate Policy Initiative (focusing on tracking climate finance flows and innovating blended climate finance solutions) and for the Climate Bonds Initiative (developing the Climate Bond Standard and tracking climate-aligned bonds). He has experience working in China and Europe and holds an MSc in Environmental Technology from Imperial College London.

Himanshu Pabreja is an India-registered lawyer who has gained a diverse work experience with law firms, NGOs, academia and think tanks. His practice essentially focused on environmental litigation, advisory opinions, ESG and grassroots-level implementation of environmental policies. He has recently completed his MSc in Environmental Policy and Regulation at the LSE, where his dissertation focused on the role of independent climate change advisory bodies on national political debates and policies. He intends to explore how policies are shaped by different actors from inception to implementation.

Richard Perkins is Associate Professor in the Department of Geography and Environment at the LSE where he is Programme Director of the MSc in Environmental Policy and Regulation. He is also Associate of the Centre for Economic Transition Expertise (CETEx) at the LSE. Richard's research examines the growing role of financial and corporate actors in governing sustainability. Within this frame, his work explores the evolution of the green and sustainability bond markets, the proliferation of voluntary net zero targets, the effectiveness of coalitions within sustainable finance and how green finance maintains its legitimacy. Richard received his PhD from the University of Cambridge.

Abi Perriman is a consultant in the Inclusive Growth and Climate Change team at Itad. She manages complex evaluations and advises on monitoring, evaluation and learning strategies for government donors, multilaterals, foundations and international organisations. Her focus is on innovative finance and private sector development. She holds an MSc in Environment and Development from the London School of Economics and Political Science (LSE).

Valeria Piani is Head of Stewardship at Phoenix Group, where she leads the in-house stewardship team and collaborates with Phoenix's asset management partners to influence the ESG performance of investee companies. She was previously Strategic Engagement Lead at UBS Asset Management (where she was responsible for climate change engagement, stewardship reporting and integration research in the industrial sector). Prior to this, she worked for the Principles for Responsible Investment (PRI) where she managed a team of 11 members responsible for coordinating investor collaborative engagement activities with companies on a range of ESG issues. In addition to being a non-executive director of the Investor Forum Board, Valeria is also a member of the CA100+ Global Steering Committee, the IIGCC Corporate Programme Advisory Group, the PRI Advance Advisory Committee and the Net Zero Asset Owner Alliance Engagement Track.

Amy Cano Prentice has conducted policy-oriented research for the OECD, the Overseas Development Institute (ODI) and the UK Government on a range of environmental and economic issues, including fiscal reform, climate risks and energy transition policy. She holds an MSc in Environmental Policy and Regulation from the London School of Economics and Political Science, and a BASc in Arts and Sciences from University College London. She regularly writes articles on cross-cutting topics related to green fiscal policy, fossil fuel reform and climate policy, and serves on the board of the journal *Indice*, edited by the Spanish National Institute of Statistics.

Chup Priovashini is Senior Analyst at Chronos Sustainability, where she is responsible for research and technical support across Chronos' projects in responsible investment, health and biodiversity. Her recent work includes aiding investors in evaluating their climate strategy and policy, assessing investors' role in managing the business risks of artificial intelligence and developing a benchmark on corporate air pollution. Chup holds a BA in Geography from the LSE and an MSc in Nature, Society and Environmental Governance from the University of Oxford.

Arjun Sanghera works as a healthcare operations consultant, advising healthcare companies, particularly dental practices, on how they can improve their sustainability practices. He is an MSc Environmental Policy and Regulation student at the LSE, and he holds a BSc in Politics and International Relations also from the LSE.

Kushal Shah is Climate Investment Specialist for a large global asset manager, where he is the subject matter expert on climate-related investment topics. His work includes conducting investment-related research, assisting investors with their climate-focused portfolio strategies and developing investment solutions. Kushal holds an MS in Financial Economics from Columbia Business School, an MBA from the Indian Institute of Management, Bangalore, and a B.Tech. in Electrical and Electronic Engineering from the National Institute of Technology, Trichy.

Meutia Riana Sukma has recently completed her MSc in Environment and Development at the LSE, with a dissertation focused on the political economy of Indonesia's national climate fund. Meutia previously worked with Rainforest Alliance, where she led the organisation's fundraising strategies in the Asia Pacific region. She holds a BA in Development Studies from the School of Oriental and African Studies, University of London.

Rory Sullivan is CEO of Chronos Sustainability and Visiting Professor in Practice in the Department of Geography and Environment at the London School of Economics and Political Science (LSE). Rory has advised government agencies and regulators – including in Peru, Colombia, South Africa, Malaysia and Thailand – on the development and implementation of sustainable finance policy. He has also advised many asset owners and asset managers on the development and implementation of their responsible investment and net zero strategies. In addition, Rory has supported the design and delivery of many key sustainable finance initiatives including Climate Action 100+, the Transition Pathway Initiative and the PRI/UNEPFI Fiduciary Duty in the 21st Century project. Rory was previously Head of ESG Research and Standards at FTSE Russell, Head of Responsible Investment at Insight Investment and, for many years, was an advisor on sustainability-related policy to organisations such as the UNFCCC, the OECD and Environment Australia. He is the author/editor of 11 books on sustainable investment, including *Responsible Investment in Fixed Income Markets* (with Joshua Kendall) and *Valuing Corporate Responsibility: How Investors Really Use Corporate Responsibility Information.* Rory holds a PhD in law, postgraduate degrees in environmental science and environmental law, and an undergraduate degree in engineering.

Krista Tukiainen is a climate finance expert and Co-founder of ClimateAligned, a start-up using artificial intelligence to evaluate the sustainability credentials of bonds, companies and countries. She has over a decade of experience in sustainable finance, including as a consultant and as Head of Market Intelligence at the Climate Bonds Initiative, where she worked with financial institutions to advance green finance and helped develop regulated taxonomies in collaboration with the EU Platform on Sustainable Finance. Krista has served on advisory groups for organisations including ICMA, LSEG and FoSDA. She holds an MSc in Environmental Policy and Regulation from the LSE.

Nora Venin is Account Manager at Adthena where she has been working for the last three years. She has recently completed her MSc in Environmental Policy and Regulation at the London School of Economics where her dissertation focused on barriers to green bonds in Mauritius. She also holds a BA in European Social and Political Studies from UCL. She previously worked as Associate at Orbit Partners and interned at the Maldives High Commission in London and in the Mauritius Mission to the United Nations in New York.

Yuqi Wang is an MSc in Environmental Policy and Regulation student at the LSE, where she contributes to projects on sustainable finance and adaptation finance. Her work includes supporting research into the performance of sustainable finance, evaluating successful cases of adaptation finance and writing policy papers on scaling up adaptation finance in the UK. She has also undertaken internships at Hubei Provincial Department of Ecology and Environment in China, at Lvdoya and at the United Nations. She holds a BSc in Environment and Development from the LSE.

Emeline Warner is Responsible Investment Analyst within the Investment Function at Just Group, an FTSE 250 financial services firm and one of the UK's leading providers of retirement financial solutions. Her key responsibilities include the classification of sustainable investments and the integration of responsible investment within investment decision-making. She completed her MSc in Environment and Development at the LSE where her dissertation focused on green bonds supporting development objectives in South Africa. She also holds a BA in Human Geography from the University of Exeter. Emeline previously interned at both CBRE and LiveWest in real estate ESG consultancy and Foodbuy (Compass Group) in sustainable food procurement.

Duo Xu has completed an MSc in Environmental Policy and Regulation at the LSE, where her dissertation focused on CSR communication and CSR reporting. She also holds Bachelor of Social Science degree in Environment and Development from Ritsumeikan Asia Pacific University.

Jisoo You is a consultant at Green Climate Fund (GCF), where she supports institutional learning by curating lessons learned from funded activities and readiness grant portfolios. Her focus is on climate finance and adaptation finance, particularly on how financial mechanisms can support vulnerable communities and strengthen resilience to climate impacts. She holds an MSc in Environmental Policy and Regulation from the LSE, as well as a BSc in Environmental Management and a BA in Western History from Seoul National University.

Hao Zhong is Carbon Asset Management Officer at Goldwind, specialising in green methanol projects. He contributes to carbon accounting, International Sustainability and Carbon Certification (ISCC) certification and carbon finance product development for these projects. With a professional background spanning both non-profit and commercial environmental sectors in China, he previously worked as Programme Officer for environmental NGOs and as Analyst for an environmental consulting firm. Hao Zhong holds an MSc in Environmental Policy and Regulation from the LSE, where his dissertation focused on the EU green bond standard. He was awarded a full scholarship for this programme. He also holds a BA in International Studies from the University of Nottingham.

Acronyms

AAHK	Airport Authority Hong Kong
ACGA	Asian Corporate Governance Association
ADF	African Development Foundation
AFOLU	Agriculture, Forestry, and Other Land Use
AI	artificial intelligence
AIGCC	Asia Investor Group on Climate Change
AOSIS	Alliance of Small Island States
APRA	Australian Prudential Regulation Authority
ASIC	Australian Securities and Investments Commission
AUM	assets under management
BIS	Bank for International Settlements
bps	basis points
BVCA	British Private Equity & Venture Capital Association
CA100+	Climate Action 100+
CBD	Convention on Biological Diversity
CBDR	common but differentiated responsibilities
CBDR-RC	Common but Differentiated Responsibilities and Respective Capabilities
CEO	chief executive officer
CETEx	Centre for Economic Transition Expertise (LSE)
CGAP	Consultative Group to Assist the Poor
COP	Conference of the Parties
CPI	Climate Policy Initiative
CSR	corporate social responsibility
CSRD	Corporate Sustainability Reporting Directive (Europe)
DB	defined benefit (pension schemes)
DC	defined contribution (pension schemes)
DFI	development finance institution
EBA	European Banking Authority
ECB	European Central Bank
ECCs	essentially contested concepts
EFRAG	European Financial Reporting Advisory Group
EGM	emergency general meeting

EIB	European Investment Bank
EIOPA	European Insurance and Occupational Pensions Authority
EMDEs	emerging markets and developing economies
ESG	environmental, social and governance (issues)
ESMA	European Securities and Markets Authority
ESRS	European Sustainability Reporting Standards
ETF	exchange traded fund
EU	European Union
FAIRR	Farm Animal Investment Risk and Return Initiative
FAO	Food and Agriculture Organization
FCA	Financial Conduct Authority (UK)
FCLT	Focusing Capital on the Long Term
FoSDA	Future of Sustainable Data Alliance
G77	Group of 77 (countries)
GBP	Green Bond Principles
GCF	Green Climate Fund
GDP	gross domestic product
GIIN	Global Impact Investing Network
GPIF	Government Pension Investment Fund (Japan)
GRI	Global Reporting Initiative
GSIA	Global Sustainable Investment Alliance
HAGCCF	United Nations Secretary-General's High-level Advisory Group on Climate Change Financing
IASB	International Accounting Standards Board
ICCR	Interfaith Center on Corporate Responsibility
ICGN	International Corporate Governance Network
ICMA	International Capital Market Association
IEA	International Energy Agency
IFC	International Finance Corporation
IFRS	International Financial Reporting Standards
IIGCC	Institutional Investors Group on Climate Change
ILO	International Labour Organisation
IMF	International Monetary Fund
IORP	Institution for Occupational Retirement Provision
IOSCO	International Organization of Securities Commissions (IOSCO)
IPCC	Intergovernmental Panel on Climate Change
IPO	initial public offering
IRENA	International Renewable Energy Agency
ISSB	International Sustainability Standards Board
KPI	key performance indicator
L&D	loss and damage
LDC	least developed country
LSE	London School of Economics and Political Science
LSEG	London Stock Exchange Group
MDB	multilateral development bank

MSMEs	micro, small and medium enterprises
NAP	National Adaptation Plan
NCQG	New Collective Quantified Goal
NDC	Nationally Determined Contribution
NGFS	Network for Greening the Financial System
NGO	non-governmental organisation
NZAOA	Net Zero Asset Owner Alliance
ODI	Overseas Development Institute
OECD	Organisation for Economic Co-operation and Development
PEFA	Public Expenditure and Financial Accountability
PPP	public–private partnership
PRI	Principles for Responsible Investment
R&D	research and development
RAN	Rainforest Action Network
ROA	return on assets
ROE	return on equity
SASB	Sustainability Accounting Standards Board
SBTi	Science Based Targets initiative
SDGs	Sustainable Development Goals
SEC	Securities and Exchange Commission (US)
SFDR	Sustainable Finance Disclosure Regulation (Europe)
SIDS	Small Island Developing States
SLB	sustainability-linked bond
SRI	socially responsible investment
SWESIF	Swedish Forum for Sustainable Investments
SWF	sovereign wealth fund
TCFD	Task Force on Climate-related Financial Disclosures
TNFD	Taskforce on Nature-related Financial Disclosures
UK	United Kingdom
UKSIF	UK Sustainable Investment and Finance Association
UN	United Nations
UNCTAD	UN Conference on Trade and Development
UNDP	United Nations Development Programme
UNEP FI	United Nations Environment Programme Finance Initiative
UNEP	United Nations Environment Programme
UNFCCC	United Nations Framework Convention on Climate Change
UNFCCC SCF	UNFCCC Standing Committee on Finance
UNGPs	UN Guiding Principles on Business and Human Rights
US	United States
USAID	United States Agency for International Development
USEPA	US Environmental Protection Agency
WEF	World Economic Forum
WFE	World Federation of Exchanges
WRI	World Resources Institute

Chapter 1

Introduction

Rory Sullivan and Richard Perkins

What Is Sustainable Investment?

Sustainable investment (often referred to as responsible investment) is an approach to investment that explicitly acknowledges the relevance of environmental, social and governance (or sustainability) factors to the investor. Organisations such as the Principles for Responsible Investment (PRI) suggest that sustainable investment complements traditional financial analysis and portfolio construction techniques as it involves considering sustainability-related issues when making investment decisions and influencing companies or assets (PRI, 2022).

These, apparently straightforward, descriptions raise complex issues which are not easy or straightforward to resolve. For example, investment is invariably associated with the expectation of generating a positive financial return. Yet these descriptions of sustainable investment provide no guidance on the relative importance of financial considerations, on the one hand, and of sustainability-related aspects, on the other. The descriptions also do not specify what actions should be taken (or even whether any actions need to be taken), nor do they explain how the needs and interests of investors concerned about financial returns can be reconciled with those of investors concerned about delivering positive sustainability outcomes. In addition, the descriptions do not clarify the timeframes over which investors should consider sustainability-related issues or explain how medium- and long-term impacts are to be reconciled with shorter-term impacts.

DOI: 10.4324/9781003467632-1

Despite this lack of clarity, sustainable investment is now a significant part of the investment market. For example, the 2022 Global Sustainable Investment Review (Global Sustainable Investment Review (GSIA), 2023) reports that around one third of global investment assets are managed in line with some form of sustainable investment strategy. Further evidence of investment's growing enmeshment with sustainability is provided by the PRI (an international network of investors who commit to incorporating sustainability issues into their investment decision-making and ownership practices) which has more than 5,000 signatories, representing over half the world's institutional assets under management (Atkin, 2024).

Various factors have underpinned the emergence and growth of sustainable investment. In part, it is a response to rising moral concerns over social and environmental issues, ranging from gender equality through to anthropogenic climate change. Sustainable investment offers the potential to enhance positive sustainability impacts or reduce negative ones through actions such as investing in companies or activities with positive social or environmental characteristics, through avoiding companies or activities with negative social or environmental characteristics, through working with company management to encourage improved social or environmental performance and through engaging with policymakers to encourage the adoption of policies, regulations or other measures that improve the sustainability performance of companies. The growth of sustainable investment has also been motivated by the belief that, by considering sustainability factors in investment analysis and decision-making, investors can achieve better financial returns. A related argument, although it has been mainly deployed by investors motivated by moral concerns, is that the generation of long-term sustainable returns is dependent on stable, well-functioning and well-governed social, environmental and economic systems.

Clients and stakeholders have also contributed to the growth of sustainable investment. Interest from clients has provided opportunities for new products and services such as green exchange-traded funds (ETFs), low carbon indices, sustainability-related data and analytics and sustainability advisory services. Pressure from clients, customers, beneficiaries and other stakeholders has prompted investors to act on sustainability. Finally, public regulation has been important, with many countries introducing regulatory requirements which directly or indirectly have stimulated growth in sustainable investment and related activities. For example, institutional investors in a growing number of jurisdictions are required to adopt policies explaining how they account for sustainability factors in their investment practices, and to report on how they implement their sustainability-related policies (see, for example, PRI (2025) and UNCTAD (2025)).

While the drivers for growth are well understood, important questions remain about the implications and impacts – both positive and negative – of 'sustainable investment'. For example: Does sustainable investment deliver superior financial returns? To what extent is sustainable investment consistent with investors' fiduciary duty? Does sustainable investment contribute to better sustainability outcomes? Which sustainable investing strategies deliver the most positive sustainability impacts? Is disclosure an effective tool for governing sustainability within the investment system? Can we distinguish between genuine sustainability and greenwashing by financial actors? Does sustainable investment properly account for justice and equity concerns? Does sustainable investment align with clients' ethical values and interests?

These questions are important. The legitimacy and continued momentum of sustainable investment relies on positive answers to many of them. Yet, in many cases, it is difficult to provide a definitive answer. There are different reasons. First, definitions are inconsistent and contested. Even the term sustainable investment encompasses a whole range of investment strategies including negative and positive screening, the integration of environmental, social and governance (ESG) issues into investment decision-making, impact investment and shareholder engagement and voting. Second, there are many issues with sustainability-related data. These include inconsistent methodologies, data gaps and inadequate understanding of which data points are material from the perspective of financial returns or social and environmental impacts. Third, findings from past studies on financial and sustainability performance are based on different geographic samples, industry samples and time periods, making it difficult to draw general conclusions. Fourth, there are many different definitions and measures of performance. Amongst others, sustainability has been assessed using process measures such as changes in management policies and practices, outcome measures such as absolute changes in emissions and impact measures such as the effects on receiving environments. Similarly, in relation to business and financial performance, the measures used, amongst many others, include asset valuation, share price, cost of capital and return on investment. These measurement and methodological choices have a major impact on research findings and, in turn, on the conclusions that can be drawn about the impacts of sustainable investment.

What Are the Objectives of This Book?

It is inevitable that sustainable investment will be subject to greater scrutiny in the coming years. It is therefore important that we critically examine and analyse sustainable investment and clearly specify what we know and what we do not know. One of the advantages of writing this book at this time is that there is now a significant and growing body of academic and practitioner work – albeit not as much as one might hope – on sustainable investment, how it is being mobilised and implemented, and some of the advantages and disadvantages of current approaches. There is also a reasonable amount of data and empirical analysis on the financial and sustainability-related outcomes associated with different sustainable investment strategies and instruments. In many areas, the evidence is mixed, but it is nevertheless possible to tease out a series of emerging insights and lessons.

About the Book: Chapter by Chapter

We begin, in Chapters 2 and 3, by providing an introduction to the investment system and to where and how sustainable investment fits within this system. In Chapter 2, Cora Buentjen, Fatima Husain and Chup Priovashini describe the key functions and features of the institutional investment system and the key actors within this system. In Chapter 3, these authors with Robert Black unpack key terms and concepts – such as materiality, timeframes and diversification – that are central to understanding investment, to understanding how sustainability-related considerations are integrated into investment processes, and to understanding whether and how sustainable investment influences investment performance and sustainability outcomes.

Chapters 4 and 5 focus on how actors' preferences, together with the legal and policy landscape, shape sustainable investment. Chapter 4, authored by Richard Perkins and Krista Tukiainen, sheds light on why sustainable investment is the subject of considerable disagreement. The authors draw attention to the importance of actors' values, beliefs and interests, and outline ways in which disagreements can be productively addressed and harnessed to advance public sustainability goals. Chapter 5 by Rory Sullivan analyses how the duties – loyalty, prudence – owed by fiduciaries such as pension funds to the people whose money they manage affect investment decision-making processes, and whether these duties enable or hinder the incorporation of sustainability-related issues into investment decision-making and into ownership practices.

We then examine the impact of sustainable investment and the determinants of this impact – drawing on both conceptual and empirical insights. Kester Low, Yuqi Wang and Kushal Shah (Chapter 6) analyse the academic literature on financial performance and ask whether sustainable investment delivers better financial outcomes. Cecilia Meinardi, Arjun Sanghera, Nora Venin and James Corah ask the same question in relation to sustainability outputs and outcomes (Chapter 7). The book then digs deeper into these questions. Amy Cano Prentice, Meutia Riana Sukma, Ferth Vandensteen Manaysay, Hao Zhong and Padraig Oliver (Chapter 8) assess whether sustainable investment can deliver on the goals of the Paris Agreement, while Emma De Fino, Emeline Warner and Rachel Crossley (Chapter 9) assess whether better disclosure – by companies or by investors – leads to better sustainability performance. Finally, Tristan Gilet, Krishnapriya J, Himanshu Pabreja and Valeria Piani (Chapter 10) critically assess the value and contribution of collective action initiatives in sustainable investment.

Questions of legitimacy, accountability and governance in sustainable investment are examined in Chapters 11. 12 and 13. In Chapter 11, Noga Natanson, Hilary Lai, Sumira Bothé and Johan Florén look at the issue of greenwashing and ask whether the information provided by investors in relation to sustainable investment can be trusted. Claudio Cichi, Áine O'Dea, Duo Xu and Valentin Jahn (Chapter 12) assess whether the information provided by companies, investors and data and ratings providers can be relied upon, and the implications of this. Lastly, Abi Perriman, Dido Gompertz and Jisoo You (Chapter 13) look at whether sustainable investment, as currently practised, meets the needs of the Global South.

In the final chapter (Chapter 14), Rory Sullivan and Richard Perkins bring some of the key themes from the book together. They reflect on the progress that has been made to date in terms of the actions taken by investment organisations and the financial and sustainability outcomes that have been achieved. They offer suggestions on the policy frameworks and the institutional structures that need to be in place for sustainable investment to make a meaningful contribution at scale to public social and environmental goals such as those set out in the Sustainable Development Goals. They conclude by reflecting on the critical role of individuals working within the investment industry, arguing that investment professionals need to proactively and assertively shape their roles and their activities to ensure that they make a meaningful, at scale contribution to positive social and environmental outcomes.

References

Atkin, D. (2024, August 8), 'Meeting Investors Where They're At: PRI Launches New Strategy', *Principles for Responsible Investment Blog*, www.unpri.org/pri-blog/meeting-investors-where-theyre-at-pri-launches-new-strategy/12636.article

Global Sustainable Investment Alliance (GSIA) (2023), *Global Sustainable Investment Review 2023*, www.gsi-alliance.org/wp-content/uploads/2023/12/GSIA-Report-2022.pdf

Principles for Responsible Investment (PRI) (2022), *What Is Responsible Investment?*, www.unpri.org/introductory-guides-to-responsible-investment/what-is-responsible-investment/4780.article

Principles for Responsible Investment (PRI) (2025), 'Regulation Database', www.unpri.org/policy/global-policy/regulation-database (last viewed 19 January 2025).

UNCTAD (2025), 'Sustainable Finance Regulations Platform', https://gsfo.org/sustainable-finance-regulations-platform (last viewed 20 February 2025).

Chapter 2

Key Actors and Their Roles in the Investment System

Cora Buentjen, Fatima Husain and Chup Priovashini

Introduction

This is the first of two chapters that set out some of the key terms and concepts that are relevant to sustainable. In this chapter we focus on the overall investment system and the actors within the system. We start by explaining, in broad terms, the purpose of the financial system as a whole and the relationship between the investment system and the wider financial system. We then look more closely at the institutional investment system, the primary focus of this book, and describe the main actors in this system, what they do and how they relate to each other. These features, roles and interactions define why sustainability issues are important to the actors, what they understand as their roles and responsibilities and how they implement their commitments to responsible investment and sustainable finance.

In a short chapter such as this, we cannot hope to cover every actor, every interaction or every motivation. Therefore, our approach throughout is to provide

 DOI: 10.4324/9781003467632-2

a framework that allows you to understand the role and the contribution of individual actors, and how these individual actors interact with and relate to each other in the context of the financial system as a whole.

What Is the Purpose of the Financial System?

In broad terms, the purpose of the financial system is to facilitate the flow of capital from those that have it to those that need it. For example, while it does not provide a formal definition of the financial system, the International Monetary Fund (IMF) notes that

> Financial markets facilitate the transfer of productive resource between entities or sectors with surplus resources to those in need of resource, and in doing so support the productive potential and development of the economy. Markets provide a setting within which financial claims can be traded under established rules of conduct, and can facilitate the management of credit, market and, other risks.
>
> (International Monetary Fund (IMF), 2019, p. 11)

Financial systems can be understood as a network of institutions that work together to exchange and transfer capital from one place to another. The IMF states that "The financial sector consists of institutional units, financial instruments and markets, and government regulation, interacting to facilitate intermediation between providers and users of funds" (IMF, 2019, p. 11). The actors relevant to the themes in this book include those entities directly involved in making or enabling financial transactions – for example institutional investors, insurance companies, stock exchanges and investment banks – as well as regulators, government treasuries and monetary authorities, standard setters, and international organisations such as the IMF and the World Bank. Useful introductory sources providing an overview of the actors in the financial system include IMF (2019) and Armour *et al.* (2016: 22–50). A comprehensive overview of the investment system is provided in Arjaliès *et al.* (2017).

The specific roles played by the financial system (and the actors within the system) include the following:

1. Making and enabling payments: The financial system provides platforms where money can be transferred and exchanged between actors in the system.
2. Mobilising savings: The financial system enables individuals and organisations to save (or accumulate) money and, if they wish, to pool and invest this money.

3. Managing risk: The financial system can help individuals and organisations manage risk through, for example, allowing them to diversify their investments and allowing them to buy insurance.
4. Providing liquidity: The finance system can provide individuals and organisations with access to their money, and the ability to exchange their assets for cash.
5. Allocating capital: As stated earlier, the financial system enables the transfer of resources (capital) between entities or sectors with surplus resources to those in need of these resources. The system can also help individuals and organisations to identify, assess (e.g. through due diligence and risk assessment) and invest in projects, assets, activities, companies or other opportunities.
6. Monitoring performance: The financial system can monitor the performance (which may include social and environmental performance in addition to financial performance) of the recipients of capital.
7. Maintaining economic stability: The financial system, often under the direction of central banks and other regulators, can adjust the supply of money and where and how money is allocated, as part of wider efforts to support economic stability and reduce the likelihood of significant economic shocks or disruptions.

The Institutional Investment System: An Overview

We start this section by providing a high-level description of the institutional investment system before delving into more detail on the key actors and key features of the system that relate to the sustainability themes that are the subject of this book.

To start with, institutional investment can be understood as the part of the financial system that allows organisations to pool money and to invest this money on behalf of others. In broad terms, the investment industry helps individuals, companies and other entities to achieve their goals by helping them grow and allowing them to receive an income from their investments. In most cases, these goals are expressed in financial terms (e.g. having enough money to live on in retirement, achieving a particular rate of return) but can also include non-financial goals such as supporting companies or projects that provide societal or environmental benefits.

Within this system, institutional investors are organisations – including pension funds, investment managers, insurance companies, investment banks and sovereign wealth funds (SWFs) – that invest and manage money for their clients, their beneficiaries (e.g. the individuals that receive a pension, the individuals that receive insurance payouts) or their members. These organisations hire investment professionals to manage the money by investing in shares, bonds, property and other assets. Institutional investors are important sources of capital and their scale means that their buying and selling of shares and other assets can cause big movements in the prices of these assets. It has been estimated that institutional investors account for about 80% of the Standard & Poor's (S&P) 500 total market capitalisation (Chen, 2024), that institutional investors account for about 80% of the volume of trades on the New York Stock Exchange (Palmer, 2024) and that the world's 50 largest institutional investors hold approximately 25% of the world's equity market capitalisation (Medina *et al.*, 2022).

These organisations can exert influence on others. For example, pension funds may include specific performance conditions in their contracts with investment managers, and investment managers may vote their shareholdings on important company matters. Therefore, the views that these organisations hold (including their views on sustainability-related issues) and the decisions that they take (e.g. on which assets to buy and sell, on whether they support or oppose management decisions) have an important influence on the behaviour of other investors and of companies.

The Institutional Investment System: Key Actors

In the investment system, capital (money) is provided by individuals, by organisations (e.g. companies) or by other entities (e.g. governments). These providers of capital can invest their money directly in shares, bonds, real estate and other assets. Alternatively, they can rely on third parties to invest their money on their behalf. Those that are of particular relevance to this book include the following:

- Pension funds, which are organisations that receive payments from individuals and from the individuals' employers, and promise to pay a retirement benefit in the future to the beneficiaries of the fund. Pension funds may invest directly in assets and/or may invest through investment companies or other entities.
- Investment managers (or asset managers), which are organisations that provide professional investment services to banks, individuals and other organisations (including pension funds) looking to invest their funds.
- Insurance companies, which are organisations that protect policyholders from various types of risk. Policyholders pay premiums which are then invested by the insurance company, with the investments chosen to reflect the types of risk being insured.
- Savings institutions (such as banks), which take deposits from customers and then make loans (e.g. mortgages, business loans) to others.
- Foundations, which are typically funded for the specific purposes or objectives of the organisation (e.g. improving the quality of public services, providing access to education or healthcare).

- SWFs, which are state-owned investment funds established to provide benefits for a country's economy and its citizens.

The investment chain ends with the recipients of the investment capital. For example, companies may use the money to invest in new projects, to access new markets, for research and development, to hire new staff, to acquire other businesses and/or to meet their financial obligations. Similarly, governments may use this money to build infrastructure, fund access to healthcare, education or other essential services and/or support key industry sectors.

In Focus: Asset Owners

Asset owners manage investments for a group of people or organisations. From a sustainability perspective, they are important because their size and their commercial relationships with investment managers mean that they may have a significant influence over the investment chain as a whole. For example, one source suggests that, as of 2023, the world's 100 largest asset owners manage $26.3 trillion in assets collectively (Thinking Ahead Institute, 2024). This influence is acknowledged by the Principles for Responsible Investment (PRI) which states, "Heading the investment chain, asset owners set the direction for markets globally. They are increasingly focused on managing their assets sustainably, as they often have long-term liabilities and investment horizons" (PRI, 2022). Asset owners can exert influence in various ways. For example, they can set sustainability-related expectations or targets for their investment portfolios, they can seek to influence corporate behaviour through voting, dialogue and collaboration, they can preferentially invest in companies with better sustainability performance (or, equally, avoid companies with poorer performance) and they can seek to exert wider influence (e.g. through working with other investors, through defining expectations of their investment managers, through engaging with policymakers).

The most significant types of asset owners, in terms of assets under management (a measure of size), are, in order, pension funds, insurance companies, SWFs and endowments and foundations (Brigandi and Ortel, 2018); we discuss each of these below. Family offices (private companies that manage investments and trusts for one or multiple wealthy families) are sometimes included in the general category of asset owners.

Pension funds are organisations established to accumulate and grow the retirement savings of the funds' participants (often referred to as beneficiaries). There are two main types of pension plans (although hybrid forms are increasingly common): defined benefit (or DB) schemes where the plan sponsor commits to paying a specified retirement benefit and defined contribution (DC) schemes where the contributions are defined but the ultimate retirement benefit is not specified or guaranteed by the plan sponsor. Pension funds, depending on the scheme and the country, receive payments from future beneficiaries and/or the beneficiaries' employer and/or government.

Insurance companies take on specific financial risks in exchange for premiums paid by policyholders. These policyholders are individuals, organisations or other entities that purchase insurance policies from the insurance company. In return for paying premiums, policyholders receive the insurer's commitment to cover specific losses or damages outlined in the policy. Insurance companies generally invest these premiums in bonds, stocks and other assets.

SWFs are state-owned funds that invest financial assets for the country's benefit. They are funded from a country's savings, from revenues from the exploitation of oil, gas and other mineral resources and/or from individual savings and pensions. Their aim is to support the short- and long-term economic development of the country in question. Their investments, therefore, generally have to meet a mix of financial and strategic (national interest) objectives.

Endowment funds and foundations aim to support the goals and objectives of the parent organisation. Organisations such as universities, museums and hospitals often have significant endowment funds, where the funding is provided by donations and bequests. Endowment funds and foundations may be time limited (e.g. all of the capital is required to be disbursed within a particular period) or may be designed to exist in perpetuity. The investment approach adopted will depend on their parent organisation's goals and timeframes.

Asset owners have features that shape their approach to sustainability issues. First, they have different time horizons although most larger asset owners have a reasonably long-term investment time horizon; we discuss time horizons in Chapter 3. Second, they can manage their investments directly, they can outsource to asset managers or they can combine both approaches. The decision on whether to outsource or keep investment management in-house depends on factors such as the size of their assets, the relative costs of in-house or outsourced investment management and the asset owner's internal capabilities. Asset owners, especially those that have a substantial portion of their assets managed externally, are reliant on their asset managers to deliver on their investment and sustainability-related objectives. Third, they – or their investment managers – may invest in different asset classes or seek to diversify their investments.

A Note on Terminology: Asset Classes and Diversification

An asset class is a group of investments that exhibit similar characteristics (Ganti, 2024). Examples of common asset classes include equities (or stocks), fixed income (or bonds), cash, commodities and real estate.

Asset classes have different financial characteristics and react differently under different market conditions, and there is often little correlation between the financial performance of different asset classes. This characteristic is important; it means that investors can diversify their investments. Diversification involves spreading investments across different asset classes, industries and geographies to reduce risk and enhance potential returns.

Over the past 20 years, in most jurisdictions, larger institutions have progressively moved away from domestic (home country) investment to being internationally diversified and have increased their investments in alternative asset classes, such as private equity and hedge funds.

In Focus: Asset Managers

Unlike asset owners who hold assets directly, asset managers act as stewards of their clients' assets without owning them outright. Their core function is to build and manage investment portfolios in line with their clients' financial objectives. These objectives could be capital preservation, providing income to meet outgoings or liabilities, delivering particular returns relative to inflation or maximising the value of investments while mitigating risks. The activities carried out by asset managers include researching and analysing different investment opportunities, selecting the investments – for example stocks, bonds and real estate – that their clients' money will be invested in (taking due account of the clients' financial and other objectives), and monitoring and managing the investment portfolio.

Depending on their clients' expectations (both formal contractual obligations and informal expectations) and on their own views on how to create investment value, asset managers should seek to maintain and enhance the long-term value of the businesses and other entities in which they invest. For example, they could actively engage with company management and could encourage better risk management, or better management of social and environmental issues and impacts.

A Note on Terminology: Traditional and Alternative Asset Managers

While there are no hard and fast rules, it is common to differentiate between investment managers based on which asset classes they invest in. 'Traditional' asset managers offer products within the more popular asset classes such as equities (shares), fixed income, money market and property. In contrast, 'alternative' asset managers invest outside these traditional asset classes, in areas that are generally seen as involving higher risk. Examples include hedge funds, quant-driven funds, private equity and venture capital, and private debt. Of course, many investment managers offer both traditional and alternative investment opportunities.

Other Actors in the Investment System

The list of actors that enable investment does not end with the core investment chain. Other actors that provide market infrastructure and enable the flow of information include the following:

- Investment banks, which are specialised financial institutions involved in complex financial transactions. They act as intermediaries between companies seeking capital and investors looking to deploy funds. Among other roles, they help companies raise capital, they advise on and help execute mergers, acquisitions and divestments and they facilitate the purchase and sale of assets.
- Stock exchanges, which are organised marketplaces where shares and other financial assets can be traded between buyers and sellers. Well-known exchanges include the New York Stock Exchange, the Nasdaq, the Shanghai Stock Exchange, Euronext, the Bombay Stock Exchange, the Hong Kong Stock Exchange, the London Stock Exchange, the Australian Securities Exchange and the Johannesburg Stock Exchange. Stock exchanges can support sustainability in a variety of ways, including promoting good governance in business practices, promoting investment in sustainable development and encouraging better reporting and disclosure (see, generally, Cleary *et al.*, 2017).
- Sustainability data and information providers are third-party companies that gather, analyse and report data on the sustainability performance of companies, governments and other entities. Some of the bigger players include MSCI, London Stock Exchange Group, Morningstar Sustainalytics and Bloomberg. These organisations are discussed in more detail in Chapter 12.
- Credit rating agencies assess borrowers' ability to repay debt and the likelihood of default and, from this analysis, provide investors with information on the creditworthiness of issuers and their debt (see, generally, Kendall and Sullivan, 2023). These agencies assess both borrowers (e.g. a government, a corporate) and debt instruments (e.g. a green bond, a specific government bond). Credit ratings agencies are highly regulated. Globally, three credit rating agencies – S&P, Moody's and Fitch Ratings – dominate the market.
- Financial market policymakers and regulators set 'the rules of the game' in the financial and investment systems. They define how market actors interact with each other, how these actors manage risk and what these actors should report. Their mandates generally focus on consumer protection and prudential regulation (i.e. ensuring that the financial system is healthy, safe and stable). Many have started to act on sustainability-related issues and have introduced measures to encourage institutional investors to adopt formal policies on sustainability-related issues, to pay greater consideration to sustainability-related issues in investment decision-making, to

engage with investee companies and to report on their sustainability-related policies, practices and performance (Miller *et al.*, 2018; PRI, 2025).

- Investment consultants (or actuarial consultants) are widely used by asset owners; in fact, in some jurisdictions, asset owners are required to obtain advice from such consultants. Investment consultants – examples include Willis Towers Watson, Mercer and Aon Hewitt – make recommendations to investors on portfolio construction, asset allocation and asset manager selection. They monitor and review investment performance, with the aim of ensuring that the chosen investment strategies and investment managers' strategies remain effective and relevant.

Investment markets, and the way these markets deal with sustainability-related issues, are also shaped by the actions and activities of other actors. Policymakers and regulators who define wider economic, social and environmental policies and regulations – for example carbon markets and technology standards – help define where investors will invest and where they will not invest. As noted by the PRI, a sustainable economy, ultimately, requires alignment between the goals of the finance system and the goals, policies and standards set for the wider economy (Pirovska *et al.*, 2022, 2023). Global standard setters – examples include the International Accounting Standards Board (IASB), the International Sustainability Standards Board (ISSB) and International Organization of Securities Commissions (IOSCO) – are important because they develop standards and frameworks that they then encourage national regulators and policymakers to adopt. Finally, non-governmental organisations, civil society organisations and trade associations (among others) seek to shape and influence the financial system through campaigns and through lobbying investors, policymakers and other actors.

Concluding Comments

In the context of this book's focus on sustainable finance, there are two important insights to be taken from this chapter. The first is to clarify that the ability of asset owners to cascade their expectations and ambitions through to the end recipients or users of their capital is shaped by the behaviours and actions of the many intermediaries and other actors in the investment system. These intermediaries can support and enable (or, conversely, can obscure and prevent) the delivery of these expectations and ambitions.

The second, which may be obvious but is important to stress, is that this is a financial system. The goals of the investment system and of the actors within this system are generally defined in financial terms. This, inevitably, means that objectives and targets are expressed in financial terms, and that financial considerations dominate decision-making. It also means that, for many actors, sustainability issues are analysed and discussed in financial terms, where the focus is on questions such as how financially significant the impacts are, whether the actions enhance or damage returns and whether it is financially worthwhile to focus on sustainability issues in investment decision-making.

Implications for Practitioners

1. Understand your organisation's position in the investment system. Specifically, you need to understand
   a. Which actors in the investment system (e.g. asset owners, beneficiaries, asset managers, companies, regulators) you can influence.
   b. How much influence you have over each of these actors. Are there particular actors that you can compel to take action (e.g. can you introduce sustainability-related considerations into contracts)? Are there actors that you can influence directly (e.g. an asset manager may engage with investee companies to improve their sustainability reporting)? Are there actors that you can persuade to take action (e.g. asset managers may encourage their asset owner clients to do more on sustainability)?
   c. What wider influence you have. For example, policymakers are often interested in the views expressed by institutional investors, and investment managers may, in response to requests from their asset owner clients, be willing to strengthen their engagement with particular companies.
2. Understand the limitations and constraints you face. For example, while asset owners sit at the top of the investment chain, they generally cannot dictate how investment managers invest or prescribe the engagement that the investment managers carry out. They can, however, encourage action through encouraging better reporting on the actions taken, through asking about the actions taken and through making sustainability performance a central part of investment manager selection, monitoring and review processes.
3. Build sustainability into your governance systems and processes. For example:
   a. Establish a clear policy on sustainability. This will help direct your activities and will also send a clear signal to clients, service providers and partners about your expectations of them.
   b. Explain – acknowledging the points above about how the financial system works – how you intend to achieve the goals set out in your policy, both the actions you will take and the actions you expect or would like others to take.

c. Monitor and report publicly on what you have done, how you have performed, the contribution made by others and the challenges or barriers to progress.

References

Arjaliès, D., Grant, P., Hardie, I., MacKenzie, D. and Svetlova, E. (2017), *Chains of Finance: How Investment Management Is Shaped* (Oxford University Press, Oxford).

Armour, J., Awrey, D., Davies, P., Enriques, L., Gordon, J., Mayer, C. and Payne, J. (2016), *Principles of Financial Regulation* (Oxford University Press, Oxford).

Brigandi, T. and Ortel, S. (2018, February 20), 'The Seven Kinds of Asset Owner Institutions', *CFA Institute*, https://blogs.cfainstitute.org/investor/2018/02/20/the-seven-kinds-of-asset-owner-institutions

Chen, J. (2024, May 23), 'Institutional Investor: Who They Are and How They Invest', *Investopedia*, www.investopedia.com/terms/i/institutionalinvestor.asp

Cleary, S., Alderighi, S., Fenner, R., Anthony, A. and Somerville, S. (2017), *The Role of Stock Exchanges in Fostering Economic Growth and Sustainable Development* (UN Conference on Trade and Development (UNCTAD) and World Federation of Exchanges (WFE)), https://sseinitiative.org/sites/sseinitiative/files/publications-files/wfe-unctad-exchanges-growth-and-sustainable-development.pdf

Ganti, A. (2024, June 12), 'What Are Asset Classes? More Than Just Stocks and Bonds', *Investopedia*, www.investopedia.com/terms/a/assetclasses.asp

International Monetary Fund (IMF) (2019), *Financial Soundness Indicators Compilation Guide*, www.imf.org/en/Data/Statistics/FSI-guide

Kendall, J. and Sullivan, R. (eds.) (2023), *Responsible Investment in Fixed Income Markets* (Routledge, London).

Medina, A., De La Cruz A. and Tang, Y. (2022), *Corporate Ownership and Concentration.* OECD Corporate Governance Working Papers No. 27 (OECD, Paris), www.oecd.org/en/publications/corporate-ownership-and-concentration_bc3adca3-en.html

Miller, A., Grabski, T. and Sullivan, R. (2018), *How Securities Regulators Can Support the Sustainable Development Goals: A Sharing of Experiences* (Sustainable Stock Exchanges Initiative), https://sseinitiative.org/sites/sseinitiative/files/publications-files/sse-regulator-report-compressed.pdf

Palmer, B. (2024, October 30), 'Institutional Investors vs. Retail Investors: What's the Difference?', *Investopedia*, www.investopedia.com/ask/answers/06/institutionalinvestor.asp

Pirovska, M., Ransome, H. and Sullivan, R. (2022), *A Sustainable Finance Policy Engagement Handbook* (Principles for Responsible Investment), www.unpri.org/download?ac=17538

Pirovska, M., Vandermosten, J., Sullivan, R. and Black, R. (2023), *Investing for the Economic Transition: The Case for Whole-of-Government Policy Reform* (Principles for Responsible Investment), www.unpri.org/download?ac=21824

Principles for Responsible Investment (PRI) (2022), *What Is Responsible Investment?*, www.unpri.org/download?ac=10223

Principles for Responsible Investment (PRI) (2025), 'Regulation Database', www.unpri.org/policy/global-policy/regulation-database (last viewed 1 February 2025).

Thinking Ahead Institute (2024), *The Asset Owner 100*, www.thinkingaheadinstitute.org/research-papers/the-asset-owner-100-2024/#:~:text=The%20most%20influential%20capital%20on%20the%20planet&text=The%20study%20reveals%20the%20world's,compared%20to%20the%20previous%20year

Chapter 3

Key Concepts in Sustainable Investment

Cora Buentjen, Fatima Husain,
Chup Priovashini and Robert Black

Introduction

In Chapter 2 we provided an overview of the investment system as a whole and of the key actors within this system. In this chapter, we focus on key concepts, ideas and definitions that are necessary to understand how sustainable investment is implemented in practice and how sustainable investment might influence investment performance and sustainability outcomes.

We start by defining sustainable investment and explaining why financial institutions might be interested in paying attention to sustainability-related issues in their investment and other activities. We then describe the main approaches to sustainable finance and the key concepts – materiality, timeframes and diversification – that shape the implementation of these approaches. We conclude by offering suggestions on how investment practitioners, specifically those charged with developing and implementing sustainable finance strategies, might navigate the pressures they face to focus on short-term drivers of financial performance.

DOI: 10.4324/9781003467632-3

Why Is Sustainable Investment Important?

Investment decisions influence the share prices, the bond prices, the insurance costs, and the availability and the cost of capital for companies, projects, assets and other entities. These costs and prices, in turn, affect the financial performance of these companies, projects, assets and other entities. If investment decisions fail to adequately account for the value of good sustainability-related performance or the costs of poor performance, investors may create incentives for companies to cause (or fail to prevent) harmful corporate impacts on society and the environment (Sullivan and Mackenzie, 2006: 22–26). Conversely, investment strategies that incorporate sustainability-related considerations may increase the availability of funding for activities aligned with sustainability goals, may restrict funding for harmful activities or practices, may encourage more sustainable corporate practices and may encourage better disclosures of sustainability risks and performance metrics in financial and corporate reporting.

As discussed in Chapter 1, there are various reasons for investors to be interested in sustainable investment. First, there is evidence that sustainable investment can improve investment performance through, for example, investing in companies that benefit from sustainability-related regulations or opportunities and avoiding companies that may be negatively affected by sustainability-related regulations (see generally Whelan *et al.*, 2021). Second, investors may be motivated by the potential to enhance the positive sustainability impacts or reduce the negative sustainability impacts of their investments through, for example, investing in companies or activities with positive social or environmental characteristics, or working with company management to encourage improved social or environmental performance. Third, investors' clients or beneficiaries may expect them to build sustainability-related matters into their investment practices and processes. Fourth, many countries have now introduced requirements for institutional investors to adopt policies explaining how they account for sustainability factors in their investment practices and processes, to engage with the companies and other entities in which they are invested and to report on how sustainability issues affect their financial performance and on how their investments impact society and the environment (see, for example, Principles for Responsible Investment (PRI), 2025).

These drivers for action do not exist in isolation. In fact, they frequently interact with and reinforce (or undermine) each other. For example, an investor may not see that a particular sustainability issue is relevant to an investment decision, but customer demand or regulatory pressures may lead it to decide that it needs to engage with the company to ensure that the issue is being effectively managed. Equally, having analysed the investment implications of an issue, an investor may decide that the issue is not relevant to the investment decision and, therefore, that no further action is required. That is, the specific actions an investor takes, the specific sustainable investment strategies adopted and the specific outcomes (financial and sustainability) that are sought are shaped and informed by the views that the investor holds about sustainability, by its investment objectives and timeframes (which we discuss further below) and by the external pressures it faces to act on these issues.

What Is Sustainable Investment? Definitions and Approaches

In broad terms, sustainable investment (or responsible investment) refers to the practice of taking sustainability-related considerations into account when making financial or investment decisions, and when engaging with companies or other stakeholders. This definition does not – as illustrated by the interpretations proposed by the European Commission, the PRI and the UK Sustainable Investment and Finance Association (UKSIF) (see Box 3.1) – provide any guidance on the relative importance of financial performance versus impacts on society or the environment, nor does it prescribe what actions should be taken (or even whether any actions need to be taken).

Box 3.1 Definitions of Sustainable (and Responsible) Investment

The European Commission states:

> Sustainable finance refers to the process of taking environmental, social and governance (ESG) considerations into account when making investment decisions in the financial sector, leading to more long-term investments in sustainable economic activities and projects ... In the EU's policy context, sustainable finance is understood as finance to support economic growth while reducing pressures on the environment to help reach the climate- and environmental objectives of the European Green Deal, taking into account social and governance aspects.
>
> (European Commission, 2025)

The PRI states:

> Responsible investment involves considering environmental, social and governance (ESG) issues when making investment decisions and influencing companies or assets (known as active ownership or stewardship). It complements traditional financial analysis and portfolio construction techniques. Responsible investors can have different objectives. Some focus exclusively on financial returns

> and consider ESG issues that could impact these. Others aim to generate financial returns and to achieve positive outcomes for people and the planet, while avoiding negative ones.
>
> (Principles for Responsible Investment (PRI), 2022)

UKSIF states:

> Sustainable finance relates to investment and finance that considers environmental, social and governance (ESG) impacts. The decision to consider ESG can be for reasons that are ethical or financial or both. The strategies investors use to consider ESG issues are wide ranging and depend on the level of positive impact an investor wants to make, if any.
>
> (UK Sustainable Investment and Finance Association (UKSIF), 2025)

One common way of describing sustainable investment is in terms of the strategies used. Table 3.1 describes the five most common strategies, as identified by the CFA Institute, the Global Sustainable Investment Alliance (GSIA), and the PRI. Data from Global Sustainable Investment Alliance (GSIA) (2023) suggest that stewardship is the most common sustainable investment strategy, closely followed by environmental, social and governance (ESG) integration and negative/exclusionary screening. Positive screening, sustainability-themed investing and impact investing are much less commonly used.

While, at the definitional level, there is a reasonably broad level of agreement that sustainable investment refers to the integration of sustainability-related issues into investment research and decision-making processes, the reality is that the approaches in Table 3.1 are not homogeneous, and the term sustainable (or responsible) investment covers a whole series of complex and potentially contradictory ideas.

Figure 3.1 provides a conceptual illustration of how different sustainable investment strategies might be described in terms of the emphasis they place on financial returns versus impact. The specific balance point between financial returns and impact will depend on the investor's overarching objectives, the expected returns from the investment strategy, the investor's timeframes, the manner in which sustainability-related impacts are considered in the investment process and the weight given to sustainability-related impacts in investment decisions. It will also depend on the specific issues that are of concern (to the investor and to its clients), the metrics and key performance indicators (KPIs) used to assess performance and the data that are available to assess performance.

Table 3.1 Major Responsible Investment Strategies

Approach	*Definition (from CFA Institute, GSIA and PRI (2023))*	*Additional Notes*
Screening	Applying rules based on defined criteria that determine whether an investment is permissible.	GSIA (2023) identifies three main approaches to screening: ■ Norms-based screening, where investments are screened against minimum standards of business or issuer practice based on international norms such as those issued by the United Nations. ■ Negative/exclusionary screening, where certain sectors, companies, countries or other issuers are excluded from investment. Exclusion criteria can refer to product categories (e.g. weapons, tobacco), company practices (e.g. animal testing, violation of human rights, corruption) or controversies. ■ Positive/best-in-class screening, where sectors, companies or projects are selected because of their positive sustainability performance relative to their industry peers.
ESG integration	Ongoing consideration of ESG factors within an investment analysis and decision-making process with the aim of improving risk-adjusted returns.	
Thematic investing	Selecting assets to access specified trends.	Thematic investing is underpinned by the belief that economic, technological, demographic, cultural, political, environmental, social and regulatory dynamics are key drivers of investment risk and return (GSIA, 2023).

Table 3.1 (Continued)

Approach	*Definition (from CFA Institute, GSIA and PRI (2023))*	*Additional Notes*
Stewardship	The use of investor rights and influence to protect and enhance overall long-term value for clients and beneficiaries, including the common economic, social and environmental assets on which their interests depend.	Stewardship approaches can include some or all of the following (GSIA, 2023): ■ Engagement with investees, where investors engage with current or potential investees or issuers with the aims of raising awareness, sharing information and insights and/or improving policies, practices, processes or performance on relevant sustainability issues. ■ Use of formal shareholder rights, where investors use their formal rights as a shareholder (e.g. to vote on company issues, to call emergency meetings, to submit proposals to be voted on at the company's annual general meeting) to address or encourage action on a specific sustainability-related issue. ■ Collaboration, where investors work with other investors to amplify their influence on a specific issue or topic. ■ Policy engagement, where investors engage with policymakers to encourage policy or regulatory changes on relevant sustainability-related issues. This can include responding to public consultations, attending government hearings and holding meetings with policymakers. ■ Engagement with the investment chain, where investors negotiate with others in the investment chain. For example, asset owners that outsource all or part of their investment function can embed sustainable investment principles into how they choose and monitor their external investment managers, consultants and other service providers.
Impact investing	Investing with the intention of generating positive and measurable social and/or environmental impacts alongside financial returns.	

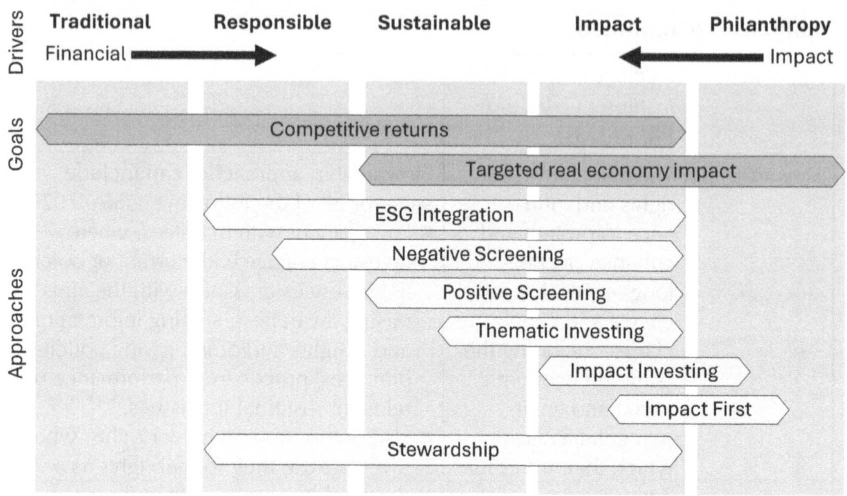

Figure 3.1 Illustration of Sustainable Investment Strategies

Source: Adapted from PRI (2013)

Later chapters in this book analyse and describe the different sustainable investment strategies in more detail. In particular, Chapter 6 reviews the links between sustainable investment strategies and financial performance literature, Chapter 7 discusses the impacts that might result from different sustainable investment strategies and Chapter 10 analyses investor collaborations and collective action.

Key Concepts

In this section we focus on three key concepts – materiality, timeframes and diversification – that shape and inform how sustainable investment is implemented in practice.

Key Concept 1: Financial Materiality

Materiality is one of the most important concepts in investment practice. In very general terms, materiality refers to the criteria used by investors to identify and prioritise those factors that are relevant to their decision-making and, as importantly, to filter out those that are not considered relevant.

In the sustainable investment literature, the terms single materiality and double materiality are widely used to describe the factors that are relevant to the decisions being made. Single materiality (or financial materiality) is widely used to describe the financial significance of a particular issue (see Box 3.2). The definition of what is financially material helps companies determine whether information about an item, transaction or other event should be provided to users of its financial statements (IFRS, 2018).

Box 3.2 Defining Financial Materiality

The IFRS Foundation sets standards used globally for financial reporting that improve the communication between companies and investors. IFRS states:

> Information is material if omitting, misstating or obscuring it could reasonably be expected to influence the decisions that the primary users of general purpose financial statements make on the basis of those financial statements, which provide financial information about a specific reporting entity.
>
> (IFRS, 2018)

There is no consensus on the precise threshold or quantitative level at which an issue becomes 'financially material.' To determine materiality, entities and auditors often specify a percentage of a key financial performance measure (e.g. profit before tax, operating income, asset valuations). These percentages differ depending on the company or sector, but typical corporate examples are 5% of gross profit (i.e. an issue is considered financially material if it has, or could have, an impact – positive or negative – of 5% or more on gross profit), or 2–3% of operating income or turnover (Muc, 2024; Sullivan, 2011). For investors, an issue could be defined as material if it could affect the value of the portfolio by 1% (Muc, 2024) or has a material impact on an individual company within the portfolio (Sullivan, 2011). Of course, in practice, financial metrics are only part of the picture and companies and investors will also be interested in other aspects of company or portfolio importance; for example, for a media company, investors may be interested in total subscriber numbers and in subscriber churn.

The limitation of the concept of single materiality is that issues considered important or significant by stakeholders (unless these issues manifest themselves as financial impacts on a business through, for example, regulation, damage to brand or reputation, increased costs) may be excluded from investment analysis and from investor-company dialogue (see, generally, Sullivan, 2011). That is, just because an issue is of concern to a particular stakeholder group does not mean that investors will conclude that the issue is or could be financially material. Investors need to understand how the issue in question might affect the company or other entity they have invested in, and to assess how financially significant these effects might be. For example, while it is possible to make an assessment of the extent to which a mining company has complied with international guidelines on resettlement, the question investors then need to ask is whether the company's approach to resettlement will affect the company's ability to obtain the licences or permits it needs, or whether mine construction will be delayed or production disrupted as a consequence of community dissatisfaction with the resettlement process.

To address the limitations of single materiality, double materiality considers both financial impacts and broader social and environmental impacts. There are clearly links between the two concepts, given that at least some of the sustainability-related impacts of an organisation may become financially material over time.

The concept of double materiality has been particularly influential in relation to the development of corporate sustainability reporting, with the European Union (see Box 3.3), the Global Reporting Initiative (Global Reporting Initiative (GRI), n.d.) and others expecting companies and other entities to report on (a) the impacts they have on society and the environment, and hence their contributions towards sustainable development, and (b) the financial implications of sustainability issues. The aim is to encourage companies to take responsibility for their impact on society and the environment (not just for those impacts that are considered to be financially material). It also acknowledges that a company's impact on the world can be significant, even if this impact does not directly affect the bottom line. Double materiality (and the expectation that companies will report in this way) reflects the reality that financial reporting (even if it requires reporting on financially material sustainability issues) is unlikely to meet the needs of stakeholders concerned about the impacts of a company on society or the environment.

Box 3.3 The European Union's View on Double Materiality

The European Union's Sustainability Reporting Standards (ESRS) state (European Union, 2023; for more detailed guidance see European Financial Reporting Advisory Group (EFRAG) (2023)):

- "Double materiality has two dimensions, namely: impact materiality and financial materiality."
- "A sustainability matter is material from an impact perspective when it pertains to the undertaking's material actual or potential, positive or negative impacts on people or the environment over the short-, medium- or long-term."
- "Information is considered material for primary users of general-purpose financial reports if omitting, misstating or obscuring that information could reasonably be expected to influence decisions that they make on the basis of the undertaking's sustainability statement."

> "A sustainability matter is material from a financial perspective if it triggers or could reasonably be expected to trigger material financial effects on the undertaking. This is the case when a sustainability matter generates risks or opportunities that have a material influence, or could reasonably be expected to have a material influence, on the undertaking's development, financial position, financial performance, cash flows, access to finance or cost of capital over the short-, medium- or long-term."

Key Concept 2: Timeframes

Discussions around materiality cannot be separated from discussions around timeframes. In practice, for most investors, the timeframe of interest is relatively short term. Most attention tends to be paid to how the company and its share price will perform over the next one or two years at most. Issues that may impact the business beyond that time tend to receive much less attention (Janicka *et al.*, 2021).

Long-term investors face pressure to balance adequate short-term returns – reflected by the emphasis on annual performance targets and quarterly reviews – with long-term objectives. In practice, most aspects of investment, from risk management measures, to investment mandates, to board and manager turnover, operate in the short term (European Securities and Markets Authority (ESMA), 2020). The practical consequence is that investors are likely to be very interested in a sustainability issue that has a material impact over the next one to two years but less interested in an issue that may have a bigger impact over a longer period (Semmler *et al.*, 2024). This is due to a number of factors: (a) investors discount the future (i.e. they use a non-zero positive discount rate to account for future impacts on the business); (b) investors frequently exclude high consequence but low probability events from their calculations (on the grounds that the likelihood of these occurring over the timeframe of interest to the investor are relatively low); (c) investors are generally sceptical that governments will act to correct market failures; and (d) investors assume that, even if governments do act, firms that are disadvantaged will be compensated in some way (Sullivan, 2011).

This does not mean that investors are unaware of or uninterested in these longer-term issues, simply that they will tend to focus on short-term factors in their investment decisions, and will often assume that long-term effects will play out over timeframes that allow companies sufficient time to adapt their strategies or business models.

Key Concept 3: Diversification

In broad terms, diversification is the process of allocating capital in a way that reduces an investor's exposure to any one particular asset or risk. This can be done through spreading investments across different asset classes such as stocks, bonds and real estate, and across different sectors and geographic regions. The benefit of diversification is that it lowers the potential for significant losses by mitigating the impact of any single investment – be that a company, a sector, a geographic region, an asset class – performing poorly. It also means that investment performance is, generally, more consistent over time as losses in one area are often counterbalanced by gains in another. For example, if a large copper mine is forced to close due to water constraints, any losses may, partially or wholly, be offset by the higher copper prices that result from the closure.

From a sustainability perspective, portfolio diversification has two implications. The first is that investors – in particular those large asset owners who can be described as 'universal owners' because their portfolios are, effectively, a representative slice of the economy (see, generally, Hawley and Williams, 2000; Urwin, 2011) – essentially depend on the performance of the economy as a whole. These investors are exposed to the consequences of systemic issues such as climate change and cannot avoid these consequences simply by selling assets or avoiding particular sectors, geographies or activities (Irvin, 2022). They, therefore, should have an interest in taking action to reduce the negative externalities (and to increase the positive externalities) associated with their investment portfolios, although the extent to which they do so will be strongly shaped by the costs of taking action and by the benefits that are likely to accrue to them (Irvin, 2022). The second implication is that while diversification may increase the number of companies or other entities in a portfolio that are exposed to these systemic issues, it may also mean that systemic sustainability-related issues and risks are seen as less material because they are, in part, managed through diversification. That is, even though these issues may be financially material to an individual company, they may not be material to a portfolio holding many hundreds of companies.

It is relevant to note that diversification is also used by companies to manage their risks. The logic is similar: by diversifying their supply chains, their operations, their business activities and their geographies, companies can achieve a degree of insulation (or protection) from many environmental and social risks. For example, if we take the case of an electricity generating company with a number of generating facilities, if a storm or extreme weather event means that one of its power stations is unable to operate, the company will generally be able to compensate for this through increasing production at other facilities. The company may also benefit from the higher wholesale electricity prices that generally follow when the available power generation capacity is reduced.

Concluding Comments

As a broad generalisation, the emphasis of financial materiality in investment analysis, the relatively short investment time horizon of most investment analysts and the use of diversification as a risk management tool may limit investors' willingness to provide financing to address global social and environmental problems. Even those pension funds and foundations with long-term, economy-wide interests tend to focus on short-term financial performance; a common refrain is that asset owners offer three-year mandates, with one-year performance targets and three-monthly performance reviews. While the intention may be to invest and think long term, in practice the way that pension fund assets are managed often emphasises short-term performance and returns, signalling to asset managers and companies that longer-term financial performance and sustainability-related impacts are of less importance.

While this is a relatively discouraging conclusion, it is only part of the picture. The fact that sustainability-related issues can be important sources of risk and of opportunity for companies means that investors are interested in how companies are managing these issues. In addition, regulation, sustainability-related reporting requirements and client expectations have all been important drivers for the growth in sustainable investment and for the number of investment organisations making commitments to sustainable investment.

Implications for Practitioners

1. Ensure that you are clear about why sustainability-related issues are seen as important by your organisation. Is it because of the financial significance of these issues, because of client demand or because of regulation?
2. Recognise that establishing a sustainable investment strategy (e.g. ESG integration, stewardship, screening) is only a start. You need to understand the internal and external factors that shape how the strategy is implemented in practice and you need to ensure that these factors do not undermine the implementation of the strategy or the delivery of your organisation's goals. Among the factors you need to consider (and, in turn, manage) are the following:
    a. The investment and other objectives for the funds and products that you manage or invest in.
    b. The importance investment analysts and portfolio managers assign to sustainability-related issues in their investment research and decision-making processes.
    c. The specific sustainability-related issues that are identified and assessed in the investment process, and the sustainability issues that are not considered to be financially material.
    d. The timeframes over which performance is assessed and managed.
    e. How trade-offs and tensions between financially material issues and significant sustainability-related issues are managed.

3. Adopt a proactive approach to communicating your organisation's views on sustainability to investment managers, to clients and to investee companies, and show interest in the sustainability-related data and information provided by clients, companies and investment managers. It is easy for these organisations to assume that sustainability-related issues are not important if these issues are not routinely and explicitly raised in meetings and in reports.

References

CFA Institute, Global Sustainable Investment Alliance (GSIA) and Principles for Responsible Investment (PRI) (2023, November), *Definitions for Responsible Investment Approaches*, www.gsi-alliance.org/wp-content/uploads/2023/10/ESG-Terminology-Report_Online.pdf

European Commission (2025), 'Overview of Sustainable Finance', https://finance.ec.europa.eu/sustainable-finance/overview-sustainable-finance_en (last viewed 6 April 2025).

European Financial Reporting Advisory Group (EFRAG) (2023), *Implementation Guidance: Materiality Assessment*, www.efrag.org/sites/default/files/sites/webpublishing/SiteAssets/IG%201%20Materiality%20Assessment_final.pdf

European Securities and Markets Authority (ESMA) (2020), *Short-Termism Pressures from Financial Markets (ESMA, Paris)*, www.esma.europa.eu/sites/default/files/trv_2020_1-short_termism_pressures_from_financial_markets.pdf

European Union (2023, December 22), 'Commission Delegated Regulation (EU) 2023/2772 of 31 July 2023 Supplementing Directive 2013/34/EU of the European Parliament and of the Council as Regards Sustainability Reporting Standards', *Official Journal of the European Union*, https://eur-lex.europa.eu/legal-content/EN/TXT/HTML/?uri=OJ:L_202302772#:~:text=Specifically%2C%20ESRS%20specify%20the%20information,(b)

Global Reporting Initiative (GRI) (n.d.), *Double Materiality. The Guiding Principle for Sustainability Reporting*, www.globalreporting.org/media/rz1jf4bz/gri-double-materiality-final.pdf

Global Sustainable Investment Alliance (GSIA) (2023), *Global Sustainable Investment Review 2022*, www.gsi-alliance.org/wp-content/uploads/2023/12/GSIA-Report-2022.pdf

Hawley, J. and Williams, A. (2000), *The Rise of Fiduciary Capitalism: How Institutional Investors Can Make Corporate America More Democratic* (University of Pennsylvania Press, Philadelphia).

IFRS (2018), *Definition of Material: Amendments to IAS 1 and IAS 8*, www.ifrs.org/content/dam/ifrs/project/definition-of-materiality/definition-of-material-feedback-statement.pdf

Irvin, D. (2022), 'Universal Owners, Shareholder Primacy, and Stakeholderism', *Emory Corporate Governance & Accountability Review*, Vol. 10, No. 1, pp. 104–143, https://scholarlycommons.law.emory.edu/ecgar/vol10/iss1/4

Janicka, M., Sajnóg, A. and Sosnowski, T. (2021), 'Short-Termism – The Causes and Consequences for the Sustainable Development of the Financial Markets', in Leal Filho, W., Krasnov, E. and Gaeva, D. (eds.), *Innovations and Traditions for Sustainable Development.* World Sustainability Series (Springer, Cham), pp. 485–501, https://doi.org/10.1007/978-3-030-78825-4_29

Muc, M. (2024, November 22), 'Materiality in IFRS Standards and Financial Reporting', *IFRS Community*, https://ifrscommunity.com/knowledge-base/materiality/#:~:text=Materiality%20is%20a%20fundamental%20concept,labels%20them%20as%20minimum%20requirements

Principles for Responsible Investment (PRI) (2013), *Understanding the Impact of Your Investments: Measuring Environmental and Social Performance*, www.unpri.org/thematic-and-impact-investing/understanding-the-impact-of-your-investments/141.article

Principles for Responsible Investment (PRI) (2022), *What Is Responsible Investment?*, www.unpri.org/introductory-guides-to-responsible-investment/what-is-responsible-investment/4780.article

Principles for Responsible Investment (PRI) (2025), 'Regulation Database', www.unpri.org/policy/global-policy/regulation-database (last viewed 1 February 2025).

Semmler, W., Lessmann, K., Tahri, I. and Brago, J. (2024), 'Green Transition, Investment Horizon, and Dynamic Portfolio Decisions', *Annals of Operations Research*, Vol. 334, pp. 265–286, https://doi.org/10.1007/s10479-022-05018-2

Sullivan, R. (2011), *Valuing Corporate Responsibility: How Do Investors Really Use Corporate Responsibility Information?* (Greenleaf Publishing, Sheffield).

Sullivan, R. and Mackenzie, C. (eds.) (2006), *Responsible Investment* (Greenleaf Publishing, Sheffield).

UK Sustainable Investment and Finance Association (UKSIF) (2025), 'What Is Sustainable Finance?', https://uksif.org/learn/what-is-sustainable-investing/ (last viewed 6 April 2025).

Urwin, R. (2011), 'Pension Funds as Universal Owners: Opportunity Beckons and Leadership Calls', *Rotman International Journal of Pension Management*, Vol. 4, No. 1, pp. 26–33, https://papers.ssrn.com/sol3/papers.cfm?abstract_id=1829271#

Whelan, T., Atz, U., Van Holt, T. and Clark, C. (2021), *ESG and Financial Performance: Uncovering the Relationship by Aggregating Evidence from 1,000 Plus Studies Published between 2015–2020* (NYU Stern, New York), www.stern.nyu.edu/sites/default/files/assets/documents/NYU-RAM_ESG-Paper_2021%20Rev_0.pdf

Chapter 4

Why Do We Disagree About Sustainable Finance?

Richard Perkins and Krista Tukiainen

Introduction

In 2022 the European Commission sparked controversy by proposing the inclusion of certain gas and nuclear activities within its EU Taxonomy Regulation, a scheme that classifies whether economic activities are environmentally sustainable. As part of a wider Sustainable Finance Package, the Taxonomy aims to steer investment towards sustainable economic activities consistent with the EU's environmental and social objectives. The Commission argued that investment in gas and nuclear could accelerate the transition to a low-carbon economy. However, non-governmental organisations (NGOs) such as Greenpeace, WWF and BUND promptly criticised the proposal, citing the negative environmental impacts of these activities. Members of the European Parliament went on to approve the Commission's proposal, only for several NGOs and at least one Member State to initiate legal action.

The intention in starting with this example is not to take sides or to pronounce on who was right or wrong. Indeed, as we argue below, such binaries can be unhelpful. Rather, the aim is to illustrate a wider point: sustainable finance is the subject of considerable disagreement.

 DOI: 10.4324/9781003467632-4

Our goal in this chapter is to lift the lid on these disagreements. We shed light on three main aspects: (1) the *what* – that is, the matters over which people disagree; (2) the *why* – the underlying reasons actors disagree; and (3) the *how* – ways to address those disagreements. Inspiration for the chapter comes from the authors' experience of sustainable finance – one of us as an academic, researcher and educator, the other as a practitioner, advocate and entrepreneur. We have both encountered a wide range of disagreements in the field. Yet we have also been struck by participants' failure to recognise the underlying causes of their differences. We have moreover observed how this can lead to seemingly intractable positions, with protagonists talking past one another, and to disagreements that do not resolve themselves in ways conducive to public sustainability goals.

It is against this backdrop that the chapter encourages a more reflexive approach. It invites readers to ask questions of themselves and of others when engaging in debates and controversies within the field of sustainable finance. A core theme – inspired by the work of Hulme (2009) – is that we are better placed to move beyond unhelpful divisions by first understanding *why* we disagree. For practitioners, grasping the roots of disagreement can help clarify strategy, reduce frictions and increase alignment with both public and private goals.

The rest of the chapter is organised as follows. We begin by unpacking the different subjects of disagreement. The next section locates disagreement as an inherent feature of sustainable finance's character as an 'essentially contested concept', followed by an examination of the implications of contestation and contestability. We then delve deeper, explaining how three underlying attributes – values, beliefs and interests – give rise to disagreements. Next, we highlight why understanding these attributes is important for moving beyond labels such as 'wrong' and 'right'. The penultimate section considers how disagreements can be addressed. The final section offers some reflections on the implications for investment practitioners.

What Do We Disagree About?

A key claim in the opening section is that sustainable finance is the subject of ongoing disagreement. This raises an important question: what exactly do we disagree about? The answer is many things! To make sense of this diversity, we identify three broad subjects of disagreement, although these may intersect in practice.

First, debate centres on *whether* financial actors should take action on sustainability issues and, if so, to what end. This is not simply a question of technical capability or regulatory requirements. Rather, it concerns the basic purpose of finance. One view is that the financial system's primary function is the efficient allocation of capital to maximise risk-adjusted returns. From this perspective, sustainability considerations are admissible – if at all – only to the extent that they are financially material (see further Chapters 3 and 5). This position remains influential in legal and regulatory interpretations of fiduciary duty and underpins resistance to sustainability mandates perceived as political or ideological. Conversely, others believe that financial actors should contribute to positive environmental and social outcomes even when the financial case is less obvious or measurable. This position supports strategies such as climate-aligned investing or capital reallocation to underfinanced sustainability goals.

At the heart of these differences lies the question of responsibilities. Should the responsibilities of financial actors include contributions to public sustainability goals, or are such concerns distractions from their core objectives? Disagreements over these issues frequently surface in debates about the relative importance of single and double materiality in sustainable finance, but they also arise in other contexts. For example, a point of contention is whether central banks should pursue climate objectives as part of their mandates and, if so, the scope of their intervention (Yates, 2024). This tension was exemplified in debates over the European Central Bank's (ECB) incorporation of climate criteria into its corporate bond purchasing programme. While some praised the move as a necessary adaptation to systemic risk, others criticised it as an overreach of the ECB's mandate.

Disagreements do not stop when actors agree on the need to incorporate sustainability concerns into decision-making. A second subject of disagreement centres on *conceptions* of sustainability. People differ in how they understand and define sustainability, and in what they deem to be, or not to be, sustainable. Rival conceptions can trigger disputes about whether a particular entity, activity or security aligns with a given definition. Green bonds illustrate these differences. Many disagreements over green bonds stem from divergent understandings – among market participants and other actors such as NGOs – of what qualifies as 'green'. The 2017 green bond issued by Repsol, a Spanish oil-and-gas firm, is instructive. Proponents of the bond justified the green label on the grounds that the bond contributed to climate goals by reducing greenhouse gas emissions. Others disputed its green credentials, arguing that financing was prolonging the life of carbon-intensive infrastructure (Cripps, 2017).

Third, actors disagree about *means* – that is, how sustainability-related objectives can, or should, be realised. Sustainable finance embodies many different, and sometimes conflicting, views on the best investment strategies, financing instruments and policies to address sustainability outcomes and/or sustainability-related financial goals. These differences about the *how* can fuel controversy. The divestment versus engagement debate illustrates these dynamics. Supporters of divestment have argued that it can be a powerful lever for achieving long-term emissions reductions, for instance, by constraining capital available to fossil-fuel firms and building support for more ambitious public policies. Critics have suggested divestment may have limited influence on real-world emissions and can run counter to fiduciary considerations. Instead, many institutional investors have advocated strategies such as engagement to achieve sustainability goals, with divestment positioned as a last resort.

Disputes over means are not only about which *types* of investment strategy, financing instrument or policies should be pursued. They also arise out of different views about how specific examples of these – say, a particular financing instrument – should be *configured*. This can be seen in debates about whether sustainability-linked bonds (SLBs) should have a step-up (i.e., rewarding issuers for meeting targets) or step-down (i.e., penalising issuers) financial structure. Here, the disagreement is about instrument design and configuration, rather than instrument choice. Controversies over means may also encompass questions of *who*. These issues have come to the fore in relation to the regulation, and self-regulation, of sustainable finance. Disagreement have arisen, for instance, about the role that governments should play in delivering on the ambitions of sustainable finance.

These three subjects – focusing on whether, what and how – are not exhaustive. Yet they capture many of the main areas of disagreement. Table 4.1 summarises the key actors involved. An important feature of sustainable finance is that disagreements do not always involve critique from voices outside mainstream finance, such as NGOs, publics or political and bureaucratic actors. In many instances, disputes arise among financial-market participants themselves or with other industry players, such as ratings agencies and portfolio companies. Disagreements may play out within the same jurisdiction but can also transcend national borders – for example between actors in the Global South and those in the Global North.

Sustainable Finance as an Essentially Contested Concept

One way of making sense of disagreements is to recognise that they may be *inherent* to sustainable finance. This is because sustainable finance can be usefully understood as an 'essentially contested concept'. Walter Gallie (1956 : 169) first introduced the notion of essentially contested concepts to describe a class of issues that are prone to 'endless dispute'. More recently, efforts have been made to link the idea of essentially contested concepts to sustainable finance (Dimmelmeier, 2023), as well as to related strategies such as impact investing (Hockerts *et al.*, 2022) and concepts such as materiality (Oll *et al.*, 2024). Several defining features of essentially contested concepts can help us understand disagreement within the field of sustainable finance:

- **Essentially contested concepts are appraisive.** They involve judgements about something that is positively valued. In this case, the 'valued achievement' (Gallie, 1956 : 171) is sustainability. Many (though not all)

Table 4.1 Actors Involved in Disagreements

Actor	*Example*
Financial intermediaries (asset managers, banks, venture capital firms etc.)	Disagreements between asset managers regarding the merits of a shareholder resolution in advancing real economy sustainability objectives.
Service providers (ratings agencies, index providers etc.)	Disagreements between an ESG ratings provider and a rated company over the ratings provider's evaluation (or assessment) of the company.
Real economy corporates (oil-and-gas companies, agribusinesses etc.)	Rejection by a company's management of a climate-related (e.g. lobbying) shareholder proposal.
Non-governmental organisations (e.g. campaigning organisations focused on particular environmental and/or social issues)	NGO criticism of third-party assessment methodologies used in finance to evaluate 1.5°C aligned pathways.
Membership initiatives (e.g. trade associations and investor coalitions)	Disagreements between a trade association and one or more of its members about the desirable stringency of environmental requirements.
Financial and other public regulators	Disagreements between financial regulators and asset managers over the content of mandatory sustainability fund labelling requirements.
Political actors (e.g. elected politicians)	Criticism by politicians about the compatibility of investors' climate commitments with investors' fiduciary duty.
Journalists	Criticism of green definitions used by banks in meeting their climate pledges.
Academics	Challenges to blended finance and de-risking approaches promoted by international financial institutions on the grounds of justice considerations.

Source: Authors

people would agree that sustainability is a good thing. Yet disagreements may arise because of differences of opinion – often value judgements – as to what constitutes 'good' or 'desirable' sustainability (Hockerts *et al.*, 2022).

- **Essentially contested concepts are internally complex.** They embody many possible elements. Sustainable finance can therefore encompass an array of environmental, social and economic features and objectives, reflecting the multivalent character of sustainability itself (Connelly, 2007).

Internal complexity, in turn, lends itself to a wide range of conceptions of sustainable finance, depending on how actors attribute importance to individual elements (Oll *et al.*, 2024). For instance, some actors may place central emphasis on economic aspects, framing sustainable finance as a strategy to maximise risk-weighted returns. Others may see it exclusively as a path to generating positive environmental or social impact. Still others may include varying combinations of economic, social and environmental components and objectives in their conception of sustainable finance. Yet, while essentially contested concepts manifest in diverse understandings, applications and evaluative criteria, they are nevertheless recognisable as belonging to the same overarching category. This helps to explain why diverse investment strategies – from ESG integration through to impact investing – are frequently bracketed under the umbrella of sustainable finance.

- **Essentially contested concepts are defined by their openness.** Simply put, the meaning and boundaries of essentially contested concepts are not fixed. Because of their openness, concepts such as sustainable finance may be reinterpreted and revised over time (Dimmelmeier, 2023; Dumas and Louche, 2016). Such changes in the conceptions of essentially contested concepts can be a source of disagreement, as actors dispute their appropriateness. For instance, attempts to bring transition finance – mobilising capital for firms in hard-to-abate sectors to become less carbon-intensive – into the sustainable-finance arena have been met with opposition from certain actors.
- **Essentially contested concepts are characterised by 'reciprocal recognition'** (Collier *et al.*, 2006). Different actors may be aware that other parties are also using the concept of sustainable finance, albeit in ways that differ from their own. Moreover, to demarcate and defend their own conception, they may employ the concept aggressively and defensively in contrast to others' usage. This can result in competition between parties seeking to advance their own specific framing of the concept. Ongoing disagreements over the meaning and boundaries of concepts such as impact investing, transition finance, materiality and green bonds can be understood in these terms (Höchstädter and Scheck, 2015; OECD, 2022; Oll *et al.*, 2024; Perkins, 2021).

When viewed as an essentially contested concept, it is unsurprising that sustainable finance is the subject of disagreement. Debate, controversy and contestation are not flaws waiting to be fixed. Rather, they are integral to sustainable finance, reflecting the complex, open and value-laden nature of the concept. While it is possible to talk about sustainable finance as a singular category, there are many different conceptions of the basic idea of integrating sustainability considerations into finance. Frictions between these conceptions lie at the heart of disagreement within sustainable finance.

What Are the Implications of Contestation?

There are different ways of interpreting sustainable finance's essentially contested nature. One is to regard it as an impediment to the normative goal of sustainability. The very malleability of sustainable finance means that it runs the risk of misuse by unscrupulous actors. Profit-driven financial institutions can exploit ambiguity through sustainability-themed products, services and assets that contribute little to public sustainability goals (see Chapter 11).

Disagreement that takes the form of public critique may also discourage financial actors from engaging with sustainable finance, for fear of reputational damage or legal challenges. The issue of greenhushing is relevant here (Falchi *et al.*, 2022). Disagreements may also serve as a 'dangerous distraction' (Fancy, 2021). For example, technical disputes about whether an asset manager's net-zero target is Paris-aligned might divert attention from more fundamental questions about the adequacy of government climate policy and its implementation.

Another way of approaching the essentially contested nature of sustainable finance is to recognise its generative potential. One upside of the flexible, open-ended nature of sustainable finance is that it can enrol a broad range of actors. Sustainable finance functions as a boundary object (Box 4.1), allowing a diversity of market, civil and state actors to work together in the shared pursuit of sustainability (Bowker *et al.*, 2016). These include actors with very different conceptions of, and appetites for, sustainability (Ahlström and Monciardini, 2022). This bridging function is important if we accept that meeting public sustainability goals will require the participation of a wide range of financial-market participants. It is also important in view of the potential for such actors to deepen their commitment to more impactful sustainability over time through engagement, reflection and learning.

Box 4.1 What Are Boundary Objects?

Boundary objects are things such as organisations, objects, categories and discourses. They are flexible enough to be adapted and applied in a range of different settings, while retaining sufficient coherence to maintain a common identity across varied applications (Star and Griesemer, 1989). Concepts such as natural capital, green buildings, resilience and environmental justice are examples of boundary objects within the domain of sustainability. Boundary objects enable actors occupying different 'social worlds' to co-operate by providing a common language, set of practices and shared space for action (Fernández Chulián *et al.*, 2025).

Sustainable finance can be interpreted as a domain in which a range of market, state and civil actors work to integrate sustainability concerns into finance. Participants may have very different interpretations of, and goals for, sustainable finance, and their practical usage and concrete applications are disparate. Yet, as a boundary object, sustainable finance allows varied individuals, organisations and institutions to participate in a shared project despite the lack of consensus on what sustainable finance is and the ends it serves.

The potential upside of interpretive flexibility can be seen in the case of green bonds – which themselves can be understood as a boundary object within the broader domain of sustainable and green finance. The market for green bonds has grown rapidly by enabling a wide range of issuers and investors to participate, including actors with very different ambitions and conceptions of what qualifies as green. One downside – from the normative perspective of advancing public sustainability goals – of such flexibility is that the green-bond space has been accommodating of very 'light green' bonds whose substantive environmental contribution may be limited (Perkins, 2021; Schutter *et al.*, 2021).

Contestation can also be instrumental in clarifying what should, and should not, be considered sustainable. Returning to the example of Repsol, the criticism evoked by its 2017 green bond helped draw boundaries around the kinds of projects oil-and-gas companies could legitimately finance through green bonds, or whether they could issue bonds considered green at all. Contestation may also be instrumental in raising the bar regarding the ambitions of sustainable finance. Criticism of the credibility of net-zero targets has led to efforts – by investor associations and coalitions such as the Net-Zero Asset Owner Alliance (NZAOA) – to revise protocols for measuring carbon emissions.

The very fact that sustainable finance is contestable, and indeed contested, is also important from the perspective of democratic principles. To consider why, imagine a situation in which there was no debate, no disagreement and no critique of sustainable finance. Who would decide what is considered sustainable? What might happen if this actor were captured by narrow, sectional interests? What if there were no means for important stakeholders – such as communities negatively affected by 'sustainable' investments – to voice their concerns? The point is that disagreement and dissensus are integral to the politics of sustainability and to competition over social, environmental and economic issues in plural, democratic societies (Baker, 2016).

This is not to downplay economic, structural and other inequalities, which mean that certain actors may be better placed to influence the outcome of democratic politics (Schütze and Stede, 2024; Tischer and Ferrando, 2024). Yet democratic considerations remind us that the ambition should not be to neuter disagreement altogether. Instead, the goal should be to engage difference productively in ways that clarify and advance public interests.

What Lies Beneath

Up to this point, we have located disagreement in sustainable finance as stemming from its nature as an essentially contested concept. Yet fully understanding the underlying reasons requires us to delve deeper. More specifically, we suggest that disagreements in sustainable finance are fundamentally rooted in three attributes: values, beliefs and interests. These may be held by individuals, organisations, governments or other collectives. The crucial point is that disagreements – which reveal themselves in critique and opposition – are invariably expressive of underlying differences in actors' values, beliefs and interests.

Values, beliefs and interests are intertwined. Values inform both beliefs and interests, while beliefs help to shape interests. In an important sense, interests can be understood as the practical embodiment of people's underlying values and beliefs. This nested relationship is depicted in Figure 4.1. While recognising their interrelatedness, this threefold division – of values, beliefs and interests – is nevertheless useful in making visible conceptually distinct attributes that might otherwise be obscured by superficial descriptors such as 'differences of opinion' or 'different ways of looking at things'. In the rest of this section, we unpack each of these attributes, explaining their role in giving rise to disagreements.

Values

Values can be understood as people's ideals about desirable goals and behaviours (Steg and de Groot, 2012). Values matter because they shape what people think is important, their priorities and their expectations of the kind of economy, society and environment to which we should aspire. Non-exhaustive examples of values

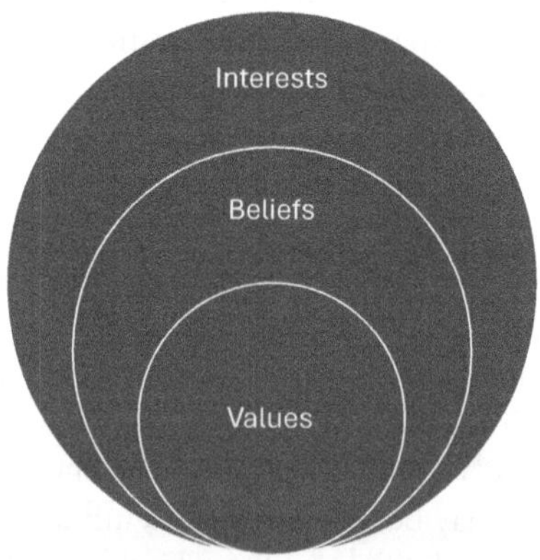

Figure 4.1 The Relationship between Values, Beliefs and Interests

Source: Authors

in the domain of sustainability include social equity, accountability, responsibility, environmental protection and economic growth.

Many disputes in sustainable finance can ultimately be traced to values. Values mean that people may identify and frame sustainability differently. This is important in view of our earlier discussion of how disagreements stem from the internally complex nature of essentially contested concepts. Because of their values, individuals may prioritise certain elements of sustainability over others. Some actors place greater importance on environmental and social aspects and goals of sustainable finance, while others place greater weight on economic aspects. Disputes rooted in these differences are sometimes presented as a clash between *values* (i.e., non-monetary goals) and *value* (i.e., monetary goals) (Starks, 2023). Yet we suggest that they are better understood as expressions of different sets of values and of the weight people attribute to them. Tensions between economic values, on the one hand, and environmental and social values, on the other, can be seen in debates over the importance of inward-impact (financial) materiality and outward-impact (environmental and social) materiality in sustainable finance. Values also lie at the heart of the ESG backlash in the United States (Baumüller and Sopp, 2021; Oll *et al.*, 2024). One way of interpreting criticism of sustainable investment by 'anti-ESG' constituencies – such as the Heritage Foundation – is therefore as a manifestation of the primacy of their economic values.

Disagreements within sustainable finance may also result from differences in the importance people ascribe to particular social or environmental aspects of sustainability. A case in point is the disagreements that have arisen over carbon credits, such as those established under Article 6 of the Paris Agreement – disagreements that are symptomatic of wider tensions within sustainable finance between environmental and social priorities. What matters for many supporters of carbon credits is that they provide a vehicle for advancing mitigation goals. Their worth is rooted in environmental values and in the importance of stabilising the climate system. One criticism of carbon credits is that they may imperil Indigenous and other communities in the Global South, who may find their land sacrificed for climate mitigation projects. At the heart of these concerns are social values and the importance of livelihoods, human rights and justice considerations. These critics may similarly value climate stabilisation, but not at the expense of social considerations.

This example further illustrates how values are evaluative, serving as guiding principles for what people regard as good and bad, and right and wrong. Different people may view the same sustainability-related investment, activity or policy through the lens of their own values. In this way, values can set the stage for disagreement by informing how people evaluate the worth, appropriateness or rightfulness of things. For instance, two investors may have different attitudes towards a sustainability fund, depending on the degree to which it aligns with their own values and with what they hold to be important.

Beliefs

Beliefs can be understood as convictions or accepted truths that people hold. They inform how people interpret and make sense of complex realities and guide their decision-making and behaviour. Beliefs can take different forms, ranging from moral beliefs through to empirical, scientific and policy beliefs about the world (Sabatier and Weible, 2007).

How people understand sustainability problems, their causes and who is to blame is shaped by their beliefs. For example, individuals may hold different causal beliefs – assumptions about the reasons for unsustainable behaviour. Take the case of climate change. One common belief is that financial actors are failing to act sufficiently on climate change because they lack adequate information. Another belief is that the inadequate pricing of greenhouse gas emissions underlies insufficient action on climate change (Ameli *et al.*, 2020). The environmental issue is the same, and it is quite possible for people to subscribe to more than one set of causal beliefs. Yet disagreements can arise when different beliefs cannot easily be reconciled, leading to competing knowledge claims and counterclaims (Sharman and Perkins, 2017).

People's convictions about causes often inform corresponding beliefs about the appropriate response. Those who believe that informational failures lie at the heart of climate inaction within finance might prioritise solutions such as enhanced or mandatory non-financial reporting. Likewise, instruments such as carbon taxes or tradable-permit schemes are likely to be among the preferred policies of actors who characterise the problem as inadequate pricing. The way problems are defined therefore has consequences for the solutions judged appropriate. Beliefs about preferred responses may be encapsulated in implicit or explicit theories of change informed by empirical, theoretical and scientific understanding. Theories of change outline how and why a desired outcome is expected to come about. They have become increasingly popular within sustainable finance but have also become the focus of disagreements, reflecting different underlying beliefs about the best way to address sustainability challenges.

Beliefs offer a valuable window onto greenwashing disputes in sustainable finance (see also Chapter 11). Some greenwashing claims result from deliberate attempts by financial actors to create a misleading impression of the true greenness of their activities, products or services. However, greenwashing disputes also arise because of disparate beliefs about the nature, requirements and criteria for sustainability. In other words, people disagree because they have different conceptions of what is sustainable or unsustainable, and of how best to categorise and measure sustainability. The case of Hong Kong Airport Authority's green bond is instructive here (Box 4.2). It reveals how greenwashing disputes can be understood as the product of differing beliefs about what should be included in the frame when evaluating sustainability.

Box 4.2 Airport Authority Hong Kong's (AAHK) Green Bond

A green bond that faced greenwashing claims was issued by Hong Kong's Airport Authority in 2022. The US$1 billion bond formed part of a larger package of financing associated with the construction of a third runway. Proceeds from the sale were earmarked for green buildings (construction of new passenger terminals and facilities and retrofitting of existing buildings); clean transportation (including an airport-wide electric-vehicle fleet and charging facilities); and energy efficiency (including an LED light-replacement programme). Reclaim Finance, a green NGO, labelled the bond 'high-flying greenwashing'. Among the criticisms was the assertion that airport expansion would only increase emissions. The project was also said to threaten endangered dolphin species in the surrounding Hong Kong waters (Reclaim Finance, 2022). Supporters, by contrast, claimed that the bond merited the green label. The activities financed met the usual eligibility criteria and would help to reduce the environmental impact of the airport's operations. None of the proceeds would go towards financing the new runway. The bond also received a Green and Sustainable Finance Certificate (pre-issuance) from the Hong Kong Quality Assurance Agency (Davis and Boey, 2022; Ng, 2022).

How can we make sense of these rival accounts? One interpretation is that Airport Authority Hong Kong's (AAHK) inaugural green bond was a self-serving attempt to curate an impression of greenery for marketing purposes – or indeed to deflect attention from the negative environmental impacts of airport expansion. Reclaim Finance, on this reading, was simply exposing the hypocrisy of the Airport Authority issuing a green bond. A different reading is that the conflicting perspectives reflect differing underlying beliefs about what legitimately qualifies as green. If you believe that what matters is the environmental credentials of the financed activities, the green label may appear justified. Conversely, if you believe that the environmental impacts associated with the issuer's wider business operations (i.e., airline travel) should enter the evaluative frame, the same bond may look more non-green than green.

Readers will no doubt have their own opinions on whether the bond qualifies as green and on the possible motives of the airport operator. The important point is that people may hold different beliefs about what counts as socially or environmentally sustainable, and these differences may, in turn, manifest themselves in greenwashing claims and counterclaims.

People's beliefs are often informed by their underlying values (Hornsey *et al.*, 2016). For example, whether people believe that carbon-intensive sectors, such as livestock agriculture, should be able to access green finance will be shaped by their values. Values also influence a third underlying reason for disagreement: interests.

Interests

Interests refer to the outcomes or goals that actors seek to realise. They are often expressive of the desire for individual or collective gain. Disagreements in sustainable finance can arise when actors pursuing different interests come into conflict with one another.

A broad distinction can be drawn between *private* and *public* interests. Private interests are benefits – often economic – that accrue primarily to specific individuals or groups. For example, government subsidies that increase corporate profits are in the self-interest of private companies (Simmons *et al.*, 2011). Public interests, by contrast, relate to the well-being or betterment of society. Examples relevant here include environmental outcomes such as biodiversity stabilisation and social goals such as gender equality.

One way in which the pursuit of private and public interests fuels disagreement is through competing economic and environmental objectives. These divisions surfaced in the controversy surrounding the EU Taxonomy. Major oil-and-gas companies such as BP and Enel lobbied in favour of including gas as a sustainable economic activity (InfluenceMap, 2022). It was in their economic self-interest to do so, given their dependence on the fuel source and their desire to retain access to a wide pool of capital for future projects. Opposition from several environmental NGOs was rooted in public interests. Their central claim was that financing new gas capacity was 'at odds' with the climate goals of the Paris Agreement and the EU (Reclaim Finance, 2021).

The distinction between private and public interests is often more complex than this example suggests. To begin with, the two may overlap. For example, investors have self-interested reasons to encourage investee companies to reduce their value chain emissions, including by reducing exposure to financially material transition risks. In this case, private interests of safeguarding financial returns are positively aligned with public interests of climate mitigation. Moreover, actors involved in sustainable finance may hold a range of interests that straddle the private–public divide. Multilateral development banks – such as the World Bank and the European Investment Bank (EIB) – seek positive social and environmental impact as well as financial returns (Erforth and Keijzer, 2025). Interests are also rarely homogeneous, even within the same sector. For example, different asset managers may have different interests, reflecting their conceptions of the relevant time horizon over which to optimise returns, beliefs about the materiality of climate risks and the preferences of their clients. Whether private, public or both, a key takeaway is that actors may have interests in particular sustainability goals,

Table 4.2 Values, Beliefs and Interests as Reasons for Disagreement

Attribute	*What is it?*	*Example*
Values	What people hold as important or desirable	Value-based disagreements about whether investors have a responsibility *only* to consider sustainability factors which are financially material in investment decision-making, or both financial *and* social/environmental impact materiality (i.e., double materiality).[1]
Beliefs	People's accepted truths or convictions about the world	Disagreements about which metrics actors believe best capture biodiversity-related risks and impacts in finance.
Interests	Outcomes or benefits which people wish to gain or secure	Disagreements between vulnerable, developing countries (with interests in securing compensation to address the negative impacts of climate change) and developed economies (with interests in limiting their financial and legal liabilities) over financing arrangement for Loss and Damage within the UNFCCC process.

Source: Authors

Note: [1] See Chapter 3 for an explanation of double materiality

policies or instruments (Colgan *et al.*, 2021; Meckling, 2015). Contestation can ensue as they seek to advance their preferred conceptions and solutions aligned with their interests.

Viewed through a rationalist lens of costs and benefits, one might conclude that most disputes in sustainable finance are ultimately rooted in diverging interests. There is a kernel of truth in this. The transition to a sustainable economy creates winners and losers. The stakes are high: large sums of money are involved; sustainability transitions can have far-reaching consequences for the competitiveness of companies, regions and countries; the health of planetary support systems depends on mobilising sufficient finance and aligning financial decision-making; and people's livelihoods – and even lives – are on the line (Nedopil, 2023; Semieniuk *et al.*, 2021; United Nations, 2024). Against this backdrop, sustainable finance is fertile territory for interests to collide.

Yet a narrow focus on interests risks obscuring the extent to which those interests – or, more accurately, *perceived* interests – are shaped by underlying values (Hay, 2011). To take a hypothetical example: someone who values the intrinsic importance of biodiversity may see their self-interest served by nature-positive finance. Table 4.2 summarises the roles of values, beliefs and interests in giving rise to disagreements.

Why Understanding the Underlying Reasons for Disagreement Matters

Taking seriously the role of values, beliefs, and interests helps us better understand controversy in sustainable finance. What may appear to be disputes over facts can mask deeper reasons for disagreement. In other words, when people disagree about sustainable finance, we may be witnessing only the tip of the iceberg.

The debate over divestment is revealing in this respect. It is not uncommon to find financial-market participants frustrated with supporters of fossil-fuel divestment (Murray, 2022). The charge is that the latter are ignoring the 'facts'. These facts are that divestment is unlikely to impact the cost of capital and may simply result in the transfer of ownership from more to less responsible investors. The result: divestment will have little impact on real-world decarbonisation. Yet to view the divestment debate exclusively through the lens of epistemic truths would be to miss an important point. Supporters of divestment may not only subscribe to different factual beliefs. Disagreements between the two sets of actors are also symptomatic of different value commitments. The divestment movement's position is rooted in the premise that it is morally *wrong* to continue to provide finance to perpetuate fossil-fuel production and consumption. This is fundamentally a deontological position whereby actions are judged right or wrong according to whether they conform to a moral norm. Conversely, supporters of alternative strategies such as engagement and voting often take a consequentialist position, wherein acts are judged according to their outcomes.

Both critics and supporters of divestment are right when viewed through the prism of their own set of values, assumptions and goals. Each brings their own logic, reasoning and even confirmatory evidence, and therefore can claim to have justification for their position. However, seen from their own vantage point, the other is wrong.

These observations show why it can be difficult to resolve – or even reconcile – many disagreements. Values and beliefs are often deeply held and not readily amenable to change (Sabatier and Weible, 2007; Steg and de Groot, 2012). Interests, too, can remain entrenched. This helps to explain the protracted nature of disputes in sustainable finance, from the merits of divestment to responsibilities for international climate finance.

Acknowledging the influence of values, beliefs and interests also reveals why seemingly objective science, data and analytics cannot always serve as neutral arbiters. The production of knowledge has a 'backstage' (Skjølsvold, 2013): scientific and related knowledge embodies assumptions and judgements that reflect the values, beliefs and philosophical commitments of its producers. These elements are frequently black-boxed – sealed off and invisible to outsiders (Latour, 1987). An important implication is that, contrary to appearances, science, data and analytics are rarely value-free. Box 4.3 illustrates these issues through the examples of ESG ratings and climate scenarios.

Box 4.3 ESG Ratings and Climate Scenarios in Perspective

ESG ratings are often presented by their providers as authoritative, objective truths. Yet beneath their proprietary methodologies lies a series of value-laden judgements about what constitutes 'good' and 'bad' sustainability practices and performance (Boiral *et al.*, 2020; Chelli and Gendron, 2013). Eccles and Stroehle (2018) show that the construction of ESG ratings – notably what they measure and how these issues are aggregated and weighted (see also Chapter 12) – is shaped by each provider's values and belief systems. These, in turn, are influenced by social origins such as founding members, guiding principles and geography. For example, with organisational roots in mainstream financial analysis and a prioritisation of economic values, MSCI's assessment methodology centrally focuses on identifying financially material sustainability-related risks. Conversely, Vigeo Eiris has its origins in, and around, organisations such as churches, charities and trade unions. With a greater emphasis on social and environmental values, its ratings give particular weight to issues such as human rights and labour, defining materiality broadly in a way that accounts for both financial and social/environmental impact. The point is that, rather than being independent of them, ESG ratings are shaped by values and subjective beliefs.

Similar issues characterise climate scenarios produced by public bodies. Scenarios model changes in technologies, policies, markets and economic aspects that are required to meet a particular emissions pathway or temperature goal. Increasingly used in finance, these scenarios carry the scientific authority of organisations such as the International Energy Agency (IEA) and the Intergovernmental Panel on Climate Change (IPCC). The modelling of climate scenarios involves a complex set of choices about possible futures. However, these are not only technical matters, but also normative ones. Decisions about, for example, the appropriate balance between emissions reduction and carbon removal in climate scenarios involve value judgements (Gaede and Meadowcroft, 2016; Täger, 2022; Tilsted *et al.*, 2023). In other words, seemingly objective scientific truths inscribed in climate scenarios may be infused with subjective, value-laden assumptions.

Another reason why science cannot be relied on to solve disagreement is that it is always possible for people to select, draw on and present specific evidence aligned with their own values, beliefs and interests. This may result from strategic manipulation, with actors consciously cherry-picking science, data and analytics to suit self-serving economic or other interests (Borie and Bracking, 2024). Yet it may also be the product of more unconscious processes. People are therefore known to filter in and filter out information according to whether it aligns with or conflicts with their existing values and beliefs (Zhou and Shen, 2022). That is, they are more likely to show an affinity with, and give greater weight to, scientific evidence, data and analysis that are compatible with their worldview. Equally, they are more likely to ignore, or even actively reject, the same information if it is incompatible with their values, beliefs and interests. People may also be unconsciously biased towards or against certain sources of scientific information, data and analysis, depending on their normative commitments and epistemological predispositions (Brewer and Ley, 2013). What kinds of science, data and analysis are accepted as the truth, or indeed who is deemed a worthy provider of knowledge, may therefore differ.

It is against this backdrop that it is naïve to assume that more or 'better-quality' science, data and analytics can always unify divisions. Indeed, science itself can be the source of disagreement and can even make disputes 'worse' (Sarewitz, 2004). This does not mean that there is no role for science in addressing disagreements. Science can be a valuable input to decision-making and dispute-resolution processes. Nor does it mean that greater weight should not be given to certain scientific claim-makers and claims over others. To take one example: the consensus around the science of anthropogenic climate change expressed by bodies such as the IPCC is more 'robust' than that put forward by dissenting voices (Oreskes, 2004a, 2004b). Yet the discussion here cautions against the idea that disagreement can be resolved by appealing to scientific or technical facts alone (Schön and Rein, 1994).

Addressing Disagreements in Sustainable Finance

What can, or indeed should, be done to move forward when confronted with disagreements in sustainable finance? How can we reduce the possibility of disagreement arising in the first place? And how can we attempt to address disputes when they are grounded in entrenched values, beliefs and interests? Answering these questions in any depth lies beyond the scope of a single chapter. We nevertheless point to two broad areas of consideration. The first centres on ways of better engaging, deliberating and decision-making in relation to actual or potential disagreements. The second focuses on the various roles that market devices – such as sustainability standards and taxonomies – can play in mitigating disagreements.

Towards More Productive Engagement

One way to address disputes in sustainable finance is to make the reasons for disagreement more visible (Carolan, 2006; Hulme, 2009). This implies participants in disputes being prepared to explain their position. Relevant questions include: What do they value? Why is the issue important to them? What motivates them to disagree? What scientific, economic, moral or other beliefs inform their position? Which sources of scientific or another knowledge are they drawing on, and why? What interests do they hold in relation to the issue?

The purpose of addressing such questions is two-fold. One is that it can help reveal the values, beliefs and goals which guide actors' different positions in disagreements. In doing so, it can foster a better shared understanding of why we disagree on a particular issue, one that goes beyond the 'facts' of the matter (Özkaynak *et al.*, 2023). Another reason is that making visible the underlying reason(s) for disagreements is that it opens-up the possibility of identifying areas of common ground. This, in turn, may provide an entry point for progressing from entrenched positions (Curnock *et al.*, 2024; Howarth and Sharman, 2015).

How such engagement should be organised will vary. Yet, particularly in more intractable controversies, the academic literature places great store on deliberative approaches (Giamporcaro *et al.*, 2023). These approaches emphasise the inclusive, reasoned discussion of issues. Deliberation seeks to promote mutual understanding by giving actors opportunities to learn about each other's positions and the reasoning behind them. Through structured, respectful dialogue, the aim is for agreement to be reached among different parties by persuasion and the force of reason, rather than by coercion or pressure. Science can play a role in these deliberations, but only alongside a discussion of people's values, rather than as an alternative to them. Scientific knowledge can usefully inform discussions, yet it should also be open to probing, questioning and challenge by participants.

The principles of open, reciprocal dialogue – involving reason-giving, listening and evaluation – can be applied in a range of settings. They are potentially relevant to addressing disagreements between, for example, investors and companies during shareholder engagement. More challenging are disputes that involve diverse sets of stakeholders, such as local communities, governments and financial actors. A core tenet of deliberative democracy is procedural justice, whereby different actors are given a fair and equitable opportunity to be heard (Habermas, 1998). Participatory forms of deliberation that meet these requirements can be difficult and costly to enact. Moreover, it may not always be realistic, or even desirable, to reach outcomes that everyone regards as legitimate when deeply held values cannot easily be reasoned away.

Nevertheless, this should not deter the pursuit of more inclusive forms of dispute resolution – particularly for complex, value-laden issues in which multiple actors have a legitimate stake (Dietz, 2013). For instance, decisions about financing mangrove-restoration projects in developing countries may require balancing local and global environmental benefits against livelihood diversity and the possible displacement of local communities. Addressing existing and potential disagreements over such issues lends itself to deliberative approaches that involve the different stakeholders concerned, including marginalised groups historically excluded from decision-making. More inclusive approaches to dispute resolution may be important in generating and safeguarding wider trust in sustainable finance. They also increase the likelihood that public interests and goals, as well as private ones, will be considered.

Mobilising Devices (e.g. Standards, Taxonomies)

Market devices is a term used to describe various frameworks, tools and instruments that allow sustainability to be embedded in finance. The range of relevant devices is potentially diverse but includes standards, sustainability indexes, taxonomies, disclosure frameworks and even artificial intelligence (AI). Devices can help reduce the possibility of disagreements arising in the first place, as well as playing a role in resolving disputes when they do arise. However, as will be explained below, they also risk depoliticising sustainability.

A central way devices can help mitigate disagreement is by defining and clarifying what is, or is not, environmentally or socially sustainable. By establishing standardised methodologies and evaluative criteria, devices provide common reference points for assessing, distinguishing and labelling sustainability. This may reduce uncertainty and ambiguity over whether, say, a company or activity qualifies as sustainable (Tettamanzi *et al.*, 2024). Examples of devices that can perform these functions include taxonomies (e.g. the EU Taxonomy), product standards (e.g. the Climate Bonds Standard) and sustainability-related evaluations (e.g. Transition Pathway Initiative assessments) (see also Chapter 11). Such devices can side-step routine disagreements – for example between buyers and sellers – that arise because actors use different, potentially idiosyncratic, criteria for sustainability.

Another way devices can reduce disagreements is by promoting transparency (see also Chapter 12). Standards – such as the International Sustainability Standards Board's (ISSB) climate-related disclosures – require the reporting of sustainability-related information using consistent methodologies. Disclosures may also be required by other standards, together with various voluntary initiatives in sustainable finance (see also Chapter 10). Providing information in standardised formats may help resolve disputes by allowing actors to adjudicate more effectively on sustainability-related claims. Devices may also prevent disagreements by guiding market actors on appropriate disclosures or by making them more cautious about their sustainability-related communications.

The very process of developing or revising devices – such as multi-stakeholder standards or public taxonomies – can also play a role in identifying and addressing potential areas of disagreement. More specifically, participatory development processes provide opportunities to learn about, and deliberate on, different actors' perspectives, knowledge and value commitments. These insights, in turn, can be incorporated into the ways devices conceptualise, measure, evaluate and certify sustainability. Participatory inclusiveness can also help to diffuse potential conflict by cultivating a sense of procedural legitimacy, shared ownership and mutual learning.

Yet two notes of caution are in order. First, there is no guarantee that devices will eliminate disagreement. In fact, devices – and the determinations they make – can themselves become the focus of controversy. Actors may take issue with how devices such as standards and ratings conceptualise, measure or qualify what is sustainable. Consider, for instance, the controversy surrounding the inclusion of gas and nuclear in the EU Taxonomy, or the criticism directed at the Science Based Targets initiative (SBTi) over its treatment of carbon removals. Some devices – and the judgements they make about what is sustainable, how sustainability should be measured and which disclosures are material – may also be viewed as more legitimate by a wider range of stakeholders. They thus have a greater capacity to avert or resolve disagreements (Bowen, 2019; Reinecke *et al.*, 2012). This may reflect, for instance, the perceived trustworthiness of the entity involved in their development or whether they are accompanied by some kind of assurance mechanism. Thus, devices are not immune from the value-, belief- or interest-based disagreements that characterise the wider sustainable finance space. They are capable of both provoking and pacifying disagreement.

Second, devices risk depoliticising sustainability by foreclosing opportunities for genuine debate. Standards, taxonomies and assessment methodologies can frame sustainability as a purely technical matter, rather than as a value-laden issue with many social, political and economic dimensions. In doing so, devices may – inadvertently or otherwise – restrict discussion to technical issues, thereby concealing criticism rooted in conflicting values, beliefs and interests. For example, net-zero targets and assessment methodologies tend to frame climate change in terms of the best way to measure emissions reductions, rather than opening up wider debate on topics such as the power structures that perpetuate climate destruction. To be clear: technical issues are not unimportant or unworthy of discussion. However, by narrowing the focus to issues deemed suitable for debate by 'experts', devices may sideline important concerns, priorities and ethical commitments (Anantharajah, 2021). They also risk excluding stakeholders with legitimate claims regarding the goals, means and responsibilities of sustainable finance.

Neither of these concerns is a reason to reject devices outright. Standards, taxonomies and sustainability-related assessments can play a valuable role in facilitating the functioning of sustainability-themed markets. They can also 'raise the bar' for the substantive requirements of sustainable finance – for example by ensuring greater alignment with public-policy goals such as the Paris Agreement. Devices can also stimulate dialogue and debate that might clarify different actors' expectations of sustainability.

Yet the depoliticisation critique nevertheless suggests a need to remain attentive to the risk that devices may constrain the scope of public debate. This, in turn, points to the importance of participatory processes – particularly for collective devices (e.g. industry standards) intended for use as shared resources in governing the sustainability-related behaviour of multiple actors. Such processes could create a deliberative space in which a range of actors can debate goals, means and responsibilities. The development critique also highlights the ongoing importance of public actors as developers and administrators. Organisations such as financial regulators and public standards agencies have democratic responsibilities to engage with, and consider the perspectives and interests of, a broad set of stakeholders. They are also more likely to open up the black box of their devices to public scrutiny.

Concluding Observations

The pursuit of sustainability involves questions about what kind of society, environment and economy we should aspire to. Sustainability also raises questions about who should define these objectives, how they should be delivered and by whom. These are fundamentally political issues which bring different values, beliefs and interests into conflict with one another and, with it, different individuals, organisations and even geographies. It is unsurprising therefore that sustainable finance itself is similarly political, and the subject of contestation, controversy and conflict.

This chapter has encouraged readers to look beneath the surface and take a more reflexive approach. Disagreements in sustainable finance may often manifest themselves in technical disputes centred on, for example, metrics, thresholds and financial penalty structures. Yet a central theme of the chapter is that an exclusive focus on *what* we disagree about can conceal the underlying reasons as to *why* we disagree. By better understanding these reasons, making visible our values, beliefs and interests, and engaging with others in a more open, deliberative manner, we should be better able to move beyond entrenched positions. We should also be better placed to harness the 'productive frictions' of disagreement in ways which help clarify common ground and collective expectations of sustainable finance.

Implications for Practitioners

Disagreement is an enduring feature of sustainable finance. As this chapter has shown, disputes over data, instruments and mandates often reflect deeper differences in values, beliefs and interests. Engaging with these disagreements reflexively – rather than treating them as mere obstacles – can help practitioners navigate complexity, improve the legitimacy of their strategies and contribute to more effective outcomes. The following points offer practical guidance for doing so:

1. Clarify what the disagreement is really about.

Disagreements may centre on definitions, strategies, or responsibilities. Before responding, practitioners should assess whether a disagreement stems from competing conceptions of sustainability, conflicting approaches or divergent views on who should act. Clarifying the basis of disagreement can help identify where progress is possible, and where divergence may need to be acknowledged.

2. Make assumptions visible – including your own.
Unspoken assumptions are a common source of confusion. Practitioners can reduce friction by being explicit about the rationale behind their own position, the objectives they prioritise and the assumptions that shape their approach. This might involve clarifying time horizons, articulating a theory of change or identifying the sources of evidence they consider most relevant. Even partial transparency can help reduce misunderstanding and foster more productive dialogue.

3. Map the perspectives of others.
Stakeholders are likely to approach sustainability from different angles, shaped by their values, beliefs and interests. Conducting informal or formal stakeholder mapping can help anticipate points of tension, clarify whose values are engaged and surface competing expectations early in a process.

4. Use scientific and technical tools with care.
Data and technical tools such as models and scenarios are essential, but they are rarely neutral and value-free. They embody choices about what to measure, how to measure it and whose perspective counts. Practitioners should consider how tools have been constructed, and whether their use aligns with broader institutional aims.

5. Involve stakeholders in design and review processes.
Early engagement with affected parties – whether investors, issuers, clients or civil society actors – can help surface disagreements before they escalate. Involving stakeholders in shaping methodologies, product design or stewardship priorities can improve both legitimacy and outcomes.

6. Plan for disagreement.
Institutions can prepare for disagreement by developing internal protocols, escalation pathways and communication strategies that allow for disagreement to be addressed constructively rather than ignored or suppressed.

Acknowledgements

We would like to thank Nikolaus Hastreiter and Rory Sullivan for helpful comments on an earlier version of the chapter. ChatGPT and Claude were used to refine ideas for this chapter and to check grammar and punctuation.

Funding

This chapter draws on research financed by the LSE Research Support Fund, London School of Economics and Political Science (LSE), UK.

References

Ahlström, H. and Monciardini, D. (2022), 'The Regulatory Dynamics of Sustainable Finance: Paradoxical Success and Limitations of EU Reforms', *Journal of Business Ethics*, Vol. 177, No. 1, pp. 193–212.

Ameli, N., Drummond, P., Bisaro, A., Grubb, M. and Chenet, H. (2020), 'Climate Finance and Disclosure for Institutional Investors: Why Transparency Is Not Enough', *Climatic Change*, Vol. 160, No. 4, pp. 565–589.

Anantharajah, K. (2021), '"But Our Lights Were Still On": Decolonizing Energy Futures Emerging from Climate Finance Regulation in Fiji', *Energy Research & Social Science*, Vol. 72, p. 101847.

Baker, S. (2016), *Sustainable Development* (Routledge, Abingdon).

Baumüller, J. and Sopp, K. (2021), 'Double Materiality and the Shift from Non-Financial to European Sustainability Reporting: Review, Outlook and Implications', *Journal of Applied Accounting Research*, Vol. 23, No. 1, pp. 8–28.

Boiral, O., Talbot, D. and Brotherton, M. (2020), 'Measuring Sustainability Risks: A Rational Myth?', *Business Strategy and the Environment*, Vol. 29, No. 6, pp. 2557–2571.

Borie, M. and Bracking, S. (2024), 'Authorising Green Finance with Claims to Science: Research Avenues to Move Beyond Sciencewashing', *Finance and Space*, Vol. 1, No. 1, pp. 494–516.

Bowen, F. (2019), 'Marking Their Own Homework: The Pragmatic and Moral Legitimacy of Industry Self-Regulation', *Journal of Business Ethics*, Vol. 156, No. 1, pp. 257–272.

Bowker, G., Timmermans, S., Clarke, A. and Balka, E. (eds.) (2016), *Boundary Objects and Beyond: Working with Leigh Star* (MIT Press, Cambridge, MA).

Brewer, P. and Ley, B. (2013), 'Whose Science Do You Believe? Explaining Trust in Sources of Scientific Information About the Environment', *Science Communication*, Vol. 35, No. 1, pp. 115–137.

Carolan, M. (2006), 'Scientific Knowledge and Environmental Policy: Why Science Needs Values', *Environmental Sciences*, Vol. 3, No. 4, pp. 229–237.

Chelli, M. and Gendron, Y. (2013), 'Sustainability Ratings and the Disciplinary Power of the Ideology of Numbers', *Journal of Business Ethics*, Vol. 112, No. 2, pp. 187–203.

Colgan, J., Green, J. and Hale, T. (2021), 'Asset Revaluation and the Existential Politics of Climate Change', *International Organization*, Vol. 75, No. 2, pp. 586–610.

Collier, D., Hidalgo, F. and Maciuceanu, A. (2006), 'Essentially Contested Concepts: Debates and Applications', *Journal of Political Ideologies*, Vol. 11, No. 3, pp. 211–246.

Connelly, S. (2007), 'Mapping Sustainable Development as a Contested Concept', *Local Environment*, Vol. 12, No. 3, pp. 259–278.

Cripps, P. (2017, June 7), 'Green Bond Comment, June – of Repsol and Reputation', *Environmental Finance*, www.environmental-finance.com/content/analysis/green-bond-comment-june-of-repsol-and-reputation.html

Curnock, M., Nembhard, D., Smith, R., Sambrook, K., Hobman, E., Mankad, A., Pert, P. and Chamberland, E. (2024), 'Finding Common Ground: Understanding and Engaging with Science Mistrust in the Great Barrier Reef Region', *PLoS One,* Vol. 19, No. 8, p. e0308252.

Davis, M. and Boey, K. (2022, January 6), 'Airport Authority HK Sells Controversial Green Bond', *IFR,* www.ifre.com/story/3196600/airport-authority-hk-prices-us4bn-144areg-s-four-tranche-senior-bond-tnp3jy9rns

Dietz, T. (2013), 'Bringing Values and Deliberation to Science Communication', *Proceedings of the National Academy of Sciences,* Vol. 110, No. Supplement 3, pp. 14081–14087.

Dimmelmeier, A. (2023), 'Sustainable Finance as a Contested Concept: Tracing the Evolution of Five Frames between 1998 and 2018', *Journal of Sustainable Finance & Investment,* Vol. 13, No. 4, pp. 1600–1623.

Dumas, C. and Louche, C. (2016), 'Collective Beliefs on Responsible Investment', *Business & Society,* Vol. 55, No. 3, pp. 427–457.

Eccles, R. and Stroehle, J. (2018), 'Exploring Social Origins in the Construction of ESG Measures', https://ssrn.com/abstract=3212685

Erforth, B. and Keijzer, N. (2025), 'Green and Global? A Policy Frame Analysis of the European Investment Bank's Re-Branding from 2018–2023', *Journal of Economic Policy Reform,* Vol. 28, No. 1, pp. 55–74.

Falchi, A., Grolleau, G. and Mzoughi, N. (2022), 'Why Companies Might Under-Communicate Their Efforts for Sustainable Development and What Can Be Done?', *Business Strategy and the Environment,* Vol. 31, No. 5, pp. 1938–1946.

Fancy, T. (2021, November 21), 'Tariq Fancy on the Failure of Green Investing and the Need for State Action', *The Economist,* www.economist.com/by-invitation/2021/11/04/tariq-fancy-on-the-failure-of-green-investing-and-the-need-for-state-action

Fernández Chulián, M., Garcia-Torea, N., Larrinaga, C. and Bebbington, J. (2025), 'Boundary Objects: Sustainability Reporting and the Production of Organizational Stability', *Accounting, Auditing & Accountability Journal,* Vol. 38, No. 2, pp. 509–536.

Gaede, J. and Meadowcroft, J. (2016), 'A Question of Authenticity: Status Quo Bias and the International Energy Agency's World Energy Outlook', *Journal of Environmental Policy & Planning,* Vol. 18, No. 5, pp. 608–627.

Gallie, W. (1956), 'Essentially Contested Concepts', *Proceedings of the Aristotelian Society,* Vol. 56, pp. 167–198.

Giamporcaro, S., Gond, J. and Louche, C. (2023), 'Deliberative Boundary Work for Sustainable Finance: Insights from a European Commission Expert Group', *Organization Studies,* Vol. 44, No. 12, pp. 1913–1938.

Habermas, J. (1998), *Between Facts and Norms: Contributions to a Discourse Theory of Law and Democracy* (MIT Press, Cambridge, MA).

Hay, C. (2011), 'Ideas and the Construction of Interests', in Béland, D. and Cox, R.H. (eds.), *Ideas and Politics in Social Science* (Oxford University Press, Oxford), pp. 65–82.

Höchstädter, A. and Scheck, B. (2015), 'What's in a Name: An Analysis of Impact Investing Understandings by Academics and Practitioners', *Journal of Business Ethics,* Vol. 132, No. 2, pp. 449–475.

Hockerts, K., Hehenberger, L., Schaltegger, S. and Farber, V. (2022), 'Defining and Conceptualizing Impact Investing: Attractive Nuisance or Catalyst?', *Journal of Business Ethics,* Vol. 179, pp. 937–950.

Hornsey, M., Harris, E., Bain, P. and Fielding, K. (2016), 'Meta-Analyses of the Determinants and Outcomes of Belief in Climate Change', *Nature Climate Change*, Vol. 6, No. 6, pp. 622–626.

Howarth, C. and Sharman, A. (2015), 'Labeling Opinions in the Climate Debate: A Critical Review', *WIREs Climate Change*, Vol. 6, No. 2, pp. 239–254.

Hulme, M. (2009), *Why We Disagree About Climate Change: Understanding Controversy, Inaction and Opportunity* (Cambridge University Press, Cambridge).

InfluenceMap (2022, February 2), 'Press Release: EU Green Deal at Risk from Pro-Gas Lobbying'.

Latour, B. (1987), *Science in Action: How to Follow Scientists and Engineers through Society* (Harvard University Press, Cambridge, MA).

Meckling, J. (2015), 'Oppose, Support, or Hedge? Distributional Effects, Regulatory Pressure, and Business Strategy in Environmental Politics', *Global Environmental Politics*, Vol. 15, No. 2, pp. 19–37.

Murray, S. (2022), 'To Engage or Divest. How Should Investors Clean Up the World's Dirtiest Companies', *Moral Money Forum*, https://forums.ft.com/s/FT-Moral-Money-Forum-How-should-investors-clean-up-the-worlds-dirtiest-companies_.pdf

Nedopil, C. (2023), 'Integrating Biodiversity into Financial Decision-Making: Challenges and Four Principles', *Business Strategy and the Environment*, Vol. 32, No. 4, pp. 1619–1633.

Ng, E. (2022, January 6), 'Sustainable Finance: "Greenwashing" Concerns Raised as Hong Kong Airport Floats US$4 Billion Bonds Package to Fund Growth, Decarbonisation', *South China Morning Post*, www.scmp.com/business/article/3162333/sustainable-finance-greenwashing-concerns-raised-hong-kong-airport-floats?module=perpetual_scroll_0&pgtype=article

OECD (2022), *OECD Guidance on Transition Finance: Ensuring Credibility of Corporate Climate Transition Plans* (OECD Publishing, Paris).

Oll, J., Theresa, S., Schiemann, F. and Akkermann, J. (2024), 'The Concept of Materiality in Sustainability Reporting: From Essential Contestation to Research Opportunities', https://ssrn.com/abstract=4323836

Oreskes, N. (2004a), 'Science and Public Policy: What's Proof Got to Do With It?', *Environmental Science & Policy*, Vol. 7, No. 5, pp. 369–383.

Oreskes, N. (2004b), 'The Scientific Consensus on Climate Change', *Science*, Vol. 306, No. 5702, pp. 1686–1686.

Özkaynak, B., Muradian, R., Ungar, P. and Morales, D. (2023), 'What Can Methods for Assessing Worldviews and Broad Values Tell Us About Socio-environmental Conflicts?', *Current Opinion in Environmental Sustainability*, Vol. 64, p. 101316.

Perkins, R. (2021), 'Governing for Growth: Standards, Emergent Markets, and the Lenient Zone of Qualification for Green Bonds', *Annals of the American Association of Geographers*, Vol. 111, No. 7, pp. 2044–2061.

Reclaim Finance (2021), *Out with the Science, in with Lobbyists: Gas, Nuclear and the EU Taxonomy*, https://reclaimfinance.org/site/wp-content/uploads/2021/07/Report-EU-taxonomy-Out-with-science-in-with-lobbyists-RF.pdf

Reclaim Finance (2022, January 4), '*Press Release: High-flying Greenwashing Around a New Green Bond for Hong Kong Airport*', https://reclaimfinance.org/site/en/2022/01/04/high-flying-greenwashing-around-a-new-green-bond/

Reinecke, J., Manning, S. and von Hagen, O. (2012), 'The Emergence of a Standards Market: Multiplicity of Sustainability Standards in the Global Coffee Industry', *Organization Studies*, Vol. 33, Nos. 5–6, pp. 791–814.

Sabatier, P. and Weible, C. (2007), 'The Advocacy Coalition Framework: Innovations and Clarifications', in Sabatier, P. (ed.), *Theories of the Policy Process* (Westview Press, Boulder), pp. 189–220.

Sarewitz, D. (2004), 'How Science Makes Environmental Controversies Worse', *Environmental Science & Policy*, Vol. 7, pp. 385–403.

Schön, D. and Rein, M. (1994), *Frame Reflection: Toward the Resolution of Intractable Policy Controversies* (Basic Books, New York).

Schutter, M., Hicks, C., Phelps, J. and Waterton, C. (2021), 'The Blue Economy as a Boundary Object for Hegemony Across Scales', *Marine Policy*, Vol. 132, p. 104673.

Schütze, F. and Stede, J. (2024), 'The EU Sustainable Finance Taxonomy and Its Contribution to Climate Neutrality', *Journal of Sustainable Finance & Investment*, Vol. 14, No. 1, pp. 128–160.

Semieniuk, G., Campiglio, E., Mercure, J., Volz, U. and Edwards, N. (2021), 'Low-Carbon Transition Risks for Finance', *WIREs Climate Change*, Vol. 12, No. 1, p. e678.

Sharman, A. and Perkins, R. (2017), 'Post-Decisional Logics of Inaction: The Influence of Knowledge Controversy in Climate Policy Decision-Making', *Environment and Planning A*, Vol. 49, No. 10, pp. 2281–2299.

Simmons, R., Yonk, R. and Thomas, D. (2011), 'Bootleggers, Baptists, and Political Entrepreneurs: Key Players in the Rational Game and Morality Play of Regulatory Politics', *The Independent Review*, Vol. 15, No. 3, pp. 367–381.

Skjølsvold, T. (2013), 'What We Disagree About When We Disagree About Sustainability', *Society & Natural Resources*, Vol. 26, No. 11, pp. 1268–1282.

Star, S. and Griesemer, J. (1989), 'Institutional Ecology, 'Translations' and Boundary Objects: Amateurs and Professionals in Berkeley's Museum of Vertebrate Zoology, 1907–39', *Social Studies of Science*, Vol. 19, No. 3, pp. 387–420.

Starks, L. (2023), 'Presidential Address: Sustainable Finance and ESG Issues–Value versus Values', *The Journal of Finance*, Vol. 78, No. 4, pp. 1837–1872.

Steg, L. and de Groot, J. (2012), 'Environmental Values', in Clayton, S. (ed.), *The Oxford Handbook of Environmental and Conservation Psychology* (Oxford University Press, Oxford), pp. 81–92.

Täger, M. (2022), *Constructing Climate Risk: How Finance Governs Its Relationship with the Planet's Climate*. Doctoral thesis, London School of Economics and Political Science.

Tettamanzi, P., Gotti Tedeschi, R. and Murgolo, M. (2024), 'The European Union (EU) Green Taxonomy: Codifying Sustainability to Provide Certainty to the Markets', *Environment, Development and Sustainability*, Vol. 26, No. 11, pp. 27111–27136.

Tilsted, J., Palm, E., Bjørn, A. and Lund, J. (2023), 'Corporate Climate Futures in the Making: Why We Need Research on the Politics of Science-Based Targets', *Energy Research & Social Science*, Vol. 103, p. 103229.

Tischer, D. and Ferrando, T. (2024), 'Shaping the Climate Transition: Multistakeholder Networks, Elites, and Sustainable Finance Policy in Europe', *Finance and Society*, Vol. 10, No. 2, pp. 113–136.

United Nations (2024), *Inter-Agency Task Force on Financing for Development, Financing for Sustainable Development Report 2024: Financing for Development at a Crossroads* (United Nations, New York), https://developmentfinance.un.org/fsdr2024

Yates, T. (2024, January 4), 'Opinion Market Insight: Climate Change Should Be Tackled by the State, Not Central Banks', *Financial Times*, www.ft.com/content/26c2d532-d6c4-4ef4-a6d9-728640a110ae

Zhou, Y. and Shen, L. (2022), 'Confirmation Bias and the Persistence of Misinformation on Climate Change', *Communication Research*, Vol. 49, No. 4, pp. 500–523.

Chapter 5

Is Sustainable Investment Consistent with Fiduciary Duty?

Rory Sullivan

Introduction

Al Gore (the Chairman of Generation Investment Management and former Vice President of the United States) and David Blood (Senior Partner of Generation Investment Management) wrote in 2015:

> Fiduciaries are tasked with the decision to buy, sell, or hold assets. There is no passive behaviour as a fiduciary; there is no 'do nothing' task … Sustainability is an important factor in the long-term success of a business. Therefore as with any other issue related to the prudent management of capital, considering sustainability is not only important to upholding fiduciary duty, it is obligatory.
>
> (Gore and Blood, 2015)

DOI: 10.4324/9781003467632-5

Fiduciary duty is one of the most important concepts in investment. It defines how those organisations or individuals (fiduciaries) charged with managing money or other assets on behalf of others are expected to behave and the factors they should consider in their decision-making. The way fiduciary duty is defined and interpreted affects the entire investment chain, not just the relationship between investment organisations and their customers, clients and beneficiaries (Principles for Responsible Investment (PRI), 2016; PRI *et al.*, 2016). It shapes the relationship between investors and companies. It informs the way in which asset owners select, appoint and monitor investment managers. It influences investment decision-making processes and ownership practices. It affects the issues, including sustainability-related issues, that investors consider in their decision-making.

The focus of this chapter is the relationship between fiduciary duty and sustainable finance and the question of whether fiduciary duty enables or hinders sustainable finance. It starts by providing an overview of the traditional definition of fiduciary duty (in particular, the duties of loyalty and care). This introduction is followed by a description of the efforts of important investor membership organisations such as the United Nations Environment Programme Finance Initiative (UNEP FI) and the Principles for Responsible Investment (PRI) to broaden the interpretation and application of fiduciary duty to encompass sustainability-related considerations. It then reviews the arguments for and against this broader definition, looking at issues such as the investment case for focusing on sustainability-related issues, on legal requirements in different countries and on prevailing investment practice. The chapter concludes by offering reflections on the actions that might be taken by investors and by policymakers.

What do We Mean by Fiduciary Duty?

Fiduciary duties exist to ensure that those who manage other people's money act responsibly in the interests of beneficiaries or savers, rather than serving their own interests (PRI *et al.,* 2019). These duties (see Box 5.1) aim to ensure that fiduciaries are loyal to their beneficiaries, that they act in the interests of beneficiaries rather than serving their own interests and that they carry out their duties in a prudent manner. These duties are of particular importance in situations where there are imbalances in expertise and where the beneficiary has limited ability to monitor or oversee the actions of the person or entity acting in their interests (Reynolds *et al.*, 2021).

Box 5.1 The Traditional Fiduciary Duties

Fiduciary duties (or equivalent obligations) exist to ensure that those who manage other people's money act in the interests of beneficiaries and do not serve their own interests (PRI *et al.*, 2019). The most important of these duties are:

- Loyalty: Fiduciaries should act honestly and in good faith in the interests of their beneficiaries, should impartially balance the conflicting interests of different beneficiaries, should avoid conflicts of interest and should not act for the benefit of themselves or a third party.
- Prudence: Fiduciaries should act with due care, skill and diligence, investing as an 'ordinary prudent person' would do.

Fiduciaries have varying degrees of discretion in terms of how they invest the funds they control. This discretion may be narrow such as in situations where the beneficiary specifies the asset profile and only the day-to-day stock selection and other management tasks are left to the investment decision-maker. Or it may be much wider such as in situations where the beneficiary specifies (or agrees to) the investment objective, and the investment decision-maker can then decide how to achieve that objective. Furthermore, some funds may be subject to specific requirements or expectations. For example, public funds may be required to invest a defined percentage of their assets in domestic industries, their investments may be tied to the specific policies or defined strategic interests of their government (see, for example, the analysis of investment practice in different Asian markets in PRI *et al.* (2016)). Within the scope of discretion left to the investment decision-maker, fiduciary duties define how they are of particular importance in situations where there are imbalances in expertise and where the beneficiary has limited ability to monitor or oversee the actions of the person or entity acting in their interests (Reynolds *et al.*, 2021).

The specific way in which these duties are framed differs between countries. They also differ between common law (where these duties are articulated in statute and in decisions of the courts) and civil law jurisdictions (where the rules tend to be code or statute-based). In common law jurisdictions, the most important fiduciary duties are the duty to act prudently and the duty to act in accordance with the purpose for which investment powers are granted (also known as the duty of loyalty) (PRI *et al.*, 2019). In civil law jurisdictions, while the term 'fiduciary duty' may not be used, similar obligations are often applied to investors. These generally include a duty to act conscientiously in the interests of beneficiaries – in terms such as 'good and conscientious manager' (Japan) or 'professionally' (Germany) (PRI *et al.*, 2019). They also generally include a duty to seek profitable investments, recognition of the portfolio approach to modern investment (i.e. investors are expected to diversify their investments) and, potentially, limits on the types of assets that may be selected for certain types of funds (PRI *et al.*, 2019).

Across the various definitions and interpretations of fiduciary duty, there are three broad points to note. The first is that the interests of beneficiaries are generally defined (or framed) in financial terms (Reynolds *et al.*, 2021). The second is that fiduciary duties are widely considered to be procedural and purposive requirements, rather than obligations to achieve specific outcomes (Sullivan *et al.*, 2017). That is, when evaluating whether an institutional investor has delivered on its fiduciary duties, courts will distinguish between the decision-making process – specifically, whether the fiduciary can demonstrate that it has applied an appropriate degree of diligence in its good-faith pursuit of beneficiaries' interests – and the outcomes of that decision-making process (Sullivan *et al.*, 2017). The third is that fiduciary duty itself is not a static concept; it evolves and adjusts in response to changes in knowledge, market practices and conventions, regulations and policies and social norms (Martindale *et al.*, 2020).

The Evolution in Thinking on Fiduciary Duty and Sustainable Investment

In 2005, UNEP FI together with the law firm Freshfields Bruckhaus Deringer published a ground-breaking report titled *A Legal Framework for the Integration of Environmental, Social and Governance Issues into Institutional Investment* (commonly referred to as the 'Freshfields Report'). The report, in what was seen as a radical conclusion at the time, argued that "integrating ESG [environmental, social and governance] considerations into an investment analysis so as to more reliably predict financial performance is clearly permissible and is arguably required in all jurisdictions" (Freshfields Bruckhaus Deringer, 2005).

This report was followed, in 2009, by another UNEP FI report, *Fiduciary Responsibility: Legal and Practical Aspects of Integrating Environmental, Social and Governance Issues into Institutional Investment* (United Nations Environmental Programme Finance Initiative (UNEP FI), 2009). This report explored legal options on how best to integration environmental, social and governance issues into investment processes, particularly with respect to investment mandates and investment management contracts.

Despite these reports and despite the growth in the number of investors making commitments to responsible investment – for example, by the end of 2014, the PRI had 270 asset owner signatories and almost 1,000 asset manager signatories (PRI, 2025a) – concerns remained that capital markets were still not properly accounting for sustainability-related risks and opportunities (PRI, 2024a). In 2015, the PRI, UNEP FI, the UNEP Inquiry into the Design of a Sustainable Financial

System and the United Nations Global Compact launched a major report on fiduciary duty. The report – informed by an in-depth analysis of investment practice and fiduciary duty in eight countries: Australia, Brazil, Canada, Germany, Japan, South Africa, the United Kingdom and the United States – argued that "Failing to consider all long-term investment value drivers, including ESG issues, is a failure of fiduciary duty" (PRI *et al.*, 2015). It also acknowledged that, despite significant progress, many investors had yet to fully integrate sustainability-related issues into their investment decision-making processes.

Following the launch of this report, the PRI, UNEP FI and The Generation Foundation launched a three-year project, *Fiduciary Duty in the 21st Century.* The aim was to clarify investors' legal obligations and duties in relation to the integration of sustainability-related issues in investment practice and decision-making. The project involved discussions with over 400 policymakers and investors, the development of almost 20 country or region-specific roadmaps on the policy and regulatory changes required to achieve full integration of sustainability-related issues into investment processes and practices, and research into the relevance of ESG issues to investment decision-making and on the role of investment consultants (see, further, PRI *et al.* (2019)). The final report from the *Fiduciary Duty in the 21st Century* project argued that the changes in the policy and legislative landscape, in investor understanding of the financial relevance of ESG issues and in investment practice and changes meant that fiduciaries should (PRI *et al.*, 2019):

1. Incorporate environmental, social and governance issues into their investment analysis and decision-making processes, consistent with their investment time horizons.
2. Encourage high standards of ESG performance in the companies or other entities in which they invest.
3. Support the stability and resilience of the financial system.
4. Understand and incorporate beneficiaries' and savers' sustainability-related preferences.
5. Report on how they have implemented these commitments.

The report argued that these expectations both aligned with and clarified the traditional duties of loyalty and prudence (PRI *et al.*, 2019). It suggested that understanding and taking account of the sustainability preferences of beneficiaries/clients, whether these preferences are financially material or not, was a central element of the duty of loyalty. It also argued the concept of prudence (i.e. acting with due skill, care and diligence) required fiduciaries to consider all financially material factors over the short and the long-term and to act effectively and appropriately to manage these factors. From this analysis, the report proposed a 'modern' definition of fiduciary duty (see Box 5.2).

Box 5.2 Modern Fiduciary Duty

"Fiduciary duties (or equivalent obligations) exist to ensure that those who manage other people's money act in the interests of beneficiaries, rather than serving their own interests. The most important of these duties are:

- Loyalty: Fiduciaries should:
  - — Act honestly and in good faith in the interests of their beneficiaries or their clients.
  - — Understand and incorporate into their decision-making the sustainability preferences of beneficiaries/clients, whether these preferences are financially material or not.
  - — Impartially balance the conflicting interests of different beneficiaries and clients.
  - — Avoid conflicts of interest.
  - — Not act for the benefit of themselves or a third party.
- Prudence: Fiduciaries should act with due care, skill and diligence, investing as an 'ordinary prudent person' would do. This includes:
  - — Incorporating financially material ESG factors into their investment decision-making, consistent with the timeframe of the obligation.
  - — Being an active owner, encouraging high standards of ESG performance in the companies or other entities in which they are invested.
  - — Supporting the stability and resilience of the financial system.

Fiduciaries should disclose their investment approach to clients and/or beneficiaries including information on how preferences are incorporated into the scheme's investment strategy and the potential risks and benefits of doing so."

Source: PRI *et al.* (2019)

By 2019, there was a consensus among a large proportion of institutional investors that the negative sustainability impacts resulting from economic activity posed growing threats to the health of the environmental and social systems on which future investment returns rely. The increasing integration of ESG factors into investment decisions was adding new dimensions to some aspects of investment risk management but had left other risks inadequately addressed if at all (particularly system-level risks). Crucially, market perceptions and practice of ESG integration had also progressed. For example, impact investing had grown substantially (albeit as a specialist market rather than as an integral part of governance and decision-making for institutional investors). Furthermore, increasing numbers of investors were starting to acknowledge that that achieving global sustainability goals on issues such as climate change would be necessary to protect long-term investments from sustainability-related financial risks but that that narrow ESG integration alone would be insufficient to ensure investors contribute sufficiently to achieving those goals and mitigating the risks (see, generally, Lukomnic and Hawley (2021)). There was a growing sense that, in order to support the development of a sustainable economy, investors would need to consider the positive and negative sustainability impacts of investments and play an active role of agents of real-world change, rather than remaining as interested spectators seeking only to understand and manage how real-world events affect investment returns.

In October 2019, as a vital step towards clarifying the legal basis for investors to consider systemic risks and take action to pursue sustainability impact goals to mitigate those risks, The Generation Foundation, UNEP FI and the PRI appointed the law firm Freshfields Bruckhaus Deringer to analyse whether and how legal frameworks across 11 jurisdictions allow or require investors to consider sustainability-related impact goals. Their conclusion, presented in *A Legal Framework for Impact*, was that investors generally have a legal obligation to consider pursuing sustainability impact goals where doing so can contribute to achieving their investment objectives (Freshfields Bruckhaus Deringer, 2021). While the report did stress that (consistent with the findings of earlier work focused on ESG risk integration) delivering financial returns is generally regarded as the primary purpose and goal of investors, it also noted that legal duties generally provide significant discretion for investors to make informed decisions about when to pursue positive sustainability outcomes in ways that support their proper investment purpose and objectives. The report argued that long-term investors who fail to consider how to manage sustainability outcomes or systemic risks may find they are failing to address factors that are highly relevant to their ability to protect the value of their beneficiaries' or clients' investments. The report also argued that changes in policy and regulation relating to issues such as climate change, sustainable development and biodiversity mean that investors need to consider a variety of steps to manage exposure to sustainability-related risks, tackle the underlying drivers of sustainability risks and pursue positive sustainability outcomes.

What Is the Case for a Definition of Fiduciary Duty That Supports Sustainable Investment?

The reports from the PRI and UNEP FI have – both because of the quality of their analysis and because of the legitimacy and credibility of PRI, UNEP FI and the other organisations involved – built a case for an expanded conception of fiduciary duty. This wider conception expects fiduciaries to incorporate financially material ESG factors into their investment decision-making, to be active owners, to support the stability and resilience of the financial system and to reflect the sustainability preferences of their beneficiaries and clients. The question is whether this conception is supported by investment practitioners and policymakers. There are three broad arguments that suggest that this new definition captures current thinking and practice on fiduciary duty: there is evidence that sustainability issues are financially material, sustainable investment is a standard practice in many markets, and policy and regulations that mean that sustainable investment is increasingly seen as consistent with the best interests of clients (PRI *et al.,* 2019).

The first argument, i.e. that sustainability issues are important drivers of investment value, is widely accepted. Other chapters in this book present this evidence. While we are not going to repeat this evidence here (a useful summary is provided by Wheelan *et al.,* (2021) and, on debt, by Bolton *et al.,* (2023)), we note that there are literatures that support the arguments that (a) there is a positive correlation between sustainability and corporate financial performance, (b) companies with better sustainability performance can have better access to finance, (c) there are significant investment opportunities associated with sustainability-related issues, (d) the consequences of failing to effectively manage ESG-related risks can be significant (e.g. as a result of fines and penalties, litigation, clean-up costs) and (e) companies with good ratings and reputations can outperformance those with poorer ratings and reputations. There is also a growing evidence that systemic factors and externalities (as opposed to the risk and return profile of individual investments) have to each individual investee can have very significant implications for the performance of investment portfolios (see, for example, Hofstetter (2020); Burckart and Lydenberg (2021); Lukomnic and Hawley (2021)).

The second argument relates to the fact that a large number of investors now pay attention to sustainability-related issues in their active ownership activities and in their investment decision-making. This has been driven both by investors' understanding the financial materiality of these issues to their investments, and the growing demand from clients and beneficiaries that they will act on sustainability-related issues. In many jurisdictions, the integration of sustainability-related issues into investment practices and processes, and into company engagement, is an increasingly established practice and can even be considered a market norm in some (see, for example, PRI *et al.* (2019)). Globally, more than 5,300 investors (asset owners and asset managers), representing over half of the world's institutional assets under management, are now signatories to the PRI (Atkin, 2024; PRI, 2025a). These signatories commit to incorporating ESG issues into their investment processes, to acting as active owners and to reporting on their activities and progress towards implementing the Principles. In a 2023 PRI signatory consultation, a majority of the respondents (63% out of the nearly 2,000 signatories that participated in the consultation) stated that they saw their commitment to responsible investment as including a combination of managing sustainability-related risks and identifying and acting on sustainability outcomes in the future. The PRI concluded that this expansive view on responsible investment suggested that there was the potential for a more evolved dialogue on how the investment community contributes to sustainable outcomes, in way that is aligned with fiduciary duties (PRI, 2023). Other evidence that sustainable finance (or responsible investment) has become a market norm include the following: (a) the FTSE Russell's 2024 asset owner survey which found that 86% of asset owners with assets under management of US$10 billion or more implemented sustainability considerations in their investment strategies, up from 50 in 2019 (FTSE Russell, 2024), (b) the Global Sustainable Investment Alliance (GSIA) global survey which suggests that around one-third of global investment assets are now managed in line with some form of sustainable investment strategy (Global Sustainable Investment Alliance (GSIA), 2023), (c) over 600 institutional investors that support Climate Action 100+, a collaborative investor initiative, to ensure the world's largest corporate greenhouse gas emitters take necessary action on climate change (Climate Action 100+, 2025), and (d) more than 500 investors support the CDP's annual disclosure requests (CDP, 2025). The fact that so many investors pay attention to sustainability-related factors is important, as courts often look to market or investment practices to understand what good practice look like and to inform their assessment around whether an actor has fallen below expected practice.

The third argument relates to regulation. Many countries have now introduced requirements for institutional investors to adopt policies explaining how they account for sustainability factors in their investment practices and processes, to engage with the companies and other entities in which they are invested and to report on how they implement their sustainability-related policies (see, for example, London Stock Exchange Group (LSEG) (2024); (PRI (2025b)). Some countries, see the examples in Table 5.1, have introduced regulations and policies clarifying investors' legal duties. As can be seen in the Table 5.1, these measures are relatively recent. As a consequence, it is not possible at the time of writing (April 2025) to offer a definitive view on how they interact with existing statutes or how they might be interpreted by courts.

The regulatory changes that are relevant to this discussion are not just those that relate to the duties and obligations of investors. Most governments have adopted policies and regulations to meet their commitments under the Paris Agreement on Climate Change and the Sustainable Development Goals (SDGs) and to address various national social and environmental priorities (see, for example, PRI (2025b)). There is growing evidence that climate change is moving from being treated as a stand-alone, sector-specific policy issue to one that is integrated into long-term economic and development policy (Investor Agenda, 2023). While the details differ, these domestic policies generally involve the setting of national targets, the development of national policy plans and implementation programmes, the adoption of regulation and other policy instruments (e.g. economic instruments, self-regulation), the allocation of responsibilities to different actors, and the creation of incentives for action. Technically, these do not alter the way in which fiduciary duty is understood by investors or by policymakers,

Table 5.1 Examples of Clarifications to Legal Duties

Jurisdiction	*Changes*
European Union	In 2021, Delegated Regulation 2021/1256 revised the EU's Solvency II rules to require insurers to take account of the potential long-term impacts of their investment strategy and decisions on sustainability factors. In 2023, the European Insurance and Occupational Pensions Authority (EIOPA) published a technical report for the review of the Institutions for Occupational Retirement Provision (IORP) II Directive for Occupational Pension Funds. The report stated, "IORPs should be required to pursue positive sustainability goals in their investment and engagement activity if it is in line with the members' and beneficiaries' preferences and it is in their long-term best interest".
Australia	In 2023, the Australian Prudential Regulation Authority (APRA) published prudential practice guides on climate change financial risk and on investment governance. The guidance sets out clear expectations that trustees demonstrate how they integrate ESG factors (including market-wide or system-level risks) into their investment analysis, decision-making and governance. The guidance also confirmed that superannuation funds could set environmental and social impact objectives where such objectives are consistent with the outcomes the funds seek for their beneficiaries.
United Kingdom	The Occupational Pension Schemes (Climate Change Governance and Reporting) Regulations, 2021 require UK pension schemes to take proper account of climate change, to address climate-related risks and opportunities in their investment decisions and to report in line with guidance from the Task Force on Climate-Related Financial Disclosures.
Japan	In 2024, Prime Minister Kishida's Cabinet Office Policy on the Grand Design and New Form of Capitalism 2024 included the provision that the Government Pension Investment Fund (GPIF) (the world's single largest pool of retirement savings) and the Federation of Mutual Aid Associations could consider non-financial factors, including impact, when making mid- to long-term investment decisions.

Source: Adapted from PRI (2024b: 40–46)

given that such policies and regulations can be understood as part of the general process of policy development in any country. However, in practice, they have reinforced the importance of investors paying attention to sustainability-related issues as an integral part of their fiduciary duties, given that these are such an important influence on national policy priorities and economic development pathways in many countries.

What Is the Case Against a Definition of Fiduciary Duty That Supports Sustainable Investment?

Despite the undoubted progress in particular areas, there are also a series of reasons for arguing that the wider conception of fiduciary duty presented in Box 5.2 is not supported by investment practitioners and policymakers.

First, the manner in which investors define or interpret materiality may mean that relatively few if any sustainability issues are considered financially material. The threshold at which issues become financially material (see Chapter 3), the relatively short timeframes over which investors assess materiality (see Chapter 3) and the general focus of investment on company-specific issues rather than portfolio-wide issues (see, for example, the critiques in Lukomnic and Hawley (2021)) mean that for most investors most sustainability-related issues will not be considered financially material most of the time. This is exacerbated by the fact that many investors are primarily interested in relative performance (e.g. compared to a benchmark, compared to industry peers) rather than absolute performance and may, therefore, not be as concerned about factors that are likely to have an effect across the market as a whole. A consequence is that, unless there are other reasons for investors to be concerned (e.g. demand from clients), investors will be less likely to raise these issues with company management and less likely to alter their investment decisions to take these issues into account. That is, the expectation that investors will consider financially material issues in their investment research and decision-making may not actually alter the decisions that are made and may not catalyse engagement between the company and its investors on sustainability-related issues.

Second, as discussed in Chapter 2, diversification is an important portfolio risk management strategy. In broad terms, diversification is the process of allocating capital in a way that reduces an investor's exposure to any one particular asset or risk. In practice, investors do this by spreading their investments across different asset classes, different sectors and different geographic regions. The rationale underpinning diversification is that it lowers the potential for significant losses by mitigating the impact of any single investment – be that a company, a sector, a geographic region, an asset class – performing poorly. From a sustainability perspective, portfolio diversification can help mitigate the implications of systemic risks for an investment portfolio. For example, if an investor has investments in a mix of sectors and geographies, the negative impacts of climate events may be compensated for by gains elsewhere. One practical consequence is that systemic sustainability-related issues and risks may be seen by investors as being less financially material and therefore of lesser importance. A similar point applies to sustainability risks that are financially material to an individual company; at the portfolio level, such risks are rarely material given that diversified portfolios often hold many hundreds of companies. The practical implication is that, where financial materiality is the primary driver of decision-making, under prevailing market practices and approaches, the incentive for investors to carefully analyse the investment implications of sustainability-related issues or to engage with company management are reduced.

Third, there is a strong argument that, despite the rhetoric, responsible investment is not a market norm or a standard practice. The reality is that, despite the large number of investors that have made commitments to responsible investment, many have yet to fully integrate sustainability-related issues into their investment processes, to engage with the companies in which they are invested or to extend their commitments to responsible investment to all asset classes. There are various reasons: the internal time and resources required to cover the full range of asset classes, gaps in the data available to assess sustainability performance, methodology questions around how to integrate these issues into investment decision-making and scepticism about the investment value of focusing on sustainability issues across all asset classes.

Fourth, while the point that sustainability-related issues can be financially material (at least for some issues in some cases) and is relatively uncontentious, it is not clear whether investors can benefit from this insight, whether the benefits of researching and acting on sustainability-related issues outweigh the research and other costs of doing so or whether investors have the ability to change sustainability practices or outcomes in ways that will improve financial risks and returns over the appropriate timescale. The answers to these questions depend strongly on the investment strategy. Very short-term strategies (where longer-term sustainability issues are discounted) or algorithmic (rules-based) strategies that do not consider sustainability-related issues may leave limited if any room for sustainability-related considerations. Even if the investment strategy does allow space for sustainability-related considerations to be included, the skill and resources of the investor will define whether that investor can and will enhance investment performance and/or sustainability-related outcomes through focusing on sustainability-related issues. Research and acting on sustainability-related issues requires time (for analysis and modelling and for internal and external discussions) and requires data (which is often purchased from third-party data providers). Finally, there may be tensions between financial and sustainability outcomes (e.g. actions to reduce greenhouse gas emissions may be expensive); that is actions to improve sustainability outcomes may not be in the financial interests of the investor. There are also questions around whether investors are particularly well placed, given the inevitable asymmetries in knowledge and information, to define what the best actions are for companies from the perspective of improving business operations, improving financial performance or improving sustainability-related outcomes.

Fifth, despite the growth in policies and regulations relating to sustainability, there has been relatively little clarification of fiduciary duties themselves or of the extent to which the duty to maximise benefits for beneficiaries may be viewed as consistent with the analysis of and action on sustainability-related issues (Freshfields Bruckhaus Deringer, 2021). Many of the policies that have been adopted have been either voluntary or 'comply or explain', and mandatory obligations have tended to emphasise disclosure rather than requiring investors to take specific actions. These criticisms should, however, be qualified by acknowledging that responsible investment-related legislation is relatively new in most jurisdictions and that the approach we are seeing is similar to that in other discipline areas, i.e. starting with voluntary approaches and then moving to disclosure-based regulation, before introducing stronger expectations over time.

Closing Reflections

The debate around whether investors should pay attention to sustainability-related issues in their investment practices and processes has developed significantly since the Freshfields' report in 2005. There are compelling reasons for investors to incorporate financially material sustainability factors into their investment decision-making, to be active owners and to encourage high standards of sustainability performance in the companies or other entities in which they are invested. There are also strong reasons for investors to actively support the stability and resilience of the financial system (e.g. through policy engagement) and for investors to understand and pay attention to the sustainability preferences of their beneficiaries and clients.

However, the argument is not won and challenges remain. These include common interpretations of financial materiality, short investment time horizons, diversification, and weaknesses in policy and regulatory frameworks. Perhaps most fundamentally, the work of organisations such as the UNEP FI and the PRI has focused on broadening the interpretation and application of fiduciary duty to encompass sustainability-related considerations. This work has not, however, sought to change the core concept of fiduciary duty but has, instead, focused on how to extend the scope of the concept within what can be considered a mainstream understanding of investment practice and prevailing definitions and approaches to financial materiality, investment timeframes and diversification. Despite the analysis and findings of *A Legal Framework for Impact*, there has been limited discussion of whether additional policy measures should be adopted to make investors are responsible for the real-world outcomes of their investment activities. The reality is that integrating consideration of ESG issues into investment practices and processes is a necessary but insufficient condition to delivering a financial sector that serves societies and individuals within existing planetary boundaries. As currently defined, fiduciary duties do not require most investor fiduciaries to account for the sustainability impacts of their investment activity beyond financial performance. More fundamental changes – to incentives, to structures, to duties, to obligations and to the broader legal frameworks within which investors operate – are needed if the financial sector is to enable economic activities and societies to prosper in a sustainable manner.

One final reflection is that this chapter has focused on institutional investors (specifically asset owners and, to an extent, asset managers) and their duties to clients and beneficiaries. These are not the only actors in or relevant to the financial system. For example, what duties are owed by other actors (e.g. insurance companies) offering pensions and pension products? What duties are owed by insurance companies, asset managers and sponsoring organisations in contract-based schemes (i.e. where the pension provider does not have fiduciary or equivalent obligations to the beneficiary in the way that a trustee would in a trust-based scheme)? What duties do investors have to deliver sustainability-related outcomes in situations where public policy measures such as trading schemes, taxes and other regulations are weak or limited? Addressing the duties and obligations of other actors in the investment system is likely to be a key focus in the years to come.

Implications for Practitioners

Investors

1. Obtain legal advice on how fiduciary duty (and similar obligations) are understood and implemented in each of the countries in which you operate.
   a. Review your sustainable investment commitments, practices and strategies in the light of this review.
2. Survey your clients to understand their views on sustainability-related issues and how they would like these to be addressed in the investments that you manage for them.
3. Recognise that fiduciary duty is generally understood as a process requirement (i.e. whether the fiduciary can demonstrate that it has applied an appropriate degree of diligence in its good-faith pursuit of beneficiaries' interests).
   a. Regularly monitor, review and assess your responsible investment activities to assess the financial and sustainability-related outcomes achieved. If the evidence suggests that the desired outcomes (in terms of impact or financial performance) are not being met, then the responsible investment strategy should be revised.
4. Recognise that definitions and interpretations of fiduciary duty evolve and are evolving.
   a. Periodically conduct a legal review of your approach to responsible investment to ensure it reflects and aligns with prevailing legal interpretations of fiduciary duty.

Policymakers

1. Adopt and effectively implement measures that support and incentivise investor action on sustainability, through:

    a. Clarifying that assessing and managing sustainability factors – in investment processes, in active ownership and voting activities and in public policy engagement – is an explicit part of investor obligations and duties.
    b. Introducing stewardship codes and corporate governance codes, and monitoring outcomes, with requirements for investors to actively engage with the companies in which they are invested, including on sustainability-related issues, and to report on this engagement.
    c. Requiring investors to disclose the processes they have in place to integrate sustainability factors into their investment research and decision-making and to monitor how such process affect the financial and sustainability performance of companies.
    d. Requiring investors to regularly engage with (or survey) their clients and beneficiaries to understand their sustainability preferences.
    e. Strengthening requirements for companies to disclose consistent, comparable and reliable information on their sustainability practices and performance.
    f. Requiring national pensions funds and sovereign wealth funds to take account of sustainability-related issues in their own investment processes and when appointing external investment managers and to report on how they are doing so.

Acknowledgement

This chapter has benefited enormously from comments and suggestions provided by Robert Nash of The Generation Foundation.

References

Atkin, D. (2024, August 8), 'Meeting Investors Where They're at: PRI Launches New Strategy', *Principles for Responsible Investment Blog*, www.unpri.org/pri-blog/meeting-investors-where-theyre-at-pri-launches-new-strategy/12636.article

Bolton, P., Buchheit, L., Gulati, M., Panizza, U., Weder di Mauro, B. and Zettelmeyer, J. (2023), 'On Debt and Climate', *Oxford Open Economics*, Vol. 2, https://doi.org/10.1093/ooec/odad005

Burckart, W. and Lydenberg, S. (2021), *21st Century Investing: Redirecting Financial Strategies to Drive Systems Change* (Berrett-Koehler Publishers, Oakland).
CDP (2025), 'About Us', www.cdp.net/en/about (last viewed 5 March 2025).
Climate Action 100+ (2025), 'Global Investors Driving Business Transition', www.climateaction100.org/ (last viewed 5 March 2025).
Freshfields Bruckhaus Deringer (2005), *A Legal Framework for the Integration of Environmental, Social and Governance Issues into Institutional Investment* (UNEP FI, Geneva), www.unepfi.org/wordpress/wp-content/uploads/2022/07/Freshfields-A-legal-framework-for-the-integration-of-ESG-issues-into-institutional-investment.pdf
Freshfields Bruckhaus Deringer (2021), *A Legal Framework for Impact* (The Generation Foundation, PRI and UNEP FI, London), www.unpri.org/download?ac=13902
FTSE Russell (2024), *8th Annual Sustainable Investment Asset Owner Survey 2024* (FTSE Russell, London), www.lseg.com/en/ftse-russell/sustainable-investing-solutions/global-asset-owner-survey#survey-highlights
Global Sustainable Investment Alliance (GSIA) (2023), *Global Sustainable Investment Review 2022*, www.gsi-alliance.org/wp-content/uploads/2023/12/GSIA-Report-2022.pdf
Gore, A. and Blood, D. (2015), 'Foreword', in PRI, UNEP FI, UN Global Compact and UNEP Inquiry into the Design of a Sustainable Financial System, *Fiduciary Duty in the 21st Century* (PRI, London), p. 5.
Hofstetter, D. (2020), *Transformation Capital: Systemic Investing for Sustainability* (EIT Climate-KIC, Amsterdam), www.climate-kic.org/wp-content/uploads/2020/08/Transformation-Capital-Systemic-Investing-for-Sustainability.pdf
Investor Agenda (2023), *The Changing Climate Policy Landscape: Considerations for Policymakers and the Needs of Investors*, https://theinvestoragenda.org/wp-content/uploads/2023/09/The-Changing-Climate-Landscape_Considerations-for-Policymakers.pdf
London Stock Exchange Group (LSEG) (2024), *Your Guide to Sustainability Reporting* (LSEG, London), www.londonstockexchange.com/raise-finance/sustainable-finance/your-guide-sustainability-reporting
Lukomnik, J. and Hawley, J. (2021), *Moving Beyond Modern Portfolio Theory: Investing That Matters* (Routledge, London).
Martindale, W., Feller, E. and Sullivan, R. (2020), 'ESG Risks and Opportunities: A Fiduciary Duty Perspective', in Fisher, P. (ed.), *Making the Financial System Sustainable* (Cambridge University Press, Cambridge), pp. 168–195.
Principles for Responsible Investment (PRI) (2016), *How Asset Owners Can Drive Responsible Investment: Beliefs, Strategies and Mandates* (PRI, London), www.unpri.org/download?ac=1398
Principles for Responsible Investment (PRI) (2023), *2022–23 Annual Report* (PRI, London), https://dwtyzx6upklss.cloudfront.net/Uploads/z/s/n/pri_ar2023_smaller_file_8875.pdf
Principles for Responsible Investment (PRI) (2024a, January 23), 'Building on Fiduciary Duty in the 21st Century: A Legal Framework for Impact', www.unpri.org/fiduciary-duty/building-on-fiduciary-duty-in-the-21st-century-a-legal-framework-for-impact/12058.article
Principles for Responsible Investment (PRI) (2024b), *A Legal Framework for Impact: Summary Report* (PRI, London), www.unpri.org/download?ac=21308

Principles for Responsible Investment (PRI) (2025a), 'Signatory Directory', www.unpri.org/signatories/signatory-resources/signatory-directory (last viewed 5 March 2025).
Principles for Responsible Investment (PRI) (2025b), 'Regulation Database', www.unpri.org/policy/global-policy/regulation-database (last viewed 19 January 2025).
PRI, UNEP FI and The Generation Foundation (2016), *Investor Duties and Obligations in 6 Asian Markets* (PRI, London).
PRI, UNEP FI and The Generation Foundation (2019), *Fiduciary Duty in the 21st Century* (PRI, London), www.unpri.org/download?ac=9792
PRI, UNEP FI, UN Global Compact and UNEP Inquiry into the Design of a Sustainable Financial System (2015), *Fiduciary Duty in the 21st Century* (PRI, London).
Reynolds, F., Fabian, N. and Sullivan, R. (2021), 'The End of the Beginning: Next Generation Responsible Investment', in Bril, H., Kell, G. and Rasche, A. (eds.), *Sustainable Investing: A Path to a New Horizon* (Routledge, London), pp. 89–107.
Sullivan, R., Martindale, W. and Feller, E. (2017), 'Fiduciary Duty', in Krosinsky, C. and Purdom, S. (eds.), *Sustainable Investing: Revolutions in Theory and Practice* (Routledge, London), pp. 224–233.
United Nations Environmental Programme Finance Initiative (UNEP FI) (2009), *Fiduciary Responsibility: Legal and Practical Aspects of Integrating Environmental, Social and Governance Issues into Institutional Investment* (UNEP FI, Geneva).
Whelan, T., Atz, U., Van Holt, T. and Clark, C. (2021), *ESG and Financial Performance: Uncovering the Relationship by Aggregating Evidence from 1,000 Plus Studies Published Between 2015–2020* (NYU Stern, New York), www.stern.nyu.edu/sites/default/files/assets/documents/NYU-RAM_ESG-Paper_2021%20Rev_0.pdf

Chapter 6

Does Sustainable Investment Deliver Better Financial Outcomes?

Kester Low, Yuqi Wang and Kushal Shah

Introduction

One of the common claims made by proponents of sustainable finance is that it not only contributes to public sustainability goals but may also deliver superior financial outcomes for investors. Belief in this claim has been central to enrolling mainstream financial institutions and professionals into the field of sustainable finance. It also underpins ongoing demand for a range of sustainability-related data, analytics, and services to help investors identify and manage financially material sustainability-related factors.

Yet the idea that sustainable finance delivers investment performance is not universally accepted and there is ongoing debate around whether, and under what conditions, better financial performance can be achieved. This chapter seeks to help the reader make better sense of this important debate. It draws on a body of academic work that has explored the relationship between sustainable investment strategies, on the one hand, and financial performance, on the other. This

DOI: 10.4324/9781003467632-6

literature is large and growing, with contributions from disciplines ranging from finance to environmental economics. It is also diverse in terms of scope, data, methods, and findings, making it difficult to draw clear generalisations. For this reason, the chapter draws heavily on several recent meta-reviews. Broadly speaking, these reviews suggest that sustainable investing does not necessarily harm financial outcomes and can deliver comparable or even superior returns under certain conditions.

The chapter is organised as follows. We start by presenting the main theoretical arguments as to why sustainable finance might or might not deliver superior financial performance. This is followed by an analysis of the empirical evidence regarding the link between sustainable investment and financial performance. The reasons why individual studies reach differing conclusions about this relationship are then examined. Finally, the chapter offers recommendations for practitioners in the field.

What Is Superior Financial Performance?

There are various ways to define superior financial performance. Financial analysts generally compare an investment's risk-adjusted returns against a market benchmark to determine which investments outperform, as opposed to those that yield lower returns (Fatemi and Fooladi, 2013). The term 'superior financial performance' is generally understood as referring to investment returns that exceed a reference benchmark such as the S&P. The term 'alpha' is used to describe the excess returns (again, generally compared to a reference benchmark) provided by an investment or portfolio beyond what would be expected based on its risk level. In that context, a higher alpha signifies that a greater degree of outperformance has been achieved (Fatemi and Fooladi, 2013).

Another important term is 'beta', which measures how much an asset's price tends to move relative to the market. A beta of 1 means the asset's price is expected to move in line with the market. A beta of greater than 1 means the asset is more volatile than the market, whereas a beta of less than 1 means the asset is less volatile than the market.

Finally, a range of metrics and ratios (e.g. Sharpe ratios) are used to assess how well investments perform against the market (or against a reference benchmark), accounting for the amount of risk taken.

Why Might Sustainable Investment Result in Superior Financial Performance?

Several theoretical arguments and mechanisms have been proposed to explain why sustainable investment might deliver superior financial outcomes. One argument is that sustainable investment may enable investors to better identify, assess, and manage risks (Fatemi and Fooladi, 2013). There is growing recognition that social and environmental issues can be financially material (Krueger *et al.*, 2020). Failing to factor material sustainability-related risks into investment decision-making may, consequently, negatively affect financial returns (Leippold and Yu, 2023).

The importance of analysing sustainability-related risks – both the likelihood of such risks eventuating and the associated consequences – is illustrated by the case of climate change. Many studies consider climate-related financial risks among the most significant threats to investors' portfolios (see, for example, Bansal *et al.* (2016) although a somewhat different view is offered by Kirk (2023)). Flammer *et al.* (2021) define climate risks as threats posed by climate-related events that could lead to damage, liability, loss, or other forms of harm. A common distinction is made between physical risks and transition risks. Physical risks arise from the direct impacts of climate change, whether acute (e.g. extreme weather events) or chronic (e.g. steadily rising temperatures and sea levels). While there is evidence that certain amounts of these effects are already being seen, there are uncertainties around the societal response to climate change, the scale of the impacts, the timing of the impacts, the location of the impacts, and the knock-on (secondary) effects of these impacts.

Transition risks are business-related threats stemming from the societal and economic shift towards a low-carbon future. There are many uncertainties around how governments will support or enable the transition with questions around the specific measures and policies they will adopt, when these measures will be adopted and implemented, which sectors and activities will be affected, and the incentives that will be provided for the transition. The literature on the transition suggests that policies and regulations introduced to combat climate change could expose some firms to legal, regulatory, and technological risks (Krueger *et al.*, 2020) and could also expose firms in carbon-intensive sectors to the risk of becoming 'sunset industries' where they experience declining asset values and potentially become stranded assets (Bauer *et al.*, 2022; Nguyen *et al.*, 2022; Semieniuk *et al.*, 2020). Investors in these sectors could, in turn, face the prospect of reduced returns and underperformance relative to the broader market (Bernardini *et al.*, 2019). Other consequences could include regulatory penalties and reputational harm (Nguyen *et al.*, 2022), increased difficulties for high-emitting firm to access capital (Javadi and Masum, 2021) and high-emitting firms being exposed to litigation (Setzer and Higham, 2024). Given the scale of these consequences and the likelihood that there will be government action to encourage the move to a low-carbon economy, investors clearly need to identify these risks and incorporate them into their analysis and investment decision-making (Allman, 2022; Hoepner *et al.*, 2024).

Another argument for sustainable investment is that it might provide an 'insurance-like effect' that safeguards investors from downside risks during social and economic downturns (Atz *et al.*, 2023). One idea is that firms with better

ESG (environmental, social and governance) performance are better equipped to respond to such shocks, partly because they tend to be more effectively managed. Another is that investors are more likely to retain holdings in firms with strong sustainability performance, resulting in greater share price resilience compared to firms with weaker sustainability credentials (Albuquerque *et al.*, 2020). The existence of this safe-haven effect finds some support in the empirical literature (Fernández *et al.*, 2019; Leite and Cortez, 2018; Wu *et al.*, 2015).

Finally, growing demand for 'sustainability' may encourage investors to place greater emphasis on sustainable investment strategies. Pástor *et al.* (2022) outline several channels through which this demand may operate. One is increasing investor appetite for sustainable assets, which may lead to higher asset prices, or lower costs of capital. Another is consumer demand for sustainable companies and their products and services. For example, such companies may be able to charge a price premium or may benefit from regulatory changes (e.g., carbon pricing), giving them a comparative advantage.

Why Might Sustainable Investment Not Deliver Better Financial Performance?

There are several reasons why sustainable investment may not yield superior financial performance and may even underperform compared to traditional investment strategies. One reason is that certain sustainable investment strategies (e.g. negative screening) may limit the available investment universe and opportunities for diversification. A central tenet of Modern Portfolio Theory is that investors can reduce their risks by holding assets with return profiles that exhibit low correlations (Markowitz, 1952). Sustainable investing strategies – such as negative or positive screening – can restrict the pool of eligible assets (Trinks and Scholtens, 2017). As a result, sustainable investors' portfolios may miss out on opportunities to benefit from higher-return investments (Aragon *et al.*, 2023).

Another reason why sustainable investment may not deliver superior financial outcomes is the frequently non-trivial transaction, compliance, and monitoring costs associated with these strategies. Sustainable investing strategies – such as ESG integration, positive screening, and shareholder engagement – often involve additional financial outlays, including payments to third-party data providers, enhanced investment analysis and due diligence, and investor-to-company transaction costs. These costs can be particularly significant for sustainability-themed financial products and services when compared to conventional alternatives (Caramichael and Rapp, 2022; Lau *et al.*, 2022).

Sustainable investing may not deliver superior financial returns because of inflated valuations. Growing demand for sustainable assets may push up their prices. Higher valuations may be rational if based on expectations of higher returns – for instance, if more sustainable companies are experiencing rising profitability. Yet, if asset prices reflect non-monetary preferences for sustainability (Agliardi and Agliardi, 2021; Barber *et al.*, 2021; Bauer *et al.*, 2022; Hornuf and Yüksel, 2023), these prices may provide a misleading guide to future returns, creating the risk that sustainability-oriented investors may 'overpay' for sustainable investments (Cornell, 2020; Pástor *et al.*, 2022). Indeed, sustainability-themed investments may be subject to considerable hype, in the sense of exaggerated claims about their future financial potential. This may result in 'green bubbles', characterised by overinflated asset values (Lehnert, 2023). Factors such as fear of missing out (FOMO), or the limited supply of sustainable assets, may play a role here. Companies with worse environmental performance may yield higher returns because investors demand a 'premium' for holding stock that is seen as carrying higher (e.g., transition) risk (Bolton and Kacperczyk, 2021).

It is also possible that sustainability-themed investments may deliver inferior financial returns in the short term. For example, companies that prioritise climate action may incur higher near-term costs, arising from expenditures on new low-carbon capital equipment or the development of new low-carbon products. They may therefore generate lower profits and returns to investors over a short-term time horizon.

Even if companies with superior sustainability performance do deliver higher profits and returns, capitalising on these opportunities depends on investors' ability to identify such firms. A combination of greenwashing and the absence of reliable data, which make it difficult to distinguish between more and less sustainable firms, could negatively impact the returns from sustainable investing strategies.

What Do Meta-Analytical Reviews and Individual Studies Tell Us about Financial Performance?

The previous sections of this chapter have set out the broad arguments for and against the idea that sustainable investment can deliver superior financial outcomes. But what does the empirical evidence tell us about this relationship? Many academic studies have sought to answer this question. It would be impossible to review all of them in a single chapter. Indeed, individual studies reach a range of conclusions, thereby defying simple generalisations. For this reason, we turn to meta-studies that draw conclusions after reviewing, standardising, and statistically analysing the findings of multiple studies. Meta-studies can be useful in helping to identify general patterns from numerous, diverse findings in the existing literature, providing statistical insights into the sign and strength of relationships. They can also help to identify how these findings vary (e.g. by asset class, by geography) and highlight biases in past work. Examples of widely cited meta-analytical reviews on the financial performance of sustainable investing include Friede *et al.* (2015), Atz *et al.* (2023), Whelan *et al.* (2021), and Hornuf and Yüksel (2023) (Table 6.1).

Table 6.1 Summary of Major Sustainable Investment Meta-Reviews

Paper	*Sample*	*Headline findings*
Atz *et al.* (2023) Title: Does Sustainability Generate Better Financial Performance? Review, Meta-analysis, and Propositions *Journal of Sustainable Finance & Investment*	The authors reviewed 1,141 primary peer-reviewed papers and 27 meta-reviews (based on approximately 1,400 studies) published between 2015 and 2020.	■ The financial performance of ESG investing has on average been indistinguishable from conventional investing. ■ One in three studies indicate that ESG investing delivers superior performance. ■ ESG integration as a strategy seems to perform better than screening or divestment.
Friede *et al.* (2015) Title: ESG and Financial Performance: Aggregated Evidence from More Than 2000 Empirical Studies *Journal of Sustainable Finance & Investment*	The authors reviewed 60 articles published between 1970 and 2014, covering more than 2,200 unique studies when adjusted for overlaps and duplication.	■ Nearly 90% of the studies presented a non-negative relationship between environmental, social, and governance performance and corporate financial performance, with the majority of studies showing a positive relationship between the two. ■ This positive relationship appears to be stable over time.
Hornuf and Yüksel (2023) Title: The Performance of Socially Responsible Investments: A Meta-Analysis *European Financial Management*	The authors conducted a systematic literature review and identified 5,845 studies relating to ESG criteria and to socially responsible investment (SRI). Of these, 153 conducted a primary empirical study, which the authors considered in a meta-analysis.	■ SRI portfolios seem to be indistinguishable from market portfolios in general, i.e. they appear to neither outperform nor underperform market portfolios. ■ Global SRI portfolios appear to outperform regional sub-portfolios. ■ The number of included factors in a capital market model is negatively correlated with the likelihood that a study will report outperformance.

(*Continued*)

Table 6.1 (Continued)

Paper	*Sample*	*Headline findings*
Whelan *et al.* (2021) Title: Uncovering the Relationship by Aggregating Evidence from 1,000 Plus Studies Published between 2015–2020 *NYU Stern Center for Sustainable Business*	The authors reviewed the relationship between ESG and financial performance in more than 1,000 research papers published between 2015 and 2020. They also conducted a meta-meta-analysis of 13 corporate meta-analysis studies (covering 1,272 unique studies) and 2 investor meta-analysis studies (covering 107 unique studies) published between 2015 and 2020.	■ 58% of 'corporate' studies that employ operational metrics, such as return on equity (ROE), return on assets (ROA) or stock price, reported a positive relationship between ESG and financial performance, with 13% reporting neutral impact, 21% finding mixed results, and 8% reporting negative impact. ■ Of the investment studies using risk-adjusted attributes, such as alpha or the Sharpe ratio, reviewed, 59% indicated similar or superior financial performance and 14% showed negative results.

What can we conclude from these meta-studies? Most importantly, they suggest that sustainable investment does not inherently impair financial outcomes. In fact, the overall weight of evidence points towards a neutral or positive relationship between sustainability and financial performance. At the same time, a degree of caution is needed, as the literature does suggest that sustainable investment strategies are not guaranteed to outperform conventional investment strategies and may sometimes result in worse financial outcomes.

This raises the question as to why individual studies might come to different conclusions, i.e., finding neutral, positive, and negative relationships. The next section seeks to answer this question, drawing from both individual and meta-studies.

Making Sense of Mixed Findings

Different Investment Strategies

As outlined in Chapter 3, sustainable investing comprises a range of distinct investment strategies (e.g. screening, sustainability-themed investment, ESG integration). The choices made by individual studies regarding how they define

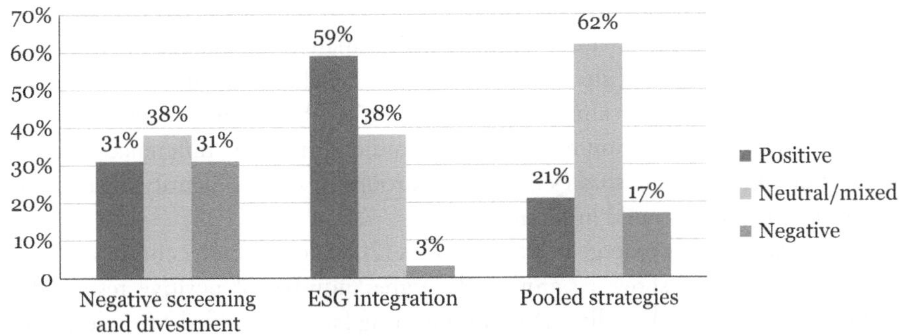

Figure 6.1 Comparing the Financial Performance of Different Portfolio Management Strategies

Source: Adapted from Atz *et al.* (2023)

sustainable investment and moreover, which investment strategies they select for examination, can significantly influence their findings. A key challenge in interpreting many existing studies is that they assess a pooled sample of portfolio management strategies (Atz *et al.*, 2023; Friede *et al.*, 2015). The findings of such studies may mask important variations in the performance of individual strategies. For example, it is possible that the positive effects of some strategies on financial outcomes are offset by the negative effects of others.

This idea receives empirical support in Atz *et al.*'s (2023) meta-review. The authors find that, across multiple studies, ESG integration performs better than exclusionary screening and divestment (Figure 6.1). This difference is unsurprising. The primary goal of ESG integration is to enhance investment performance by incorporating sustainability-related data into financial analysis, thereby improving risk management in specific portfolios and allowing investors to account for sustainability-related opportunities in their investment decision-making. In contrast, the primary goal of exclusionary screening is to give weight to the ethical values and preferences of investors. It imposes constraints on investors which might – depending on the sector and time period – lead to lower returns (Pedersen *et al.*, 2021; Zerbib, 2022).

Different Performance Measures

How studies measure financial outcomes and sustainability aspects can also have significant implications. Performance metrics vary widely among research studies. These do influence the conclusions that are drawn about the outcomes of sustainable investing. In Whelan *et al.*'s (2021) meta-analysis, the authors differentiate between (1) 'corporate' studies, which analyse the relationship between the ESG-related performance of firms and their financial performance using metrics such as return on equity (ROE), return on assets (ROA), and stock market price and (2) 'investor' studies, which analyse the financial performance of sustainability-related investments (e.g., in ESG funds or indices) using risk-adjusted metrics such as alpha or the Sharpe ratio. They found a higher incidence of mixed or negative results in investor studies, and clear differences between investor and corporate studies in the proportions of studies identifying a positive correlation (as illustrated in Figure 6.2).

Similar findings emerge in Friede *et al.*'s (2015) meta-study: corporate ('non-portfolio') studies show a significantly higher number of positive results than financial ('portfolio') studies. One complicating factor identified by these authors is that while the investor studies consider management fees and other costs, corporate studies tend to calculate financial performance without factoring in such expenses. Correlations and trends may therefore be distorted, making it difficult to draw straightforward comparisons across these studies. Meta-analyses of corporate studies have also acknowledged the importance of how corporate financial performance is operationalised (e.g. market-based versus accounting measures) in explaining the heterogeneity of findings (Wang *et al.*, 2016). The important point is that there are multiple ways of measuring financial outcomes – such as corporate-level versus portfolio-level returns, and risk-adjusted versus raw returns – which can affect the observed empirical relationship between sustainable investing and financial performance.

A further issue with the published studies is that there are many ways to measure sustainability performance, and a lack of clarity in controlling for

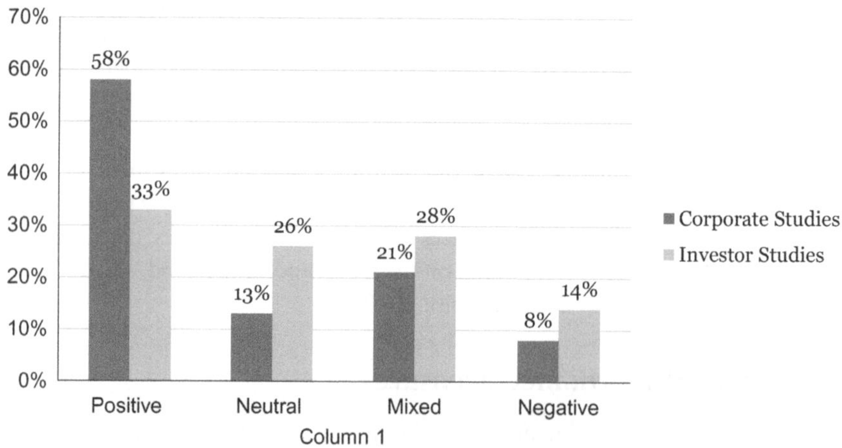

Figure 6.2 Assessing the Relationship between ESG Performance and Financial Performance

Source: Adapted from Whelan *et al.* (2021)

availability and inconsistency in the quality of ESG metrics has been shown to influence the findings of studies (Atz *et al.*, 2023; Wang *et al.*, 2016). Whelan *et al.* (2021: 3) draw attention to the 'lack of standardisation with ESG data'. For example, a significant number of studies rely on third-party ESG ratings that may be characterised by substantial biases – primarily from the definitions and measurements of the categories (Berg *et al.*, 2022; see also Chapter 12). For example, Berg *et al.* (2023) suggest that the choice of rating can have significant implications for findings regarding portfolio returns, with scores from some ESG providers exhibiting consistently positive returns, while others show negative returns in certain regions. Of course, sustainability is a multi-dimensional construct that can be defined and operationalised in many ways. It would be surprising if performance across all these different dimensions exhibited a uniform relationship with financial outcomes – particularly given that some sustainability issues are likely to be more financially material than others.

Different Scopes: Time, Geography, and Asset Classes

Another factor that influences conclusions about the relationship between sustainable investment and financial outcomes is the scope of studies – specifically, their analytical focus and boundaries. One key element is the timeframe of analysis. Widely cited studies, such as Hartzmark and Sussman (2019), have employed relatively brief periods – 11 months in their case – to conclude that there is no evidence for the superior financial performance of more sustainable funds. As the authors themselves acknowledge, there are limitations in using such truncated timeframes to establish definitive causal relationships. Whelan *et al.* (2021: 7) report that studies 'with an implied long-term focus are 76% more likely to find a positive or neutral result'. Similar conclusions are drawn in other meta-reviews (Hang *et al.*, 2019). This aligns with the preferences of sustainable investors for assessing financial returns over extended durations; for example, Cao *et al.* (2023) report that socially responsible institutions tend to have a longer average investment horizon – 4.26 quarters – compared with their non-socially responsible counterparts, at 2.63 quarters.

Timeframes are also important because of the influence of sociopolitical or economic disruptions, such as financial crises and pandemics (Agoraki *et al.*, 2023). Kölbel and Lambillon (2023) observed that, while there is evidence of a sustainability pricing premium for sustainability-linked bonds (SLBs), this has fluctuated over time. For example, they highlighted that a statistically significant unconditional premium of –31 basis points (bps) for SLB issuances in 2021 was no longer present in 2022, possibly due to 'the more volatile market in the aftermath of the Ukraine invasion, and rising inflation and interest rates' (Kölbel and Lambillon, 2023: 2). Changes in pricing or in risk premia are not only consequences of one-off events but also reflect the broader context and strategies surrounding sustainable investing. Caramichael and Rapp (2022: 14–15) noted that a statistically significant 'greenium' only emerged in 2019 following the 'maturation of the market' and widespread acceptance of green bonds as a 'mainstream investment vehicle'. Cornell (2020) and Pástor *et al.* (2022) both caution that empirical findings from past time periods – including those showing a positive relationship – may not necessarily be replicated in future ones.

Choices over geographic scope have also been shown to exert an influence on the relationships found between sustainable investment strategies and investment performance. For example, Hornuf and Yüksel's (2023) meta-analysis found significantly lower probabilities of socially responsible investment (SRI) outperformance in studies examining regional portfolios from Europe compared to global portfolios. Friede *et al.* (2015) also found evidence of geographic variations. Among other findings, they reported a greater number of positive results for emerging markets than for developed markets.

There are many possible explanations as to why the relationship between sustainable investing and financial outcomes may vary between countries and regions. These include differences in environmental regulations, the sectoral composition of industry, the variation in ESG data, and cultural preferences. For example, in relation to cultural preferences, Durand *et al.* (2013: 912) found that countries that are more collectivist and culturally distant from the United States – they cited examples such as Japan and South Korea – were more likely to favour sin stocks and hence overvalue them. These preferences may, in turn, have profound implications for the investment characteristics and investment performance of sustainable investment products in different geographies.

A further factor that can impact findings is the choice of asset classes. Most existing investor studies focus on public equities. However, the available evidence points to variations in the proportion of positive, neutral, and negative findings across different asset classes (Friede *et al.*, 2015; Whelan *et al.*, 2021). Therefore, care is required when seeking to extend the conclusions from listed equity studies to other asset classes.

Different Evaluation Frameworks

Whilst not the primary focus of this chapter, it is important to recognise that the models used to quantify the impact of sustainable investment strategies on financial outcomes also influence the findings of studies. The assumptions made in models, the factors that are included or excluded – e.g. Wang *et al.* (2016) highlight that the omission of variables such as management quality and investment in R&D can lead to spurious findings – from the analysis, and the modelling approach can all affect results (see, for example, Humphrey and Lee, 2011; Hornuf and Yüksel, 2023).

The other important point to note, albeit a less technical one, is that performance against financial benchmarks is not the only reason why people pursue sustainable investment strategies. Investors often have non-monetary preferences and may wish to invest in strategies that reflect these preferences. For example, impact investors may be willing to forgo higher returns in favour of environmental or social benefits (Barber *et al.*, 2021; Eccles *et al.*, 2017). These investors may also evaluate the financial performance of investments over different timeframes. For example, some sustainability-focused investors have a longer-term orientation than more conventional investors (Fatemi and Fooladi, 2013).

Conclusions

Sustainable investment is diverse. It can be underpinned by different motives, expectations, and conceptions of materiality. It involves various investment strategies, the implementation of which can vary markedly between investors. Sustainable investment can take place in different contexts, over different time periods, and encompass different dimensions of sustainability. There are also many ways of measuring and operationalising performance, as well as different approaches to empirically identifying the relationship between sustainable finance and financial outcomes. It is unsurprising, therefore, that studies have reached different conclusions about whether sustainable investing 'pays'.

Despite the heterogeneity in the academic literature, the evidence provides some degree of reassurance to those concerned about the financial impact of sustainable investing. It suggests that sustainable investing is likely to deliver comparable, if not better, returns than conventional strategies. This comes with a caveat: some sustainable investments, in certain asset classes, regions, and time periods, may well deliver inferior financial returns. However, in many cases, investors may be willing to accept such outcomes if these strategies are consistent with their goals and motivations, allowing them to support and to demonstrate their commitment to social and environmental goals.

Implications for Practitioners

When reviewing studies on the financial outcomes from sustainable investment strategies (or, indeed, studies on any investment strategy) you should:

1. Avoid overgeneralising the findings of individual studies.
    a. Studies may focus on different sustainable investment strategies, may use different temporal, sectoral, or geographic samples, and may rely on different metrics, statistical models, and techniques.
2. Recognise the distinction between investor- and company-level studies.
    a. Just because a company in the real economy benefits from sustainability-related activities does not automatically mean that investors in that company will also benefit financially. For example, these benefits may already be priced into the company by the time

of purchase, or the market may have failed to recognise the financial benefits of these activities.

3. Recognise that there is an investment case for sustainable investing.
   a. The existing academic evidence suggests that sustainable investing is more likely to deliver comparable or superior investment returns and, therefore, that sustainable investing is compatible with fiduciary duty. However, not all sustainable investment strategies will deliver comparable or superior returns.
4. Recognise that some sustainable investing strategies appear more likely to yield superior financial returns than others.
   a. ESG integration strategies appear to be more consistently associated with positive financial outcomes, whereas a lower rate of positive financial outcomes has been found for screening approaches.
5. Assess investment strategies on a case-by-case basis.
   a. The financial outcomes achieved from specific investment strategies (e.g. shareholder engagement) or product categories (e.g. green bonds) vary depending on how the strategy is implemented and other contextual factors.
6. Recognise that clients and beneficiaries have different motivations and interests.
   a. The case for sustainable investment cannot be reduced to financial returns alone. Investors may have other reasons to consider social and environmental objectives and outcomes alongside economic ones.

References

Agliardi, E. and Agliardi, R. (2021), 'Corporate Green Bonds: Understanding the Greenium in a Two-Factor Structural Model', *Environmental and Resource Economics*, Vol. 80, pp. 257–278, https://doi.org/10.1007/s10640-021-00585-7

Agoraki, M., Aslanidis, N. and Kouretas, G. (2023), 'How Has COVID-19 Affected the Performance of Green Investment Funds?', *Journal of International Money and Finance*, Vol. 131, p. 102792, https://doi.org/10.1016/j.jimonfin.2022.102792

Albuquerque, R., Koskinen, Y., Yang, S. and Zhang, C. (2020), 'Resiliency of Environmental and Social Stocks: An Analysis of the Exogenous COVID-19 Market Crash', *The Review of Corporate Finance Studies*, Vol. 9, No. 3, pp. 593–621, https://doi.org/10.1093/rcfs/cfaa011

Allman, E. (2022), 'Pricing Climate Change Risk in Corporate Bonds', *Journal of Asset Management*, Vol. 23, pp. 596–618, https://doi.org/10.1057/s41260-022-00294-w

Aragon, G., Jiang, Y., Joenvaara, J. and Tiu, C. (2023), 'Responsible Investing: Costs and Benefits for University Endowment Funds', *SSRN Electronic Journal*, https://doi.org/10.2139/ssrn.3446252

Atz, U., Van Holt, T., Liu, Z. and Bruno, C. (2023), 'Does Sustainability Generate Better Financial Performance? Review, Meta-Analysis, and Propositions', *Journal of Sustainable Finance & Investment*, Vol. 13, No. 1, pp. 802–825, https://doi.org/10.1080/20430795.2022.2106934

Bansal, R., Kiku, D. and Ochoa, M. (2016), 'Price of Long-Run Temperature Shifts in Capital Markets', *SSRN Electronic Journal*, https://papers.ssrn.com/sol3/papers.cfm?abstract_id=2827447

Barber, B., Morse, A. and Yasuda, A. (2021), 'Impact Investing', *Journal of Financial Economics*, Vol. 139, No. 1, pp. 162–185, https://doi.org/10.1016/j.jfineco.2020.07.008

Bauer, M., Huber, D., Rudebusch, G. and Wilms, O. (2022), 'Where Is the Carbon Premium? Global Performance of Green and Brown Stocks', *Journal of Climate Finance*, Vol. 1, p. 100006, https://doi.org/10.1016/j.jclimf.2023.100006

Berg, F., Kölbel, J. and Rigobon, R. (2022), 'Aggregate Confusion: The Divergence of ESG Ratings', *Review of Finance*, Vol. 26, No. 6, pp. 1315–1344, https://doi.org/10.1093/rof/rfac033

Berg, F., Lo, A., Rigobon, R., Singh, M. and Zhang, R. (2023), 'Quantifying the Returns of ESG Investing: An Empirical Analysis with Six ESG Metrics', *MIT Sloan Research Paper No. 6930-23*, https://doi.org/10.2139/ssrn.4367367

Bernardini, E., Di Giampaolo, J., Faiella, I. and Poli, R. (2019), 'The Impact of Carbon Risk on Stock Returns: Evidence from the European Electric Utilities', *Journal of Sustainable Finance & Investment*, Vol. 11, No. 1, pp. 1–26, https://doi.org/10.1080/20430795.2019.1569445

Bolton, P. and Kacperczyk, M. (2021), 'Do Investors Care About Carbon Risk?', *Journal of Financial Economics*, Vol. 142, No. 2, pp. 517–549, https://doi.org/10.1016/j.jfineco.2021.05.008

Cao, J., Titman, S., Zhan, X. and Zhang, W. (2023), 'ESG Preference, Institutional Trading, and Stock Return Patterns', *Journal of Financial and Quantitative Analysis*, Vol. 58, No. 5, pp. 1843–1877, https://doi.org/10.1017/s0022109022000916

Caramichael, J. and Rapp, A. (2022), 'The Green Corporate Bond Issuance Premium', *International Finance Discussion Paper No. 1346*, pp. 1–46, https://doi.org/10.17016/IFDP.2022.1346

Cornell, B. (2020), 'ESG Preferences, Risk and Return', *European Financial Management*, Vol. 27, No. 1, pp. 12–19, https://doi.org/10.1111/eufm.12295

Durand, R., Koh, S. and Tan, P. (2013), 'The Price of Sin in the Pacific-Basin', *Pacific-Basin Finance Journal*, Vol. 21, No. 1, pp. 899–913, https://doi.org/10.1016/j.pacfin.2012.06.005

Eccles, R., Kastrapeli, M. and Potter, S. (2017), 'How to Integrate ESG into Investment Decision-Making: Results of a Global Survey of Institutional Investors', *Journal of Applied Corporate Finance*, Vol. 29, No. 4, pp. 125–133, https://doi.org/10.1111/jacf.12267

Fatemi, A. and Fooladi, I. (2013), 'Sustainable Finance: A New Paradigm', *Global Finance Journal*, Vol. 24, No. 2, pp. 101–113, https://doi.org/10.1016/j.gfj.2013.07.006

Fernández, M., Abu-Alkheil, A. and Khartabiel, G. (2019), 'Do German Green Mutual Funds Perform Better Than Their Peers', *Business and Economics Research Journal*, Vol. 10, No. 2, pp. 297–312, https://doi.org/10.20409/berj.2019.169

Flammer, C., Toffel, M. and Viswanathan, K. (2021), 'Shareholder Activism and Firms' Voluntary Disclosure of Climate Change Risks', *Strategic Management Journal*, Vol. 42, No. 10, pp. 1850–1879, https://doi.org/10.1002/smj.3313

Friede, G., Busch, T. and Bassen, A. (2015), 'ESG and Financial Performance: Aggregated Evidence from More Than 2000 Empirical Studies', *Journal of Sustainable Finance*

& Investment, Vol. 5, No. 4, pp. 210–233, https://doi.org/10.1080/20430795.2015.1118917

Hang, M., Geyer-Klingeberg, J. and Rathgeber, A. (2019), 'It is Merely a Matter of Time: A Meta-Analysis of the Causality between Environmental Performance and Financial Performance', *Business Strategy and the Environment*, Vol. 28, No. 2, pp. 257–273, https://doi.org/10.1002/bse.2215

Hartzmark, S. and Sussman, A. (2019), 'Do Investors Value Sustainability? A Natural Experiment Examining Ranking and Fund Flows', *The Journal of Finance*, Vol. 74, No. 6, pp. 2789–2837, https://doi.org/10.1111/jofi.12841

Hoepner, A., Oikonomou, I., Sautner, Z., Starks, L. and Zhou, X. (2024), 'ESG Shareholder Engagement and Downside Risk', *Review of Finance*, Vol. 28, No. 2, pp. 483–510, https://doi.org/10.1093/rof/rfad034

Hornuf, L. and Yüksel, G. (2023), 'The Performance of Socially Responsible Investments: A Meta-Analysis', *European Financial Management*, Vol. 30, No. 2, pp. 1012–1061, https://doi.org/10.1111/eufm.12439

Humphrey, J. and Lee, D. (2011), 'Australian Socially Responsible Funds: Performance, Risk and Screening Intensity', *Journal of Business Ethics*, Vol. 102, pp. 519–535, https://doi.org/10.1007/s10551-011-0836-7

Javadi, S. and Masum, A. (2021), 'The Impact of Climate Change on the Cost of Bank Loans', *Journal of Corporate Finance*, Vol. 69, p. 102019, https://doi.org/10.1016/j.jcorpfin.2021.102019

Kirk, S. (2023, November 2), 'Why I Want Me Some Transition Risk', *Financial Times*, www.ft.com/content/2832f1b8-6b01-4a0d-8953-cb6dec8cc94e

Kölbel, J. and Lambillon, A. (2023), *Who Pays for Sustainability? An Analysis of Sustainability-Linked Bonds. Swiss Finance Institute Research Paper No. 23-07* (Swiss Finance Institute, University of Geneva, Geneva), https://doi.org/10.2139/ssrn.4007629

Krueger, P., Sautner, Z. and Starks, L. (2020), 'The Importance of Climate Risks for Institutional Investors', *The Review of Financial Studies*, Vol. 33, No. 3, pp. 1067–1111, https://doi.org/10.1093/rfs/hhz137

Lau, P., Sze, A., Wan, W. and Wong, A. (2022), 'The Economics of the Greenium: How Much Is the World Willing to Pay to Save the Earth?', *Environmental and Resource Economics*, Vol. 81, pp. 379–408, https://doi.org/10.1007/s10640-021-00630-5

Lehnert, T. (2023), 'The Green Stock Market Bubble', *Circular Economy and Sustainability*, Vol. 3, pp. 1213–1222, https://doi.org/10.1007/s43615-022-00223-4

Leippold, M. and Yu, T. (2023), *The Green Innovation Premium: Evidence from U.S. Patents and the Stock Market', Swiss Finance Institute Research Paper No. 23-21* (Swiss Finance Institute, University of Geneva, Geneva), https://doi.org/10.2139/ssrn.4391444

Leite, P. and Cortez, M. (2018), 'The Performance of European SRI Funds Investing in Bonds and Their Comparison to Conventional Funds', *Investment Analysts Journal*, Vol. 47, No. 1, pp. 65–79, https://doi.org/10.1080/10293523.2017.1414911

Markowitz, H. (1952), 'Modern Portfolio Theory', *Journal of Finance*, Vol. 7, No. 1, pp. 77–91, https://doi.org/10.2307/2975974

Nguyen, Q., Diaz-Rainey, I. and Kuruppuarachchi, D. (2022), 'In Search of Climate Distress Risk', *International Review of Financial Analysis*, Vol. 85, p. 102444, https://doi.org/10.1016/j.irfa.2022.102444

Pástor, L, Stambaugh, R. and Taylor, L. (2022), 'Dissecting Green Returns', *Journal of Financial Economics*, Vol. 146, No. 2, pp. 403–424, https://doi.org/10.1016/j.jfineco.2022.07.007

Pedersen, L. H., Fitzgibbons, S. and Pomorski, L. (2021), 'Responsible Investing: The ESG-Efficient Frontier', *Journal of Financial Economics*, Vol. 142, No. 2, pp. 572–597, https://doi.org/10.1016/j.jfineco.2020.11.001

Semieniuk, G., Campiglio, E., Mercure, J., Volz, U. and Edwards, N. (2020), 'Low-Carbon Transition Risks for Finance', *WIREs Climate Change*, Vol. 12, No. 1, p. e678, https://doi.org/10.1002/wcc.678

Setzer, J. and Higham, C. (2024), *Global Trends in Climate Change Litigation: 2024 Snapshot* (Grantham Research Institute on Climate Change and the Environment), www.lse.ac.uk/granthaminstitute/publication/global-trends-in-climate-change-litigation-2024-snapshot/

Trinks, P. and Scholtens, B. (2017), 'The Opportunity Cost of Negative Screening in Socially Responsible Investing', *Journal of Business Ethics*, Vol. 140, pp. 193–208, https://doi.org/10.1007/s10551-015-2684-3

Wang, Q., Dou, J. and Jia, S. (2016), 'A Meta-Analytic Review of Corporate Social Responsibility and Corporate Financial Performance', *Business & Society*, Vol. 55, No. 8, pp. 1083–1121, https://doi.org/10.1177/0007650315584317

Whelan, T., Atz, U., Holt, T. and Clark, C. (2021), *Uncovering the Relationship by Aggregating Evidence from 1,000 Plus Studies Published between 2015–2020* (NYU Stern Center for Sustainable Business), www.stern.nyu.edu/sites/default/files/assets/documents/NYU-RAM_ESG-Paper_2021%20Rev_0.pdf

Wu, J., Lodorfos, G., Dean, A. and Gioulmpaxiotis, G. (2015), 'The Market Performance of Socially Responsible Investment during Periods of the Economic Cycle – Illustrated Using the Case of FTSE', *Managerial and Decision Economics*, Vol. 38, No. 2, pp. 238–251, https://doi.org/10.1002/mde.2772

Zerbib, O. (2022), 'A Sustainable Capital Asset Pricing Model (S-CAPM): Evidence from Environmental Integration and Sin Stock Exclusion', *Review of Finance*, Vol. 26, No. 6, pp. 1345–1388, https://doi.org/10.1093/rof/rfac045

Chapter 7

Does Sustainable Investment Deliver Better Sustainability Outcomes?

Cecilia Meinardi, Arjun Sanghera,
Nora Venin and James Corah

Introduction

One of the key questions to be asked about any sustainable investment strategy is whether and to what extent the strategy does or could deliver sustainability outcomes. Addressing this question requires that attention is paid to four areas: (1) the objectives of the strategy; (2) the theory of change around how the strategy is expected to deliver these outcomes; (3) the actual design and execution of the strategy; and (4) the actual outcomes achieved from the strategy.

The aim of this chapter is to help readers think in a systematic and critical way about how sustainable investment strategies might deliver better sustainability outcomes. We present a theory of change for five – although we acknowledge we could have chosen others – different strategies (shareholder engagement, divestment, impact investment, ESG (environmental, social and governance) integration and capital allocation, negative screening). We

 DOI: 10.4324/9781003467632-7

use these theories of change to reflect on the potential for each strategy to deliver positive sustainability outcomes, and on the factors that affect the specific outcomes that might be achieved. We conclude by offering some practical suggestions for investment practitioners charged with designing and implementing these strategies.

Some Important Concepts

This chapter uses the concept of 'theory of change' – an explicit theory of how and why a particular action or intervention is expected to lead to outcomes and impacts – to draw connections between investment strategies and the outcomes they produce. Formally, a theory of change describes how an actor or organisation's actions deliver specific outcomes which are measured through target parameters (Heeb *et al.*, 2022). Theories of change are useful for identifying and assessing the linkages between investor activities, company practices and real-world outcomes. They provide a means of challenging and connecting the causal links between sustainable investment strategies and the outcomes they deliver at a firm, portfolio and societal level. By explicitly integrating critical assumptions into causal chains, theories of change also enable practitioners to better understand the nuanced conditions under which these strategies can deliver positive outcomes.

While theories of change can help explain how sustainable investment strategies can be effective in achieving sustainable outcomes, they also have limitations. A particular issue in the context of this chapter relates to the practical difficulties involved in measuring the actual outcomes and impacts that result from sustainable investment strategies, due to the wide range of metrics used to assess performance, outcomes and impacts. For example, a company's sustainability performance (or improvements in performance) can be assessed through its ESG ratings, but the different methods used in calculating these ratings can make it difficult to properly measure whether and how performance has changed (Fichtner *et al.*, 2024; see also Chapter 12 of this book).

Outcome or impact assessment is complicated by the fact that outcomes can be measured at different levels (e.g. at a company level, at an investment portfolio level, at a regional or country level, at a global level). For example, if we are interested in greenhouse gas emissions, a company's performance may be assessed on the basis of whether or not its total greenhouse gas emissions have changed and by how much. However, when we look at an investment portfolio, changes in greenhouse gas emissions from the portfolio may be driven by, for example, changes in company performance, changes in how emissions are accounted for or changes in the actual companies held in the portfolio. When we move to the regional or country level, changes in emissions could be driven by, for example, changes in company performance, changes in emissions accounting or changes in the activities conducted within the region. That is, an assessment that substantive outcomes have been achieved at one level of analysis does not necessarily mean that equivalent outcomes are achieved at other levels (Bauckloh *et al.*, 2023).

The fact that an outcome has been observed does not mean that the outcome is due to the action or intervention of the investor. An example could be where a company decides to reduce its greenhouse gas emissions. This decision may be due to an individual investor's engagement, collective engagement by investors, a threat of divestment by one or multiple investors, current or impending regulations, customer demand or consumer expectations.

Another consideration when assessing outcomes and impacts is that investors often use their own preferred measures of outcome or impact. This is particularly important when it comes to assessing the aggregate impact of sustainable investment strategies. Ideally, investors' theories of change should be explicitly located in the context of frameworks that provide globally recognised objectives for sustainable finance, such as the United Nations Sustainable Development Goals (SDG) and the Paris Agreement (Fichtner *et al.*, 2024). While such a framing would not address all of the issues around outcome measurement, it would help address at least some of the issues around comparability and assessing the aggregate impact or contribution of sustainable finance strategies.

Five Sustainable Investment Strategies: A Critical Analysis

Strategy 1: Shareholder Engagement

Shareholder engagement (often referred to as active ownership) is one of the major sustainable investment strategies employed to deliver sustainability outcomes (Braun, 2022). In broad terms, it involves shareholders using their formal rights (e.g. to vote their shareholdings, to call emergency general meetings (EGMs)) and informal influence (e.g. direct dialogue with companies, collaborating with other investors and stakeholders) to encourage changes in companies' ESG practices and performance (Kölbel *et al.*, 2020; Marti *et al.*, 2023).

The theory of change underpinning shareholder engagement is that the views expressed by investors are important influences on company decision-making and that, when investors communicate these views, companies will respond positively and constructively to these views. In the specific context of sustainability-related issues, the expectation is that shareholder engagement will lead to improvements in company practice and performance on the issues that are the subject of the engagement.

A further element of many investors' theory of change for shareholder engagement is that the signalling effect is important. By raising issues with companies, investors signal both to the company and to other investors that these issues are important and that action is needed to ensure that they are effectively managed (Gifford, 2010). Shareholder engagement may also create peer pressure for other companies to re-evaluate their practices and performance and may even lead to the development of new industry-wide norms (Kölbel *et al.*, 2020). That is, the signalling effect of engaging with one company can have knock-on effects across a group of companies.

Various factors influence the effectiveness of shareholder engagement strategies. Successful shareholder engagement is more likely to occur in companies that have stronger commitments to corporate social responsibility (CSR), in companies when board members support action on the issues being raised by shareholders and in companies with stronger track records on sustainability-related issues (Gifford, 2010: Kölbel *et al.*, 2020; Marti *et al.*, 2023). Shareholder salience is also important, with the extent to which shareholders possess power, legitimacy and urgency being key determinants of the likely success or failure of specific proposals (Gifford, 2010). As noted by Dimson *et al.* (2015), the presence of shareholders possessing larger shares of a company or from the same country as the engaged company means that ESG proposals to the board are more likely to succeed, and thus that sustainability outcomes are more likely to occur.

The substance and substantive implications of proposals are also important determinants of their likelihood of success. Proposals that impose significant costs on companies have a greater likelihood of being opposed by management, of being partially or inadequately implemented or of being disregarded (Dimson *et al.*, 2015). Such proposals are also less likely to be supported by investors, weakening the pressure on companies to implement the proposals.

Strategy 2: Divestment

Divestment strategies generally involve selling stocks in a company or a sector whose business practices have been tarnished due to their controversial nature (Plantinga and Scholtens, 2024). Divestment strategies have become an increasingly prominent and widely promoted responsible investment strategy. For example, the global fossil fuel divestment movement has grown rapidly with over US$14 trillion in divestment pledges made by 2020 (Cojoianu *et al.*, 2021; Schwartz *et al.*, 2024). This strategy has gained particular attention – although it remains to be seen how significant the strategy will be – in debt markets. Examples include calls to 'deny the debt' (where investors are asked not to provide debt to large greenhouse gas emitting activities) and pressure not to provide financial support to new carbon-intensive assets. Even though divestment shares many commonalities with negative screening, we define the latter (see below) as a criteria-driven approach that excludes companies or sectors that do not meet the investor's ethical or other objectives.

The theory of change underpinning divestment strategies is that the threat of divestment (or 'exit') creates an incentive (e.g. through the share price, through the cost of capital, through damage to the company's reputation) for companies to improve their ESG performance (Braun, 2022; Plantinga and Scholtens, 2024).

The effectiveness of divestment strategies depends on the ability of investors to widely communicate their views (and the reasons for divesting), on the credibility of the reasons advanced and on the existence of a significantly large cohort of investors willing to divest at a scale that demonstrably affects share price, the cost of capital or other financial metrics. There is evidence (see, for example, Gantchev *et al.* (2022)) that negative sustainability-related news can influence investors' willingness to divest, and that firms do experience negative short-term abnormal returns following such news. There is also evidence that companies with a higher proportion of investors concerned about sustainability-related issues are more likely to make substantive improvements to company practices following threats of divestment (Gantchev *et al.*, 2022). Furthermore, the greater the number of investors divesting or willing to divest, the greater the likelihood that such an investment strategy will encourage companies to take action (Schwartz *et al.*, 2024).

The effectiveness of divestment strategies also depends on the views of company management (specifically, whether they agree that the recommended course of action is in the best interests of the company), the incentives provided to company management and the views of the company's other investors. There is some evidence that linking managerial compensation to stock performance encourages companies to improve their corporate practices. In the context of negative news about social and environmental issues and the presence of investors concerned about sustainability-related issues, managers are incentivised to make improvements to reduce the risks of divestment (and investor exodus) (Edmans *et al.*, 2012; Gantchev *et al.*, 2022). For example, Gantchev *et al.* (2022) argue that managers who receive equity compensation often make substantive and genuine improvements in a variety of business areas, including resource use, emissions, workforce, community and product responsibility.

The empirical evidence on the effectiveness of divestment – most of which relates to greenhouse gas emissions and the low carbon transition – provides a mixed picture on the potential for divestment to significantly alter and improve corporate practices. For example, Plantinga and Scholtens (2024) argued that divestment has a limited impact on global emissions and the energy transition. However, Glomsrod and Wei (2018) concluded that divestment does have a notable impact on reducing coal consumption and increasing the global share of non-fossil electricity and Rohleder *et al.* (2022) established a causal link between divested firms experiencing a stock price decline and a subsequent reduction in company carbon emissions relative to non-divested firms. What is clear is that divestment has allowed individual investors to reduce the carbon exposure and intensity of their own financial portfolios, especially when adopting strategies which target multiple industries (Hunt and Weber, 2018). What is less clear, however, is whether these divestments have had a material effect on global greenhouse gas emissions or have simply involved selling high-emitting assets to other investors. Expressed another way, the question is whether the overall effect of divestment has simply been to shift pollution elsewhere. For example, while there is evidence that strong domestic fossil fuel divestment movements can incentivise domestic energy companies to increase their share of renewables, there is also evidence that investment banks in countries with strong divestment movements may actually increase their investments in foreign oil and gas companies (Cojoianu et al., 2021). Cojoianu *et al.* (2021) suggest that this carbon leakage may partly explain why divestment has so far played a limited role in reducing actual global greenhouse gas emissions, pointing to the fact that oil and gas financing had risen by 8% per year since 2008 despite the growth of divestment movements.

Strategy 3: Impact Investing

The Global Impact Investing Network (GIIN) defines impact investing as 'investments made with the intention to generate positive, measurable social and environmental impact alongside a financial return' (Global Impact Investing Network (GIIN), 2019: 1). In this context, Roor and Maas (2024) define impact as 'the result of an organisation's activities on individual stakeholders, society, and the environment, including intended and unintended, positive and negative, and short-term and long-term effects'.

Impact investing often focuses on specific sectors, such as renewable energy, sustainable agriculture, microfinance or conservation. Investments can be made through a variety of means, including direct investments, impact funds and thematic or cause-based investing strategies such as thematic bonds and microfinance (Penna *et al.*, 2021).

The key feature of impact investment that differentiates it from, for example, thematic investment, is that investment strategy needs to be underpinned by the explicit intention to deliver a positive social and/or environmental impact (Brest and Born, 2013; Caldecott *et al.*, 2024; Findlay and Moran, 2019; Freireich and Fulton, 2009; Jackson, 2013). Furthermore, the investor needs to measure and communicate the impacts of the investments that have been made.

The theory of change that underpins impact investment is that it will lead to increased investment in areas such as biodiversity conservation, renewable energy, sustainable agriculture practices, innovations that aim to reduce environmental impact, affordable housing and access to healthcare and education. The other key element of impact investment's theory of change is that, through measuring and reporting on impact performance, the investment strategy will demonstrate the contribution that investors can make to addressing social and performance issues (and thereby encourage others to follow) and will build capacity and expertise in impact assessment, monitoring and reporting.

The literature on impact investment suggests that it will be more successful in achieving sustainability outcomes if impact-related considerations are integrated throughout each step of the investment process, from strategy-setting all the way to exit. This explicit integration is seen as important to preventing mission drift and preventing investment processes getting decoupled from positive impacts (Cetindamar and Ozkazanc-Pan, 2017; Roor and Maas, 2024). Other factors that influence the scale of impact include the specific issues (or themes) that are targeted, the type of investor involved (e.g. fund managers, pension funds, development finance institutions, banks, private foundations) and their return objectives and timeframes and the stage at which investment is made.

Impact investment faces practical challenges. The first is that investors may not be willing or able to make impact investments, in particular where the investment performance of those investments is not as good as that from non-impact investments. While the impact investment market is significant and growing, it remains a very small proportion of the broader investment market (Hand *et al.*, 2024). Second, measuring impact is complex and investors may be reluctant – because of the risk of being accused of greenwashing (see, for example, Roor and Maas (2024) – to commit to impact investment strategies if they are not confident that they can demonstrate the positive impact or contribution that they have made. The third is that the credibility (and, in turn, the potential value) of impact investment relies on investors being able to demonstrate the positive impact that they have made. There is evidence of investors using impact-labelling a marketing tool to raise capital or for reputational reasons, instead of delivering real-economy social or environmental outcomes (Caldecott *et al.*, 2024).

Strategy 4: ESG Integration and Capital Allocation

In broad terms, capital allocation refers to 'the investor activity of allocating capital to particular financial assets' (Kölbel *et. al.*, 2020: 558). ESG integration refers to the explicit assessment of ESG-related issues in investment research and decision-making. It is important to stress that ESG integration and capital allocation are not homogenous strategies. There are multiple ways in which sustainability-related issues can be captured in decision-making at the stock (or asset) and portfolio level. Furthermore, different investors will have different views about what is financially material, reflecting their beliefs and relevant investment time horizons. The degree to which ESG integration and capital allocation affect or deliver sustainability outcomes will be shaped by these and other differences.

Formally, neither ESG integration nor capital allocation strategies target a particular set of social or environmental outcomes (i.e. as noted by Heeb *et al.* (2022), the focus is primarily, if not exclusively, on investment performance). However, investors may supplement their investment objectives with particular sustainability-related objectives.

Given that the primary purpose of ESG integration is to improve investment performance, the question is whether it actually is or should be considered a sustainable finance strategy. From a sustainability outcomes perspective, the theory of change is that, by explicitly considering ESG factors in their investment research and decision-making, investors signal to companies that these factors are important. The assumption is that companies will conclude that if they do a better job of managing these aspects (e.g. through better managing these, through accessing sustainability-related opportunities), investors will have a more positive view of the company and will, therefore, be more likely to invest in the company's equity or debt.

The empirical evidence supporting this theory of change remains limited. It is difficult to disaggregate the effects of this strategy from the other factors that shape investor and company decision-making. However, we can make a number of general observations.

The first is that the signalling effects of ESG integration are only likely to work if investors explicitly state that they look at these aspects of company performance and that they preferentially invest in good performers and/or invest less in poorer performers. The fact that so many investors have committed to the Principles for Responsible Investment (PRI) (with the associated commitment to ESG integration and active ownership) means that companies cannot be unaware that investors look at financially material sustainability issues in their investment research. However, the reality is that companies are unlikely to be convinced of an investor's commitment simply because the investor is a signatory to PRI or to other similar initiatives. Therefore, the success of this strategy is likely to depend on the extent to which investors – publicly and through their dialogue with companies – explain how they account for these factors in their investment decision-making, how good performance is a positive (and poor performance a negative) and how much weight is given to these aspects of performance in investment decision-making. While the direct signalling effects may be limited, ESG integration may alert companies to the financial implications of particular sustainability-related issues. In turn, companies may decide to address these issues if doing so provides financial or other benefits such as improved efficiency or reduced exposure to reputational risks.

The second observation is that investors need to be aligned in their understanding of what good and poor performance look like. Without this alignment, companies will not receive a clear signal on what is expected of them. The good news is that there is broad consensus on what good performance looks like from a governance and management system perspective, irrespective of whether a company is being assessed from an investment risk or an impact perspective (Sullivan, 2011). In broad terms, companies are expected to have robust board oversight processes, clear management accountabilities, clear policies, sustainability-related objectives, targets and key performance indicators, and reporting on their performance against these targets and on how the company expects its performance to evolve over time (see, for example, Sullivan, 2011). However, there is much less consensus on the performance or impact expectations of companies. Investors may not have a common view on, for example, whether a company should have a net zero target, on the extent and rate at which the company should reduce its emissions or on whether the company should operate in conflict zones or regions with poor governance.

The third observation is that the wider goals and commitments made by investors shape the signals sent to companies. If investors supplement their commitments to ESG integration (which is essentially a process measure) with explicit goals such as net zero, reducing their portfolio-related climate or biodiversity impacts or improving gender diversity, they send much stronger signals to companies about what is expected of them and of the company practices that are likely to be rewarded or penalised.

The fourth observation is that the greater the importance or weighting given to sustainability-related issues in investment decisions, the stronger the signal that is sent (see, further, Heeb *et al.*, 2022). It is important to recognise that the emphasis placed on sustainability-related factors by investors is just one influence on company management decisions. Others include the wider views held by the company's investors (e.g. do they place a significant weight on ESG-related factors?) (Gollier and Pouget, 2014; Kölbel *et al.*, 2020), the financial significance of ESG-related risks and opportunities (i.e. are they important to the future success of the company), and the manner in which company management is incentivised and rewarded.

The fifth observation, reflecting the points made above about the other strategies, is that ESG integration relies on the adequacy of the information provided by companies and by ratings and other data providers. If a company's disclosures or its sustainability ratings do not accurately reflect actual business practices, there is a risk that investors will not make robust investment decisions (i.e. they risk rewarding poorer performers or penalising good performers).

Strategy 5: Negative Screening

Negative screening involves avoiding (i.e. not investing in) companies on the basis of fixed, specified criteria. These criteria can be defined in a range of ways: by product (e.g. alcohol, tobacco), by activity (e.g. gambling), by sector (e.g. oil, mining, banking), by reference to international norms (e.g. non-compliance with international standards or principles such as those from the United Nations) or by management practice (e.g. the absence of human rights policies).

The theory of change is that screening reduces the number of investors willing to support a company (thereby reducing share price or increasing the cost of capital). Screening also sends signals to the company and to wider society about the investor's views about the company and the issue in question (Marti *et al.*, 2023). These effects, in turn, incentivise companies to take action to ensure that they are not screened out of investor's portfolios. Moreover, the adoption of screening criteria by one investor may encourage other investors to adopt similar criteria.

While ethical screening is widely used by faith-based and mission-driven investors, it is not clear how much influence it has had on company practices. Most investors – because of fiduciary obligations and a lack of consensus among their clients – either do not apply screens or only apply these to a small proportion of their investment portfolios. This has the effect of limiting the signal sent to companies. Even in areas where large segments of the market have adopted screens (e.g. tobacco, controversial weapons), it is not clear that these have materially affected companies' share prices or ability to access capital. Another factor that limits the influence of screening is that, because these screens tend to be rigidly applied, companies may decide that there is limited value in engaging with these investors because this engagement is very unlikely to change the investors' views or the way they define and apply their screens.

Conclusions

This chapter has presented a conceptual framework for thinking about and assessing the sustainability outcomes (or impacts) associated with sustainable investment strategies. The five examples presented here, which are summarised in Table 7.1, demonstrate that for any sustainable finance strategy, it is possible to develop a clear theory of change and to identify the factors that make it more or less likely that the desired outcomes will be achieved.

A number of common themes emerge from this analysis. The first is that the actual outcomes achieved will depend on the strategy (or strategies adopted) and the manner in which these are implemented. The fact that an investor has committed to, for example, ESG integration does not tell us very much about the outcomes that will result from that strategy.

The second is that an explicit focus on outcomes is important. From the discussion above, sustainable finance is more likely to deliver positive social or environmental outcomes if these are explicitly identified as part of the process of developing and implementing the strategy. Explicit outcomes also help ensure the accountability of investors to their stakeholders.

The third is that scale and alignment of expectations are important to ensure that companies receive clear, consistent signals and know that these are backed by multiple investors.

The fourth is that there are practical challenges, in particular around the specification of outcomes and ensuring that the goals and outcomes sought at the company and portfolio level lead to meaningful outcomes at the societal or global level. Despite good intentions, many of the strategies, if poorly designed or implemented, run the risk of delivering limited wider benefits or even creating harm for society or the environment.

Table 7.1 An Overview of the Sustainability Outcomes from Different Sustainable Investment Strategies

Sustainable Investment Strategy	*Summary of Empirical Insights*	*Contextual and Strategic Factors Shaping the Outcomes Achieved*
Shareholder engagement	Strong and growing body of evidence demonstrating positive effects on sustainability-related practices, in particular in situations where investor influence is effectively exerted, and companies are responsive.	■ Investor salience. ■ Proportion of shares or proportion of entity held by participating investors. ■ Materiality of the sustainability-related issue to the company or entity. ■ Management attitudes. ■ Feasibility and cost of proposed actions.
Divestment	Evidence is mixed. Some studies suggest that there are links between divestment and sustainability-related performance improvements, but broader systemic effects are debated.	■ Coherence of investor rationale. ■ Feasibility of corporate action (including the availability of strategic options). ■ Managerial incentives in relation to sustainability-related concerns. ■ Degree of coordination among participating investors. ■ Scale of capital that is or could be moved.
Impact investing	Evidence that can deliver positive sustainability outcomes when impact intent is embedded across the full investment life-cycle. Challenges remain around investors' willingness to adopt impact investment (scale), measurement and verification.	■ Degree of strategic alignment of company or entity with social or environmental goals. ■ Robustness of impact measurement frameworks. ■ Type and mission of capital providers (investors).
ESG integration and capital allocation	Limited direct evidence that these strategies lead to change in companies, although the mechanisms of influence (market signalling) are plausible and continue to be researched.	■ Weight allocation to sustainability-related considerations in decision-making. ■ Consistency and clarity of sustainability-related expectations. ■ Quality and comparability of sustainability-related data and ratings.
Negative screening	Limited empirical evidence for firm-level behavioural change. Stronger effects observed in cases of widespread or coordinated exclusionary practice.	■ Market coverage and consistency of screening criteria. ■ Perceived legitimacy and reputational impact. ■ Investor willingness to change their views (about the way they interpret and apply screens, about the company or entity) over time.

Reflections for Practitioners

1. Having a clear theory of change for sustainable investment strategies is vital. A clear theory of change helps ensure that the value and impact of particular strategies – both *ex post* and *ex ante* – are clearly defined and provide a framework for tracking actions, progress and outcomes.
2. Sustainable investment strategies need to be explicit about the outcomes and impacts they are trying to achieve, including the scale of outcomes and impacts, and the level (i.e. company, portfolio, societal). These outcomes should be used to track and assess progress and impact.
3. Relying on financial materiality or improved financial performance to deliver better sustainability outcomes is unlikely to be an effective strategy. There are multiple ways that companies can achieve desired financial outcomes, but not all are necessarily aligned with the goals of investors concerned about sustainability-related issues.
4. Investors need to work with others to deliver impact at scale. This means working to build consensus around processes and outcomes and to ensure that the signals being sent to companies – irrespective of the strategies being adopted – are consistent and are continually reinforced.

References

Bauckloh, T., Klein, C., Pioch, T. and Schiemann, F. (2023), 'Under Pressure? The Link between Mandatory Climate Reporting and Firms' Carbon Performance', *Organization & Environment*, Vol. 36, No. 1, pp. 126–149, https://doi.org/10.1177/10860266221083340

Braun, B. (2022), 'Exit, Control, and Politics: Structural Power and Corporate Governance under Asset Manager Capitalism', *Politics & Society*, Vol. 50, No. 4, pp. 630–654, https://doi.org/10.1177/00323292221126262

Brest, P. and Born, K. (2013), 'When Can Impact Investing Create Real Impact?', *Stanford Social Innovation Review*, Vol. 11, No. 4, https://ssir.org/up_for_debate/article/impact_investing

Caldecott, B., Clark, A., Harnett, E. and Liu, F. (2024, May 23), 'How Sustainable Finance Creates Impact: Transmission Mechanisms to the Real Economy', *Review of World Economics*, https://doi.org/10.1007/s10290-024-00541-9

Cetindamar, D. and Ozkazanc-Pan, B. (2017), 'Assessing Mission Drift at Venture Capital Impact Investors', *Business Ethics: A European Review*, Vol. 26, No. 3, pp. 257–270, https://doi.org/10.1111/beer.12149

Cojoianu, T., Ascui, F., Clark, G., Hoepner, A. and Wójcik, D. (2021), 'Does the Fossil Fuel Divestment Movement Impact New Oil and Gas Fundraising?', *Journal of Economic Geography*, Vol. 21, No. 1, pp. 141–164, https://doi.org/10.1093/jeg/lbaa027

Dimson, E., Karakaş, O. and Li, X. (2015), 'Active Ownership', *The Review of Financial Studies*, Vol. 28, No. 12, pp. 3225–3268, https://doi.org/10.1093/rfs/hhv044

Edmans, A., Goldstein, I. and Jiang, W. (2012), 'The Real Effects of Financial Markets: The Impact of Prices on Takeovers', *The Journal of Finance*, Vol. 67, No. 3, pp. 933–971, https://doi.org/10.1111/j.1540-6261.2012.01738.x

Fichtner, J., Jaspert, R. and Petry, J. (2024), 'Mind the ESG Capital Allocation Gap: The Role of Index Providers, Standard-Setting, and "Green" Indices for the Creation of Sustainability Impact', *Regulation & Governance*, Vol. 18, No. 2, pp. 479–498, https://doi.org/10.1111/rego.12530

Findlay, S. and Moran, M. (2019), 'Purpose-Washing of Impact Investing Funds: Motivations, Occurrence and Prevention', *Social Responsibility Journal*, Vol. 15, No. 7, pp. 853–873, https://doi.org/10.1108/SRJ-11-2017-0260

Freireich, J. and Fulton, K. (2009), *Investing for Social and Environmental Impact: A Design for Catalyzing an Emerging Industry* (Monitor Institute), www2.deloitte.com/az/en/pages/financial-services/articles/investing-for-socialandenvironmentalimpact.html

Gantchev, N., Giannetti, M. and Li, R. (2022), 'Does Money Talk? Divestitures and Corporate Environmental and Social Policies', *Review of Finance*, Vol. 26, No. 6, pp. 1469–1508, https://doi.org/10.1093/rof/rfac029

Gifford, E. (2010), 'Effective Shareholder Engagement: The Factors that Contribute to Shareholder Salience', *Journal of Business Ethics*, Vol. 92, pp. 79–97, https://doi.org/10.1007/s10551-010-0635-6

Global Impact Investing Network (GIIN) (2019), *Core Characteristics of Impact Investing (GIIN)*, https://thegiin.org/publication/post/core-characteristics-of-impact-investing/

Glomsrød, S. and Wei, T. (2018), 'Business as Unusual: The Implications of Fossil Divestment and Green Bonds for Financial Flows, Economic Growth and Energy Market', *Energy for Sustainable Development*, Vol. 44, pp. 1–10, https://doi.org/10.1016/j.esd.2018.02.005

Gollier, C. and Pouget, S. (2014), *The "Washing Machine": Investment Strategies and Corporate Behavior with Socially Responsible Investors. TSE Working Paper No 14-457s* (Toulouse School of Economics (TSE)), www.tse-fr.eu/sites/default/files/medias/doc/wp/fit/wp_tse_457.pdf

Hand, D., Ulanow, M., Pan, H. and Xiao, K. (2024), *Sizing the Impact Investing Market 2024* (GIIN), https://s3.amazonaws.com/giin-web-assets/giin/assets/publication/giin-sizingtheimpactinvestingmarket-2024.pdf

Heeb, F., Kellers, A. and Kolbel, J. (2022), *Does ESG Integration Impact the Real Economy? A Theory of Change and Review of Current Evidence* (Center for Sustainable Finance and Private Wealth, University of Zurich), www.csp.uzh.ch/dam/jcr:aeea438a-ed4c-4565-b269-e7dc07f3cc07/BAFU%20Report_DIGITAL_spreads.pdf

Hunt, C. and Weber, O. (2018), 'Fossil Fuel Divestment Strategies: Financial and Carbon-Related Consequences, *Organization & Environment*, Vol. 32, No. 1, pp. 41–61, https://doi.org/10.1177/1086026618773985

Jackson, E. (2013), 'Interrogating the Theory of Change: Evaluating Impact Investing Where it Matters Most', *Journal of Sustainable Finance & Investment*, Vol. 3, No. 2, pp. 95–110, www.tandfonline.com/doi/abs/10.1080/20430795.2013.776257

Kölbel, J., Heeb, F. and Busch, T. (2020), 'Can Sustainable Investing Save the World? Reviewing the Mechanisms of Investor Impact', *Organization & Environment*, Vol. 33, No. 4, pp. 554–574, https://doi.org/10.1177/1086026620919202

Marti, E., Fuchs, M., DesJardine, M., Slager, R. and Gond, J. (2023), 'The Impact of Sustainable Investing: A Multidisciplinary Review', *Journal of Management Studies*, Vol. 61, No. 5, pp. 2181–2211, https://doi.org/10.1111/joms.12957

Penna, C., Schot, J. and Steinmueller, W. E. (2021), *The Promise of Transformative Investment: Mapping the Field of Sustainability Investing. Deep Transitions Working Paper DT2021-11* (Utrecht University Centre for Global Challenges), https://deeptransitions.net/wp-content/uploads/2021/11/DT-Working-Paper-Transformative-Investments_final.pdf

Plantinga, A. and Scholtens, B. (2024), 'The Finance Perspective on Fossil Fuel Divestment', *Current Opinion in Environmental Sustainability*, Vol. 66, p. 101394, https://doi.org/10.1016/j.cosust.2023.101394

Rohleder, M., Wilkens, M. and Zink, J. (2022), 'The Effects of Mutual Fund Decarbonization on Stock Prices and Carbon Emissions', *Journal of Banking & Finance*, Vol. 134, p. 106352, https://doi.org/10.1016/j.jbankfin.2021.106352

Roor, A. and Maas, K. (2024), 'Do Impact Investors Live Up To Their Promise? A Systematic Literature Review on (Im)proving Investments' Impacts', *Business Strategy and the Environment*, Vol. 33, No. 4, pp. 3707–3732, https://doi.org/10.1002/bse.3644

Schwartz, J., Lendway, P. and Nuri, A. (2024), 'Fossil Fuel Divestment and Public Climate Change Policy Preferences: An Experimental Test in Three Countries', *Environmental Politics*, Vol. 33, No. 1, pp. 1–24, https://doi.org/10.1080/09644016.2023.2178351

Sullivan, R. (2011), *Valuing Corporate Responsibility: How Do Investors Really Use Corporate Responsibility Information?* (Greenleaf Publishing, Sheffield).

Chapter 8

Are Public and Private Climate Finance Delivering on the Goals of the Paris Agreement?

Amy Cano Prentice, Meutia Riana Sukma, Ferth Vandensteen Manaysay, Hao Zhong and Padraig Oliver

Introduction

In December 2015, world leaders adopted the Paris Agreement, a landmark international accord that aims to limit global warming to well below 2°C above pre-industrial levels, with efforts to further restrict the increase to 1.5°C. Achieving these ambitious goals requires a massive mobilisation of financial resources, as both mitigation (i.e., efforts to reduce greenhouse gas emissions) and adaptation (i.e., measures to manage the physical impacts of climate change) require a significant investment lift.

The Climate Policy Initiative (CPI) *Global Landscape of Climate Finance 2024* report indicates that annual global climate finance flows reached approximately US$1.46 trillion in 2022. While this represents significant growth, these flows

DOI: 10.4324/9781003467632-8

still fall far short of the US$6.7–10 trillion needed annually through 2050 to achieve the goals of the Paris Agreement (Climate Policy Initiative (CPI), 2024). In the area of adaptation finance, current levels meet only about one-third of the required US$212 billion annually for emerging markets and developing economies (EMDEs)[1] until 2030 (CPI, 2024). Private finance accounts for a growing proportion of total flows – 54% of mitigation finance in 2022 – but needs to be scaled further to address constraints on public sector budgets and to mobilise resources for both mitigation and adaptation (CPI, 2024).

The question that this chapter explores is whether, and under what conditions, public and private climate finance might fill the gaps in annual climate finance flows, particularly for developing countries. We start by defining the key terms and concepts that form the foundation of climate finance. From this, we define how much capital is needed to meet global climate objectives, and we examine the gap between current public and private capital flows and what is needed. We then discuss the reasons for this gap and the role that might be played by governments and public bodies to close this gap. We conclude with some reflections for investment practitioners on how they can understand the landscape of climate finance and on the role they might play in addressing some of the gaps in climate finance.

We want to highlight one important caveat to our analysis, which is that we focus on capital flows to meet the goals of the Paris Agreement. We are acutely aware that there are important ethical debates around climate finance that fall outside this scope, including the structure of the global finance system as a whole, historic responsibilities and liabilities for climate impacts, and the right to development versus the responsibility to protect the environment. Some of these themes are covered in Chapter 13 of this book, and this current chapter should be read and understood in that wider context.

Defining and Mapping Climate Finance

Climate finance refers to the financial flows directed towards activities that mitigate or adapt to the impacts of climate change, supporting the transition to a low-carbon economy, enhancing climate resilience, and achieving the goals of the Paris Agreement (UNFCCC Standing Committee on Finance (UNFCCC SCF), 2020). The term climate finance can encompass funding from local, national, and transnational sources, and funding derived from public, private, and alternative sources (Ackom and Motty, 2019). While often conflated with sustainable finance, climate finance is a specific subset of sustainable finance, focused directly on funding activities that address climate change through mitigation and adaptation strategies (Migliorelli, 2021; Cunha *et al.*, 2021). In recent years, as climate impacts have escalated, particularly in developing countries, some consider that climate finance should also encompass finance to address losses and damages from climate impacts (Songwe *et al.*, 2022).

Box 8.1 Climate Finance and the Paris AgreementMitigation, Adaptation, and Loss and Damage

Article 9 of the Paris Agreement stipulates the obligation of developed country Parties to provide finance to developing country Parties with respect to mitigation and adaptation. This is in continuation of the existing obligations of Annex II countries under Article 11 of the United Nations Framework Convention on Climate Change (UNFCCC). Other Parties are encouraged to continue to provide climate finance voluntarily.

At COP15 (held in 2009), developed countries agreed to collectively mobilise US$100 billion every year for climate action in developing countries by 2020, later delayed to 2025. At COP29 (in 2004), the successor climate finance goal, also known as the New Collective Quantified Goal (NCQG), was formalised at US$300 billion per year by 2035.

Article 8 of the Paris Agreement recognises the importance of averting, minimising, and addressing loss and damage (L&D) associated with the adverse effects of climate change. In the lead-up to the Paris Agreement, the 2010 Cancun Adaptation Framework introduced the conceptual distinction between L&D and adaptation. In broad terms, mitigation addresses the causes of climate change (e.g. the need to reduce greenhouse gas emissions), adaptation addresses the impacts of climate change (e.g. the need to build flood defences), and L&D is concerned with the unavoidable and irreversible impacts of the climate crisis. This is particularly important to EMDEs, who are least likely to have the resources or the capacities to respond effectively to these impacts.

While the implementation of the Common but Differentiated Responsibilities and Respective Capabilities (CBDR-RC) is enshrined in the Paris Agreement's designation of Annex I and non-Annex I countries, its application to L&D remains unaddressed. The Paris Agreement's lack of explicit mention of liability for compensation limits the scope for finance of L&D, although several avenues remain open through its legal endorsement of the Warsaw International Mechanism on L&D.

Article 2, Paragraph 1(c), of the Paris Agreement emphasises the need to make finance flows consistent with a pathway towards low greenhouse gas emissions and climate-resilient development (United Nations Framework Convention on Climate Change (UNFCCC), 2015). The United Nations Framework Convention on Climate Change's (UNFCCC's) Standing Committee on Finance Biennial Assessment and Overview of Climate Finance Flows has mapped the different actors that could be relevant to this process (UNFCCC SCF, 2021). A summary of this mapping is presented in Table 8.1.

Table 8.1 Actors Relevant to Article 2.1(c) of the Paris Agreement

Category	*Key Actors*	*Role*
Public finance	■ Government finance ministries ■ Bilateral agencies ■ Development finance institutions (DFIs) ■ Multilateral climate funds ■ Multilateral development banks (MDBs)	Public finance entities can channel funds towards climate initiatives through measures such as budget allocations, taxes, subsidies, and market mechanisms. They can also encourage private sector participation through providing foundational funding, through de-risking investments and through offering concessional financing and guarantees (UNFCCC SCF, 2021: 133).
Regulatory authorities	■ Central banks ■ Supervisory authorities ■ Government departments and policymakers (e.g. finance, treasury, energy, industry, agriculture)	Regulatory authorities, including central banks and supervisory authorities, oversee the financial system, ensuring stability and compliance with climate policies. Regulatory authorities and policymakers create the enabling environment necessary for climate finance. They do this through, for example, establishing regulations that incentivise investments in low-carbon technologies and through measures to ensure market transparency and integrity (UNFCCC SCF, 2021: 136).
Private finance	■ Businesses ■ Corporations ■ Commercial and investment banks ■ Institutional investors (see Chapter 2) ■ Venture capital and private equity	Private finance actors mobilise capital for climate projects, although – as we discuss below – their willingness and ability to do so is influenced by regulatory frameworks and by market conditions.
Market operators	■ Stock exchanges ■ Financial centres	Market operators, such as stock exchanges, facilitate the flow of financial resources by providing platforms for trading and investment.
Contributors	■ Civil society organisations ■ Research institutions	Civil society organisations and research institutions contribute by advocating for policy changes, conducting research, and promoting transparency in climate finance.

Source: Adapted from UNFCCC SCF (2021)

The interactions between different actors in the climate finance landscape are dynamic and multifaceted. For example, public finance often serves as a catalyst for private investments, with government funds being used to de-risk projects and attract private capital; for instance, public–private partnerships (PPPs) have been widely used to leverage private sector efficiency and public sector support (UNFCCC SCF, 2021: 155). Another example of such interactions are regulatory frameworks established by regulatory authorities to ensure that financial flows are transparent, accountable, and directed towards sustainable outcomes (see Gordon(2023: 24) for a specific example in the context of local government financing, see Sullivan *et al.* (2013)).

How Much Capital Is Needed? And What Is It Needed for?

The understanding of how much investment is needed for adaptation and mitigation is evolving, shaped by improvements in data and estimation methods, by evolving understanding of climate impacts and their financial requirements, by changes in the costs of technology, and by the balance being sought (and being achieved) between mitigation and adaptation.

There continue to be significant uncertainties in estimates due to data gaps, inconsistencies in methodologies, and variations in transparency across reporting systems (Chapagain, 2020, UNFCCC SCF, 2021; CPI, 2023a). The Enhanced Transparency Framework under the Paris Agreement is expected to improve the information reported by countries on climate finance, particularly regarding funding provided by developed countries and climate finance needs and received by developing countries, especially in the context of Nationally Determined Contributions (NDCs) and National Adaptation Plans (NAPs) (UNFCCC Standing Committee on Finance (UNFCCC SCF, 2021).

Notwithstanding the issues with estimating financial flows, the overarching conclusion is clear: the investment gap remains massive. While the specific numbers can be different, top-down models (which consider aggregate global investments in climate mitigation and adaptation) and bottom-up calculations based on funding needs identified by countries to reach their national targets as stipulated in their NDCs consistently provide similar conclusions regarding the scale of finance needed. Analysis by the CPI suggests that the total amount of capital needed to mitigate and adapt effectively to climate change globally is between US$6.7 trillion and US$10 trillion annually until 2050 (CPI, 2024).

While the estimates from top-down and bottom-up methods are broadly similar in terms of scale, the estimates based on submissions of needs by developing countries tend to be lower than top-down estimates. The reason is that many current national targets do not currently align with the goal of keeping global temperature rise below 1.5°C (or even 2°C) (CPI, 2023a; Energy Transitions Commission, 2024). As countries enhance their NDCs, the estimates of investment requirements derived using bottom-up estimation methods are likely to increase.

Current estimates suggest that mitigation-related activities have the greatest needs, with projected needs at US$7.2 trillion on average annually by 2030 (CPI, 2024). Investment is particularly needed in energy (in particular the low-carbon transition of energy systems) and in Agriculture, Forestry, and Other Land Use (AFOLU) (given its high mitigation potential) (CPI, 2023a). Significant investment is also needed in Transport, Buildings and Infrastructure and in Industry, with all these sectors needing considerable investments in decarbonisation technologies, such as electric vehicles, low-carbon industrial processes, low-carbon construction materials and efficient heating and cooling (CPI, 2023a) (Figure 8.1).

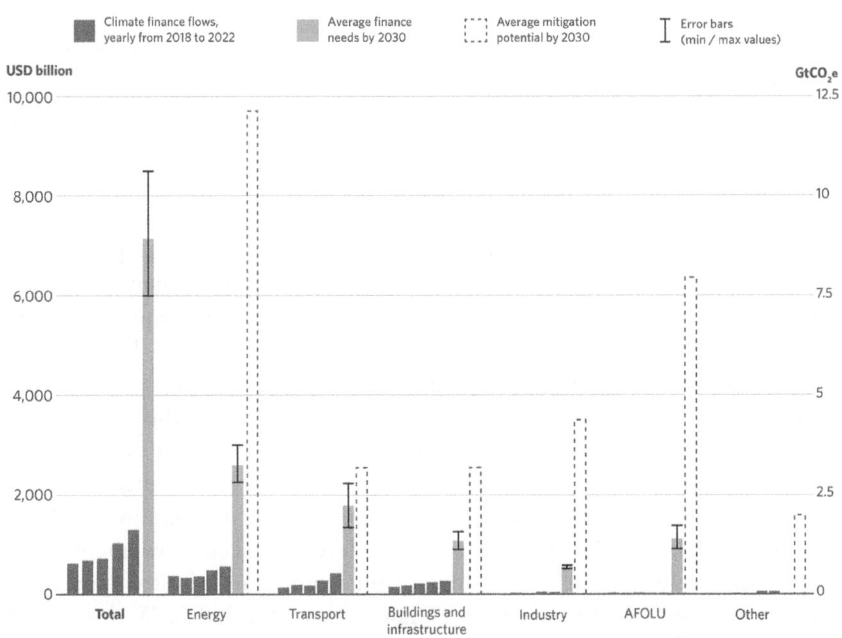

Figure 8.1 Climate Finance Flows and Needs in Key Mitigation Sectors, and Mitigation Potential (Data visualisation courtesy of Climate Policy Initiative. © 2024)

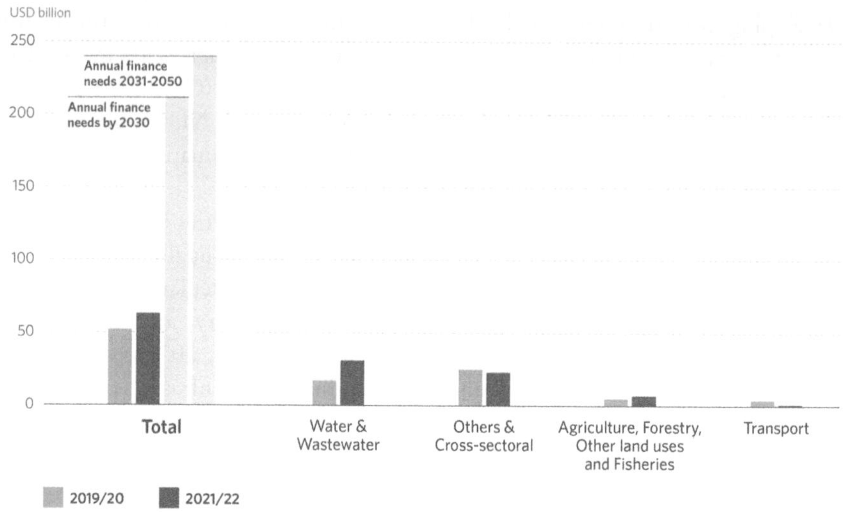

Figure 8.2 Adaptation Finance Flows and Needs by Sector (Data visualisation courtesy of Climate Policy Initiative. © 2023)

The scale of investment needed for adaptation remains significantly lower than for mitigation, although the needs are substantial, and the estimates of the amount of capital needed continue to grow. CPI estimates (see Figure 8.2) that developing countries alone require US$212 billion annually for adaptation by 2030, and US$239 billion annually in the following two decades.

When looking at adaptation needs, it is important to highlight the varying per capita adaptation needs across different income levels. As highlighted by the 2023 UNEP Adaptation Gap Report (United Nations Environment Programme (UNEP), 2023), upper-middle and high-income countries require more per capita (an annual average of US$81 per capita) compared to lower-middle-income countries (US$51 per capita) and low-income countries (US$22 per capita). However, in terms of percentage of gross domestic product (GDP), low-income countries have the highest adaptation finance needs, at 3.1% of GDP (Wignarajah *et al.*, 2023). This difference highlights the importance of targeted financial investments that consider the economic burden of adaptation on lower-income nations. Adaptation finance needs for developing countries are substantial and sector-specific, with the most investment required in infrastructure, coastal protection, and flood management (Wignarajah *et al.*, 2023). With the escalating impact of climate change, adaptation costs are projected to increase, which underscores the necessity of mobilising sufficient and timely adaptation finance to enhance the resilience of vulnerable areas.

What Is the Gap between Capital Needs and Supply?

The picture of how climate capital is spent is uneven across climate themes, sectors, technologies, and geographies (Organisation for Economic Cooperation and Development (OECD), 2023a). As shown in Figure 8.3, finance is concentrated in renewable energy and energy efficiency projects. Climate adaptation finance accounted for less than 10% of total climate finance in 2021–2022, although this is in line, proportionally, with how the current assessment of needs breaks down (CPI, 2023a).

The difference between the quantities of mitigation and adaptation finance is, in part, a function of how each type of finance is categorised and described. Whereas mitigation finance can often be attributed to whole projects or activities, adaptation finance tends to be seen as a mainstreaming activity, integrated into a country's development plans or into a company's operational activities (Richmond *et al.*, 2020). The consequence is that adaptation-related investments are often not explicitly identified or are accounted for as incremental expenditures on capital investments that would have occurred anyway. Much of the adaptation

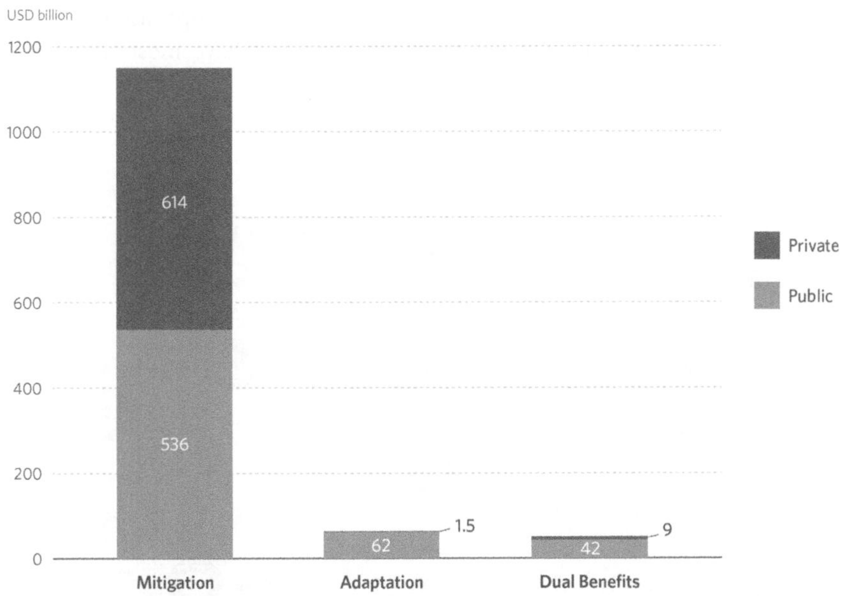

Figure 8.3 Uses of Climate Finance by Source, 2021–2022 Average, USD Billion (Data visualisation courtesy of Climate Policy Initiative. © 2023)

finance that may be occurring is therefore not tracked in project-level tracking exercises, particularly by private sector entities. While companies do spend money on adaptation-related activities, these investments tend to be focused on protecting their own assets and operations, and these expenditures are rarely classed as adaptation-related (as, for example, multilateral development banks (MDBs) and bilateral aid providers would report).

Notwithstanding the calculation issues, it is clear that the level of adaptation finance still falls short of estimated needs. Despite reaching an all-time high of US$63 billion in 2021–2022 (with public finance accounting for 98% of this total), adaptation finance falls far short of the estimated need of US$212 billion per year from all sources by 2030 for developing countries alone (CPI, 2023a). The main reason for this shortfall is that most adaptation measures are not sufficiently attractive to private investment. While there are often clear economic or societal reasons to support such investments, it is often the case that relatively few of the benefits from adaptation finance accrue directly to the entity providing the investment. Even if there are private benefits, these are often long-term (see, further, Carney's (2015) discussion of the tragedy of the horizon, as well as Stout (2022)).

As with global finance flows, climate finance is geographically concentrated, and most financing remains in its country of origin. Figure 8.4 shows the size of climate finance from each region, as well as the composition of public versus private finance. Developed countries appear to have most successfully

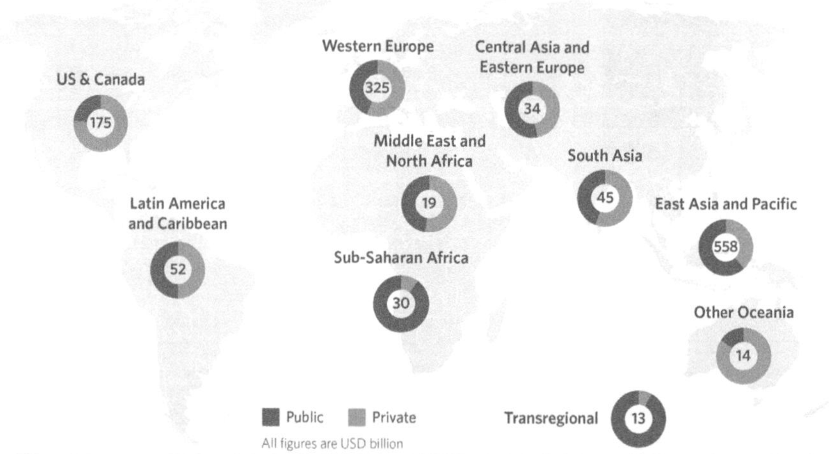

Figure 8.4 Public versus Private Climate Finance by Region, 2021–2022, USD Billion (Data visualisation courtesy of Climate Policy Initiative. © 2023)

mobilised domestic private finance (owing in large part to the extant pools of capital and to financial markets with the ability to quickly allocate capital given the right incentives). It is also relevant to note that China's domestic climate finance mobilisation was greater than that of all other countries combined, accounting for 51% of all domestic climate finance globally (Climate Policy Initiative (CPI), 2023a).[2] Globally, the largest driver of private sector growth is household spending, composing 31% of total private finance in 2021–2022, for example, due to the growth of electric vehicle sales (Climate Policy Initiative (CPI), 2023a).

How Might the Gap between Capital Need and Supply in Developing Countries Be Addressed?

Given that capital allocation in the global economy is currently dominated by developed countries (acknowledging that some other countries, such as China, also have significant domestic resources to draw on), a key challenge is ensuring that developing countries[3] have access to affordable capital to realise their NDCs and adaptation plans.

In the context of financing climate action in developing countries, high risks and low returns are widely identified as key obstacles affecting the availability of project finance. Private investors in developing countries face relatively high financial risks, particularly in the least developed and fragile states (Overseas Development Institute (ODI), 2019; OECD, 2023a, 2023b). These risks include a lack of transparency (where insufficient data availability and quality can lead to inaccurate risk assessments), weaknesses in legal frameworks and enforcement processes, and political and macroeconomic instability. In relation to investment returns, the issues include the small size of many projects and the low returns of some climate-related projects, especially adaptation projects ODI, 2019; OECD, 2023a).

To address the financial gap mentioned above, it is also necessary to understand the characteristics of financing sources, which may include public and private sources, equity, debt and other sources, and domestic and capital sources. Understanding the characteristics of public and private capital, as well as the distinct risk profiles and return expectations of each, can help with the design and delivery of policies and measures that can bridge the gap between capital need and supply. Tables 8.2 and 8.3 present high-level assessments of the features, the risk tolerances, and the return expectations of different types of public and private investors. These features, in turn, influence the willingness and ability of these different investors to support specific types of investments.

Table 8.2 Public Climate Finance Investment Risk and Return Profiles

Public Finance	*Features*	*Risk Tolerance*[4]	*Return Expectations*[5]
Donor Government Aid Agencies and Ministries	**Definition:** These are government bodies, often tied to finance ministries or foreign affairs ministries, that allocate public funds to support development initiatives through grants, subsidies or concessional loans **Objective:** To support development goals (poverty reduction, climate action, and capacity-building) in low- and middle-income countries.	**High**: Donor agencies primarily fund projects in fragile or low-income countries with high socio-economic and political risks (OECD, 2023a).	**Low:** These agencies primarily focus on non-financial objectives such as poverty alleviation, capacity-building, and climate adaptation. Their objectives are explicitly non-commercial (OECD, 2023a).
Development Finance Institutions (DFIs)	**Definition:** Government-backed financial institutions established at the national or regional level to provide financing (equity, debt, guarantees) for private-sector projects in developing or underserved markets. **Objective:** To catalyse private-sector investment through de-risking projects and demonstrating the commercial viability of projects in emerging markets to promote economic growth and development.	**Medium to High:** DFIs, such as the CDC Group and Proparco, have mandates to operate in markets that private-sector investors consider too risky. They aim to de-risk private investments while maintaining financial sustainability (Attridge and Novak, 2022; WEF, 2024; IFC, n.d.).	**Medium:** DFIs are often referred to as "impact-first" institutions in blended finance literature, aiming for moderate financial returns while prioritising development outcomes (Attridge & Novak, 2022; WEF, 2024; IFC, n.d.)
Bilateral and Multilateral Development Banks (MDBs)	**Definition:** Large, international financial institutions owned by multiple governments that provide long-term financing and technical assistance for public and private sector projects. **Objective:** To provide financing and expertise to support large-scale infrastructure, public policy reforms and social projects that drive sustainable development and poverty alleviation	**Medium to High**: MDBs such as the World Bank often operate with sovereign guarantees, which mitigate risks. However, they also engage in or support high-risk projects (e.g., infrastructure in fragile states) through concessional finance mechanisms (OECD, 2023a).	**Low to Medium:** While MDBs aim for financial sustainability to reinvest in future projects, their primary objective is development impact (ODI, 2019).

Table 8.3 Private Climate Finance Investment Risk and Return Profiles

Private Finance	*Features*	*Risk Tolerance*[6]	*Return Expectations*[7]
Institutional investors	**Definition:** Organisations such as pension funds, insurance companies, and sovereign wealth funds that manage large pools of money for long-term investments. **Objective:** To achieve stable, risk-adjusted financial returns for their beneficiaries. Increasingly, many also have sustainability-related objectives that sit alongside their financial return objectives.	**Low to Medium:** These funds have fiduciary responsibilities to their beneficiaries, meaning that they tend to have a preference for lower-risk investments with stable, long-term returns (Schanzenbach and Sitkoff, 2020). Some investors are willing to take moderate risks, particularly when investing in areas related to sustainability (Bank of America, 2023).	**Medium:** Empirical studies on institutional investors show that they have a preference for stable, risk-adjusted financial returns, and that they have limited appetite for below-market returns (CPI, 2023a; Schanzenbach and Sitkoff, 2020).
Private equity investors	**Definition:** Investment firms that provide capital to companies or projects in exchange for equity stakes, often focusing on start-ups, growth-stage companies, or buyouts. **Objectives:** To generate high financial returns by scaling businesses, optimising operations, and exiting investments through sales or IPOs.	**High** Private equity investors deliberately pursue high-risk opportunities to achieve outsized returns, especially in emerging markets or innovative sectors. Their business models, based on capital appreciation and profitable exits, demand high financial returns (BVCA, 2015; Feil, 2023).	**High**
Commercial banks	**Definition:** Traditional financial institutions that provide debt financing through loans, credit and other banking products to businesses and individuals. **Objective:** To profit from interest income and fees while offering financial services for infrastructure, trade and corporate activities.	**Low to Medium:** Commercial banks are guided by risk management regulations and typically avoid high-risk investments (BIS, n.d.). However, case studies on project financing (e.g., green bonds) show that some are willing to take moderate risks with appropriate risk-sharing mechanisms (Alliance for Green Commercial Banks, 2023).	**Medium:** Banks focus on consistent profitability through interest and fee income (CPI, 2023a; Alliance for Green Commercial Banks, 2023).

(*Continued*)

Table 8.3 (Continued)

Private Finance	*Features*	*Risk Tolerance*[6]	*Return Expectations*[7]
Multinational Corporations	**Definition:** Companies and businesses that invest in projects or innovations, either internally or externally, often as part of their wider sustainability initiatives. **Objective:** To support business growth, innovation, and brand enhancement while contributing to social and environmental goals	**Low to High**	**Low to High**
		Corporate risk appetite varies and often links to strategic goals. Corporations are primarily focused on financial returns but, on occasion, may prioritise other outcomes such as positive social or environmental impacts, or better stakeholder relationships (Gelb *et al.*, 2023; CPI, 2023b)	
Households/ Individuals	**Definition:** Private individuals or families who contribute to financial markets through savings, investments (e.g., mutual funds, stocks), or philanthropy **Objectives:** To achieve personal financial security, grow wealth or contribute to societal causes through impact investing or charitable giving	**Low to High**	**Low to High**
		Households and individuals exhibit strong heterogeneity in green investments. Some are willing to take on additional risk due to the nonpecuniary benefits, whereas others require higher financial returns to compensate for the perceived higher risk or potential costs. This variation in attitudes means that there is significant diversity in investment behaviour across different demographic and wealth groups (Aron-Dine *et al.*, 2024)	

Source: Authors

Tables 8.2 and 8.3 suggest that different actors may be more or less suited to providing different types of financing or financial support. It must be stressed that this is not simply an assertion that public bodies should fund those projects that are not attractive to private capital. Rather, it is a suggestion that public finance may have a role to play in leveraging or encouraging private finance through financial de-risking mechanisms (CPI, 2022; UNEP, 2022; World Economic Forum (WEF), 2024; World Resources Institute (WRI), 2022). In practice, public finance institutions such as development finance institutions (DFIs) and MDBs often provide guarantees, insurance, or blended finance structures to help lower the perceived risks for private investors; an example is first-loss capital, which absorbs initial losses in a partnership or co-financing arrangement. The World Bank (2024) suggests that every dollar of concessional finance not only generates 7 dollars in additional investment but also helps create markets in multiple sectors. Public bodies can also offer revenue-enhancing tools, such as tax incentives, subsidies, and public grants, to make projects more attractive to private capital, ensuring that the potential returns align with the risks undertaken (Mooij and Keen, 2012; Songwe *et al.*, 2023; United Nations Development Programme (UNDP), 2022). This is particularly critical in sectors like renewable energy, where upfront costs are high, but long-term returns are significant, and where private investment often requires both a risk buffer and policy certainty.

Recognising the opportunities presented by climate finance, many commercial participants have sought support from development actors to help tilt the risk-return calculations in favour of investment. As reported by the OECD (2023a: 44), financial institutions, primarily commercial banks, accounted for the largest proportion (43%) of climate blended finance transactions on average between 2019 and 2022, followed by corporations and institutional investors, each contributing 26%. Key leverage mechanisms included direct investments, guarantees, and syndicated loans, which collectively mobilised 77% of total private climate finance (OECD, 2023a: 20).

Beyond providing direct financial support to specific projects or initiatives, government agencies can also support climate finance by integrating climate policy into wider economic policy, rather than treating climate change as a standalone issue confined to specific sectors (Principles for Responsible Investment (PRI), 2024a, 2024b; Sullivan, 2024; Investor Agenda, 2024). Examples of such interventions include the US Inflation Reduction Act, the EU's Fit for 55 and RePowerEU plans, Japan's Green Transformation (GX) policy, and China's 1+N framework. From an investor perspective, a stable and integrated policy framework helps reduce uncertainty and risk, which in turn boosts investor and business confidence and boosts the private sector's willingness to invest (Sullivan *et al.*, 2013).

As part of wider policy action on climate change, policy instruments such as carbon pricing and carbon taxes have been supported because they both raise revenue and provide incentives for mitigation actions (United Nations Secretary-General's High-level Advisory Group on Climate Change Financing (HAGCCF), 2010). Furthermore, given the systemic nature of climate change, these policy instruments can help optimise resource allocation across sectors – including energy, transport, agriculture, and manufacturing – through finding economically efficient solutions (PRI, 2024a, 2024b). While economic instruments (such as carbon trading and carbon taxes) have been widely supported on efficiency grounds, it is important to recognise that they could also have adverse or unintended impacts. For example, they may increase costs for consumers, increase government debt and be seen by some investors as having a negative effect on the country's future prospects (see, for example, S&P Global, 2024).

Governments can also provide guarantees that help mitigate political and commercial risks, such as credit, contractual, and regulatory uncertainties (OECD, 2023a). Guarantees are particularly prevalent in low- and middle-income countries, representing approximately 24% of mobilised amounts, compared to only 5% in higher-income developing countries (OECD, 2023a: 24). These are particularly relevant to large projects that require substantial upfront investment and have long investment return cycles. For instance, renewable energy projects, which constitute the largest share of clean energy investment needs, often face significant investment barriers during the development and construction phases (OECD, 2022). From 2016 to 2021, public climate finance providers extended loans to the energy sector with an average maturity of 20.8 years (OECD, 2023a: 53). Publicly initiated and developed projects can transfer ownership to the private sector as soon as the projects pass the most hazardous phases (i.e., development and construction) and begin to generate returns, thereby freeing up public funds for other climate or broader development interventions.

Beyond their financial and policy roles, governments can also support climate finance through acting as leaders and coordinators, through ensuring that key stakeholders, including private investors, align their efforts and collaborate on low-carbon initiatives, through supporting PPPs and other risk-sharing mechanisms, through providing political support for projects, and through supporting fundraising by companies (Sullivan *et al.*, 2013).

The analysis presented in Tables 8.2 and 8.3 also highlights the importance of mobilising more domestic and local financial resources to expand the pool of private capital. Approximately half of the climate finance required by emerging markets could come from local sources by enhancing public financial policies, institutions, and domestic capital markets (Songwe et al., 2022). However, the involvement of domestic commercial investors in climate finance is often limited, with key obstacles being their concerns about the immaturity of the domestic regulatory framework and their views on the investment risks (in particular for those investments requiring large upfront capital investment) (World Bank, 2020). The importance of involving domestic investors in climate finance is not just about increasing the amount of capital available. The literature suggests that local investors, with their comprehensive grasp of the domestic investment and regulatory landscape, are well-positioned to assess local risks and conduct due diligence. Their capacity to invest in local currency can help mitigate investment risks, offering more flexible and suitable financing solutions for projects that generate local currency revenue (Convergence, 2021). Data from the World Bank suggests that private capital mobilisation projects involving domestic investors achieve a success rate of 80%, compared to 64% for projects relying solely on international investors (World Bank, 2020: 30).

Concluding Remarks

The scale of capital required to meet the goals of the Paris Agreement is immense, with trillions of dollars needed annually to fund mitigation and adaptation measures globally. Despite a doubling of climate finance flows in recent years, current investments fall drastically short of what is required, especially in developing countries and for adaptation efforts. Although progress is being made in key areas such as renewable energy and electrified transport, there remain major financing gaps in agrifood and averting deforestation, in the built environment and infrastructure, and in adapting to and becoming resilient to oncoming climate impacts.

This shortfall persists even when accounting for uncertainties in data and methodologies, underscoring the urgent need for transformative action to bridge the gap. The challenge is exacerbated by the unequal distribution of finance, with the least developed countries receiving only a fraction of the necessary funds, and private sector participation in adaptation remaining minimal.

Governments alone cannot close this financial gap, but they have a critical role in enabling and leveraging finance. Public resources can act as a catalyst for private investment through mechanisms like de-risking and blended finance, while also helping create stable policy environments that attract private capital. Governments can also utilise their convening power to coordinate stakeholders, establish regulatory frameworks, and integrate climate objectives into broader economic strategies. By combining these approaches, public actors can unlock the potential of private finance to address the monumental challenge of funding climate action.

Implications for Practitioners

1. Recognise that achieving the goals of the Paris Agreement will limit the catastrophic impacts of climate change on political and economic growth and stability. This, in turn, will benefit investment returns. Private financial institutions and investors should, therefore, proactively allocate capital towards the deployment of solutions that bring greenhouse gas emissions to zero and towards solutions that make the systems we rely on more resilient to the impacts of climate change.
2. Recognise that public policy and public financial institutions have key roles to play in mitigating greenhouse gas emissions and in supporting effective adaptation to the unavoidable impacts of climate change. Climate solutions have been successfully deployed at scale in countries and regions where there are clear long-term policy signals supporting action on climate change, regulations and incentives that support these actions, and public capital has been targeted at specific solutions and outcomes. However, such examples have yet to be replicated in developing countries where blended finance initiatives have not reached scale.
3. Be prepared to clearly explain to the government what is needed to increase the level of private financing for mitigation and adaptation, in particular in EMDEs. Investors need to explain what is expected from, for example, blended finance and first loss instruments, what is needed in terms of project size (or the aggregation of smaller projects into larger funds), what is needed in terms of investment risk/return profiles, what is needed in terms of the climate-related outcomes to be achieved, what other support is needed from government and regulatory agencies.

Notes

1 The designation of countries as either "developed" or "developing" is varied and can be a source of contention. The UN Framework Convention on Climate Change (UNFCCC) classifies countries as Annex I, non-Annex I, and Annex II. While this classification has been raised as being outdated by Parties, it serves as the organising principle for responsibilities under the Convention. CPI adopted in 2023 an updated classification of countries according to income level and development status, which differs from the UNFCCC's classification (see Appendix 1 to this chapter). Since this chapter relies on data from CPI, we use this classification.

2 It is important to caveat this analysis by noting that when lenders are not known, CPI (2023a) assumes that they are domestic lenders. The consequence is that this figure may be an overestimate.

3 In this context, the term "developing countries" refers to countries with limited domestic resources and capital allocation capacities, such as the least developed countries in Sub-Saharan Africa and members of the Alliance of Small Island States (AOSIS). However, for consistency, the term "developing countries" will continue to be used throughout this text.

4 Risk tolerance refers to the maximum level of risk that an investor is willing to accept when supporting a specific project or investment. This generally refers to the investor's tolerance for both the loss of principal and the uncertainty in expected interest or dividend returns. Based on this, three broad levels of risk tolerance can be defined:

- Low risk tolerance: The investor is unable to accept the loss of principal and has low tolerance for uncertainty in expected interest or dividend returns.
- Medium risk tolerance: The investor is unable to accept the loss of principal but can tolerate uncertainty in expected interest or dividend returns.
- High risk tolerance: The investor is willing to accept the loss of principal.

5 Return expectations refer to the investor's expectations regarding the financial returns on an investment. From this, three broad levels of expectation can be defined:

- Low return expectation: The investor is willing to accept returns below market benchmarks or no financial returns at all.
- Medium return expectation: The investor seeks returns that are aligned with market benchmarks.
- High return expectation: The investor seeks returns significantly above market averages.

6 See Note 4.

7 See Note 5.

References

Ackom, E. and Motty, M. (2019), 'Climate Finance: Unlocking Funds toward Achievement of Climate Targets Under the Paris Agreement', in Leal Filho, W., Azul, A., Brandli, L., Özuyar, P. and Wall, T. (eds.) (2019), *Climate Action. Encyclopedia of the UN Sustainable Development Goals* (Springer), https://doi.org/10.1007/978-3-319-71063-1_104-2

Alliance for Green Commercial Banks (2023), *Defining an Ambitious Climate Strategy of Green Banking: A Case Study,* www.allianceforgreencommercialbanks.org/sites/greenbanks/files/reports/Defining%20an%20Ambitious%20Climate%20Strategy%20of%20Green%20Banking_A%20Case%20Study.pdf

Aron-Dine, S., Beutel, J., Piazzesi, M. and Schneider, M. (2024), *Household Climate Finance: Theory and Survey Data on Safe and Risky Green Assets* (Stanford University and Deutsche Bundesbank), https://stanford.edu/~piazzesi/SafeGreenAsset.pdf

Attridge, S. and Novak, C. (2022), *An Exploration of Bilateral Development Finance Institutions' Business Models.* ODI Working Paper (Overseas Development Institute (ODI), London), https://odi.org/documents/8445/ODI_Working_paper_An_exploration_of_bilateral_development_finance_institutions_x0AEs0S.pdf

Bank for International Settlements (BIS) (n.d.), 'Basel III: International Regulatory Framework for Banks', www.bis.org/bcbs/basel3.htm?m=76No

Bank of America (2023), *What Is Blended Finance, and Why It Matters*, https://about.bankofamerica.com/en/making-an-impact/blended-finance

British Private Equity & Venture Capital Association (BVCA) (2015), *Risk in Private Equity*, www.bvca.co.uk/Portals/0/library/documents/Guide%20to%20Risk/Risk%20in%20Private%20Equity%20-%20Oct%202015.pdf

Carney, M. (2015), 'Breaking the Tragedy of the Horizon – Climate Change and Financial Stability' (Bank of England), www.bankofengland.co.uk/speech/2015/breaking-the-tragedy-of-the-horizon-climate-change-and-financial-stability (accessed 21 June 2024).

Chapagain, D., Baarsch, F., Schaeffer, M. and D'haena, S. (2020), 'Climate Change Adaptation Costs in Developing Countries: Insights from Existing Estimates', *International Journal of Sustainable Development*, Vol. 17, pp. 1234–1245, https://doi.org/10.1080/17565529.2020.1711698

Climate Policy Initiative (CPI) (2022), 'Blog: Ways to De-Risk Climate Finance', www.climatepolicyinitiative.org/blog-ways-to-de-risk-climate-finance/

Climate Policy Initiative (CPI) (2023a), Global Landscape of Climate Finance 2023, www.climatepolicyinitiative.org/publication/global-landscape-of-climate-finance-2023/

Climate Policy Initiative (CPI) (2023b), The Corporate Climate Finance Playbook, www.climatepolicyinitiative.org/wp-content/uploads/2023/09/2023-corporate-climate-finance-playbook.pdf

Climate Policy Initiative (CPI) (2024), Global Landscape of Climate Finance 2024: Insights for COP29, climatepolicyinitiative.org/publication/global-landscape-of-climate-finance-2024

Convergence (2021), The State of Blended Finance 2021, www.convergence.finance/resource/the-state-of-blended-finance-2021/view

Cunha, F., Meira, E. and Orsato, R. (2021), 'Sustainable Finance and Investment: Review and Research Agenda', *Business Strategy and the Environment*, Vol. 30, No. 8, pp. 3795–3813, https://doi.org/10.1002/bse.2847

Energy Transitions Commission (2024), *Credible Contributions: Bolder Plans for Higher Climate Ambition in the Next Round of NDCs*, www.energy-transitions.org/publications/credible-contributions-bolder-plans-for-ndcs/

Feil, C. (2023, November 7), 'The Untapped Potential of Private Equity in Emerging Markets', *Impact Entrepreneur*, https://impactentrepreneur.com/the-untapped-potential-of-private-equity-in-emerging-markets/

Gelb, J., McCarthy, R., Rehm, W. and Voronin, A. (2023, September 15), 'Investors Want to Hear from Companies about the Value of Sustainability', *McKinsey & Company*, www.mckinsey.com/capabilities/strategy-and-corporate-finance/our-insights/investors-want-to-hear-from-companies-about-the-value-of-sustainability

Gordon, N. (2023), 'Climate Finance: An Overview', *Environment: Science and Policy for Sustainable Development*, Vol. 65, No. 4, pp. 18–26, https://doi.org/10.1080/00139157.2023.2205347

International Finance Corporation (IFC) (n.d.), 'How Blended Finance Works', www.ifc.org/en/what-we-do/sector-expertise/blended-finance/how-blended-finance-works (accessed 19 April 2025).

Investor Agenda (2024), '2024 Global Investor Statement to Governments on the Climate Crisis', https://theinvestoragenda.org/wp-content/uploads/2024/08/2024-Global-Investor-Statement-to-Governments-on-the-Climate-Crisis.pdf

Migliorelli, M. (2021), 'What Do We Mean by Sustainable Finance? Assessing Existing Frameworks and Policy Risks', *Sustainability*, Vol. 13, No. 975, pp. 1–17, https://doi.org/10.3390/su13020975

Mooij, R. and Keen, M. (2012), 'Chapter 7. Fiscal Instruments for Climate Finance', in *Fiscal Policy to Mitigate Climate Change* (International Monetary Fund), www.elibrary.imf.org/display/book/9781616353933/ch07.xml

Organisation for Economic Cooperation and Development (OECD) (2022), *OECD Blended Finance Guidance for Clean Energy*. OECD Environment Policy Papers, No. 31 (OECD, Paris), https://doi.org/10.1787/23097841

Organisation for Economic Cooperation and Development (OECD) (2023a), *Scaling Up the Mobilisation of Private Finance for Climate Action in Developing Countries* (OECD, Paris), https://doi.org/10.1787/17A88681-EN

Organisation for Economic Cooperation and Development (OECD) (2023b), *Private Finance Mobilised by Official Development Finance Interventions: Opportunities and Challenges to Increase Its Contribution towards the SDGs in Developing Countries* (OECD, Paris), www.oecd.org/dac/2023-private-finance-odfi.pdf

Overseas Development Institute (ODI) (2019), *Blended Finance in the Poorest Countries* (ODI, London), https://cdn.odi.org/media/documents/12666.pdf

Principles for Responsible Investment (PRI) (2024a), *Climate Policy Roadmap 2024/25* (PRI, London), www.unpri.org/policy-reports/climate-policy-roadmap-2024/25/12836.article

Principles for Responsible Investment (PRI) (2024b), *Investing for the Economic Transition: The Case for Whole of Government Policy Reform* (PRI, London), www.unpri.org/download?ac=21824

Richmond, M., Meattle, C., Micale, V., Oliver, P. and Padmanabhi, R. (2020), *A Snapshot of Global Adaptation Investment and Tracking Methods*, https://climatepolicyinitiative.org/wp-content/uploads/2020/04/A-Snapshot-of-Global-Adaptation-Investment-and-Tracking-Methods-April-2020.pdf

Schanzenbach, M. and Sitkoff, R. (2020, October), 'ESG Investing: Theory, Evidence, and Fiduciary Principles', *Journal of Financial Planning*, www.financialplanningassociation.org/article/journal/OCT20-esg-investing-theory-evidence-and-fiduciary-principles

Songwe, V., Bhattacharya, A., Soubeyran, E. and Stern, N. (2023), *A Climate Finance Framework: Decisive Action to Deliver on the Paris Agreement – Summary* (Grantham Research Institute on Climate Change and the Environment, London School of Economics and Political Science, London), www.lse.ac.uk/granthaminstitute/wp-content/uploads/2023/11/A-Climate-Finance-Framework-IHLEG-Report-2-SUMMARY.pdf

Songwe, V., Stern, N. and Bhattacharya, A. (2022), *Finance for Climate Action: Scaling up Investment for Climate and Development* (Grantham Research Institute on Climate Change and the Environment, London School of Economics and Political Science, London), www.lse.ac.uk/granthaminstitute/wp-content/uploads/2022/11/IHLEG-Finance-for-Climate-Action-1.pdf

S&P Global (2024, January 18), 'Colombia Outlook Revised to Negative on Subdued Economic Growth Prospects; 'BB+/B' Foreign Currency Ratings Affirmed', https://disclosure.spglobal.com/ratings/en/regulatory/article/-/view/type/HTML/id/3113898

Stout, S. (2022), *Unlocking Private Sector Adaptation Finance* (Climate Policy Initiative), www.climatepolicyinitiative.org/unlocking-private-sector-adaptation-finance/

Sullivan, R. (2024), 'Three Priorities for Scaling Private Climate Finance', *SDG Action*, https://sdg-action.org/three-priorities-for-scaling-private-climate-finance/

Sullivan, R., Gouldson, A. and Webber, P. (2013), 'Funding Low Carbon Cities: Local Perspectives on Opportunities and Risks', *Climate Policy*, Vol. 13, No. 4, pp. 514–529, https://doi.org/10.1080/14693062.2012.745113

UNFCCC Standing Committee on Finance (UNFCCC SCF) (2020), Executive Summary by the Standing Committee on Finance on the First Report on the Determination of the Needs of Developing Country Parties Related to Implementing the Convention and the Paris Agreement (Vol. 6), https://unfccc.int/topics/climate-finance/workstreams/determination-of-the-needs-of-developing-country-parties/first-report-on-the-determination-of-the-needs-of-developing-country-parties-related-to-implementing

UNFCCC Standing Committee on Finance (UNFCCC SCF) (2021), *Biennial Assessment and Overview of Climate Finance Flows 2020*, https://unfccc.int/sites/default/files/resource/54307_1%20-%20UNFCCC%20BA%202020%20-%20Report%20-%20V4.pdf

United Nations Development Programme (UNDP) (2022), *A Global Climate Public Finance Review*, www.undp.org/sites/g/files/zskgke326/files/2022-09/UNDP-Global-Climate-Public-Finance-Review-2022.pdf

United Nations Environment Programme (UNEP) (2022), *Blended Finance: The Key to De-Risk Investments in Climate Adaptation*, www.unep.org/ndc/news-and-stories/story/blended-finance-key-de-risk-investments-climate-adaptation

United Nations Environment Programme (UNEP) (2023), *Adaptation Gap Report 2023*, www.unep.org/resources/adaptation-gap-report-2023

United Nations Framework Convention on Climate Change (UNFCCC) (2015), *The Paris Agreement*, https://unfccc.int/sites/default/files/english_paris_agreement.pdf

United Nations Secretary-General's High-level Advisory Group on Climate Change Financing (HAGCCF) (2010), *Report of the Secretary-General's High-Level Advisory Group on Climate Change Financing*, www.cbd.int/financial/interdevinno/un-climate-report.pdf

Wignarajah, D., Richmond, M., Stout, S., Martinez, G., Schell-Smith, K. and Padmanabhi, R. (2023). *State and Trends in Climate Adaptation Finance 2023* (Climate Policy Initiative), www.climatepolicyinitiative.org/wp-content/uploads/2023/12/State-and-Trends-in-Climate-Adaptation-Finance-2023_.pdf

World Bank (2020), *World Bank Group Approaches to Mobilize Private Capital for Development. An Independent Evaluation*, https://ieg.worldbankgroup.org/sites/default/files/Data/Evaluation/files/PrivateCapitalMobilization.pdf

World Bank (2024), '5 Ways to Unlock Private Capital to Tackle Climate Change', https://blogs.worldbank.org/en/voices/5-ways-to-unlock-private-capital-to-tackle-climate-change

World Economic Forum (WEF) (2024), *How De-Risking Renewable Investments can Bridge the $1.2 Trillion Gap in Developing Countries*, www.weforum.org/stories/2024/02/financial-instruments-key-to-hitting-1-trillion-in-green-investments/

World Resources Institute (WRI) (2022), *De-Risking Low-Carbon Investments*, www.wri.org/insights/de-risking-low-carbon-investments

Appendix 1
Country Classification Used for the Analysis of Climate Finance Flows

Classification	Country or Territory
Least Developed Countries	Afghanistan, Angola, Bangladesh, Benin, Bhutan, Burkina Faso, Burundi, Cambodia, Central African Republic, Chad, Comoros, Congo, Democratic Republic, Djibouti, Eritrea, Ethiopia, Gambia, Guinea, Guinea-Bissau, Haiti, Kiribati, Lao PDR, Lesotho, Liberia, Madagascar, Malawi, Mali, Mauritania, Mozambique, Myanmar, Nepal, Niger, Rwanda, São Tomé and Principe, Senegal, Sierra Leone, Solomon Islands, Somalia, South Sudan, Sudan, Tanzania, Timor-Leste, Togo, Tuvalu, Uganda, Vanuatu, Yemen, Zambia
Emerging Markets and Developing Countries	Algeria, Antigua and Barbuda, Argentina, Armenia, Aruba, Azerbaijan, Bahamas, Bahrain, Barbados, Belize, Bolivia, Botswana, Brazil, Brunei, Cameroon, Cape Verde, Chile, China, Colombia, Congo Republic, Costa Rica, Côte d'Ivoire, Cuba, Ecuador, Egypt, El Salvador, Equatorial Guinea, Fiji, Gabon, Georgia, Ghana, Guatemala, Honduras, Hong Kong, India, Indonesia, Iran, Iraq, Jamaica, Jordan, Kazakhstan, Kenya,, Korea, Democratic People's Republic Korea, Kuwait, Kyrgyzstan, Lebanon, Libya, Malaysia, Maldives, Marshall Islands, Mauritius, Mexico, Micronesia, Mongolia, Morocco, Namibia, Netherlands Antilles, Nicaragua, Nigeria, Oman, Pakistan, Panama, Papua New Guinea, Paraguay, Peru, Philippines, Puerto Rico, Qatar, Saint Helena, Saint Kitts and Nevis, Saint Lucia, Saint Vincent and the Grenadines, Samoa, Saudi Arabia, Seychelles, Singapore, South Africa, Sri Lanka, State of Palestine, Suriname, Swaziland, Syria, Taiwan, Tajikistan, Thailand, Trinidad and Tobago, Tunisia, Turkmenistan, United Arab Emirates, Uruguay, Uzbekistan, Venezuela, Vietnam. Zimbabwe

Classification	Country or Territory
Developed Countries	Albania, Andorra, Australia, Austria, Belarus, Belgium, Bermuda, Bosnia and Herzegovina, Bulgaria, Canada, Croatia, Cyprus, Czech Republic, Denmark, Estonia, European Union, Finland, France, Germany, Greece, Hungary, Iceland, Ireland, Israel, Italy, Japan, Jersey, Latvia, Lithuania, Luxembourg, North Macedonia, Malta, Mayotte, Moldova, Montenegro, Netherlands, New Zealand, Norway, Poland, Portugal, Romania, Russia, San Marino, Serbia, Slovakia, Slovenia, Spain, Sweden, Switzerland, Turkey, Ukraine, United Kingdom, United States of America

Source: Climate Policy Initiative (CPI) (2023a)

Chapter 9

Does Better Company Reporting Deliver Better Environmental Performance?

Emma De Fino, Emeline Warner and Rachel Crossley

Introduction

Over the past two decades, the number of companies disclosing environment-related information has grown significantly. Concurrently, the quantity of this information has also increased (La Torre *et al.*, 2020). As just one illustration of this change, when the CDP (previously the Carbon Disclosure Project) conducted its first annual survey to collect data on companies' greenhouse gas emissions in 2003, just 228 companies responded to the survey. By 2024, that number had increased to more than 22,000 companies (CDP, 2025).

A key driver for the increased disclosure of environment-related information has been demand from stakeholders. For example, investors, business customers and NGOs have all pressed companies to provide more information on the social and environmental impacts associated with their activities, operations and products and how they manage these (see, for example, Ilhan *et al.* (2023)

DOI: 10.4324/9781003467632-9

and Baumüller and Sopp (2021)). Governments have also introduced a range of non-financial reporting requirements – which have expanded in scope over time. For their part, companies have identified the potential for the reporting process (i.e., the collection, collation and analysis of data on their social and environmental performance) to identify opportunities to improve business practices and efficiency, and to better manage social and environmental-related risks and opportunities.

This chapter examines the extent to which companies' non-financial disclosures (in particular those related to environmental practices and performance) can contribute to better environmental performance. It begins with a brief introduction of environment-related disclosures. Next, it presents arguments supporting the idea that environment-related disclosures might lead to corporate environmental performance improvements, before reviewing arguments against. We then discuss past empirical work which has sought to explore the relationship between disclosure and corporate environmental performance. Following this, we provide a discussion of the data-related factors which might influence whether, and to what extent, non-financial disclosures drive or enable decision-making supporting corporate environmental performance improvements. The chapter concludes by offering lessons for practitioners.

A Brief Primer on Environment-Related Disclosures

Various terms have been used to describe the disclosure – also known as 'reporting' – of information on corporations' sustainability performance (Baumüller and Sopp, 2021). One commonly deployed term is non-financial reporting. This refers to all the 'information disclosed by companies about their non-financial performance and how they manage social and environmental challenges' (Hahn *et al.*, 2023: 3). The term non-financial is used because the information has traditionally not been captured in the financial statements required under regulated accounting standards. Environment-related disclosures can be understood as a subset of non-financial reporting, emphasising environmental aspects.

Environment-related disclosures are highly diverse in terms of their focus, format and audience. They can encompass a wide range of topics such as climate change, non-greenhouse gas pollution, biodiversity and land use, water use and waste. Disclosures frequently include data on corporate environmental 'performance' such as Scope 1 carbon emissions. They also cover information on policies, practices and systems to manage environment-related issues. Capital or operating expenditures on environmental issues may form part of non-financial disclosures.

The primary entities involved in non-financial reporting are companies in the real economy. Their disclosures may be made in a standalone environment, sustainability or integrated reports. They may also report directly to actors such as environmental, social and governance (ESG) ratings agencies, investors and financial and other regulators. Financial actors such as asset managers and financial advisors also disclose non-financial information, although the focus of this chapter is on disclosures by real economy corporates.

When discussing and analysing disclosures, it is important to distinguish between mandatory and voluntary disclosure. Voluntary disclosures are discretionary. Companies choose whether and, if so, how and what to report. In disclosing information, actors may make use of voluntary reporting frameworks such as the Global Reporting Initiative (GRI) (Aluchna *et al.*, 2023). These frameworks provide guidance to organisations on which topics to report on and can include protocols for compiling and disclosing data. Voluntary reporting may be motivated by a range of factors. Internally, the drivers may include a desire to improve a firm's reputation and managerial commitment to transparency. Externally, voluntary reporting may be the result of stakeholder pressures (e.g., from NGOs), or explicit requirements from actors such as investors, buyers in supply chains or stock exchanges (Ali *et al.*, 2024; Blowfield and Murray, 2019). Thus, whilst nominally voluntary, a degree of coercion may underpin some voluntary disclosures.

Mandatory disclosures are required by law. The origins of such reporting can be traced back to the 1970s, when governments in several countries began to require companies to report on aspects such as pollution expenditure (Blowfield and Murray, 2019). A large and growing number of jurisdictions across the world now require companies to disclose environment-related information. Mandatory reporting typically requires disclosing entities to report on specific metrics – often accompanied by specific requirements on data quality, materiality assessments and assurance (Tang and Demeritt, 2018). Mandatory requirements have often been built on voluntary reporting frameworks such as those produced by the Task Force on Climate-related Financial Disclosures (TCFD) and the Sustainability Accounting Standards Board (SASB) (Aluchna *et al.*, 2023).

A central objective for governments and regulators in mandating non-financial disclosure schemes has been to inform investors. As explained elsewhere (see Chapters 3 and 5), social and environmental issues may be financially material to firms, potentially impacting their costs, revenues, and, ultimately, profitability. By incorporating information on these sustainability-related risks and opportunities into their decision-making, investors should be better placed to safeguard or even enhance their returns in line with their fiduciary duties. Considerations of social and environmental impact have also underpinned mandatory disclosure requirements, although these have often been secondary to financial considerations. Nevertheless, schemes such as the European Union's Corporate Sustainability Reporting Directive (CSRD) have placed growing emphasis on disclosures material to understanding companies' impact on social and environmental issues.

Why Might Disclosures Lead to Improved Environmental Performance?

Within the present context, environmental performance broadly refers to how well a firm manages its impact on the environment. The relationship between non-financial performance and environmental performance is, in the words of one recent commentator, 'complicated' (Hahn *et al.*, 2023). It is nevertheless possible to identify several pathways through which disclosures could lead to improved environmental performance. We focus on two broad channels here: (a) heightened external scrutiny, pressure and rewards and (b) self-monitoring and management.

Heightened External Scrutiny, Pressure and Rewards

Increased non-financial reporting opens corporations up to heightened scrutiny from external actors such as investors, NGOs, regulators and customers. By helping to address so-called information asymmetries, disclosure can inform such stakeholders about the absolute and relative environmental performance of firms. For example, as part of their stewardship activities, investors can use data to identify investee companies, which are 'laggards', engage with them using the disclosed information, and exert pressure to address important shortcomings. Reporting of non-financial information thus provides enhanced opportunities for stakeholders to monitor and hold companies to account.

For their part, companies may respond to these pressures by improving their environmental performance, not least because doing so can be in their economic self-interest. For example, companies that fail to address environment-related concerns from investors may face negative consequences, possibly including shareholder resolutions or even divestment (Marti *et al.*, 2024). Likewise, companies that fail to act on pressure from NGOs risk damaging their 'social licence', which can lead to several negative repercussions (Bauckloh *et al.*, 2022). As well as reactive responses, disclosure can animate anticipatory ones. Fearing stakeholder reactions to disclosed information, corporations may proactively seek to improve their environmental performance.

More positively, disclosures offer firms an opportunity to 'signal' their superior environmental performance to external stakeholders (Mahoney *et al.*, 2013). This may allow better performing companies to add value by, for instance, cultivating brand loyalty, accessing new markets or lowering the cost of capital (Dhaliwal *et al.*, 2011). Companies may strategically anticipate and respond to these incentives by seeking to improve their underlying environmental performance, potentially giving rise to a positive feedback loop (Downar *et al.*, 2021).

Self-monitoring and Management

Another (related) way in which disclosure may prompt environmental performance improvements is by animating processes, self-monitoring and management.

That is, the collection, processing and analysis of environment-related information can influence management decision-making and lead firms to make internal improvements. For example, through an improved understanding of environmentally significant inputs, a company may identify potentially profitable opportunities to reduce its energy consumption (Tang and Demeritt, 2018). Disclosure may thus function as a managerial tool to help firms learn about environment-related inefficiencies, weaknesses and potential liabilities. It may also empower managers with information to begin to address these issues, catalysing processes of continuous improvement (Fiechter *et al.*, 2022).

Relatedly, disclosure can prompt benchmarking. Because of the availability of – to a greater or lesser extent – comparable information, companies may 'benchmark' their environmental performance against their peers. Managers may be concerned about the implications of lagging behind their competitors, possibly leading them to institute measures to learn from their peers, bringing their environmental performance closer in line with industry norms (see, for example, Cao (2019) and Tomar (2023)). These predictions are consistent with work on corporate responsibility, which suggests that firms' sustainability-related behaviour may be strongly influenced by the ambitions and performance of their peers (Berger-Schmitz *et al.*, 2023).

Why Might Disclosures *Not* Lead to Performance Improvements?

The idea that disclosure could drive improvements in environmental performance is intuitively plausible. Yet, despite its obvious appeal, there are several possible reasons why this may not happen in practice. We cover three here: misleading disclosures, user embeddedness and discloser embeddedness.

Misleading Disclosures

Information disclosures may not drive improvements in environmental performance if they do not provide a true measure of companies' underlying sustainability (impact) performance. One commonly discussed factor which might contribute to misleading disclosures is greenwashing (see Chapter 11). Specifically, it is suggested that firms may strategically disclose information in ways which create a misleading impression of their true sustainability performance (Callery, 2023; Kim and Lyon, 2011). This could involve the selective disclosure of positive environment-related information and the omission of negative information. It could also involve outright deception, for instance, a firm falsely reporting its water consumption. Greenwashing potentially allows firms to cultivate a favourable opinion of their environmental credentials among stakeholders without having to incur the costs of making changes to their sourcing, production processes or products. It ought to be noted that not all misleading disclosures are the result of deliberate deception. Some companies may simply lack the knowledge or resources to provide material and accurate disclosures.

Misleading disclosures can have consequences. If firms can substitute true environmental performance with false environmental disclosures, then the incentives to improve their underlying sustainability performance are likely to be diminished. Misleading disclosures make it more difficult for external stakeholders to hold firms to account. They may also reduce the pressure on firms, or entire sectors, to improve their performance by deflecting the attention of critical stakeholders. Within the context of sustainable finance, misleading disclosures may also result in capital misallocation, with capital flowing to firms with better disclosures rather than better underlying environmental performance (European Securities and Markets Authority (ESMA), 2024).

User Embeddedness

According to Weil *et al.* (2005), disclosure is more likely to be effective when the information is 'embedded' into the decision-making of information users. Embeddedness implies that information is relevant to users and can help them improve their decision-making in relation to organisational goals. Yet this condition may not always be met when it comes to non-financial reporting.

Potential users may not see disclosed information as useful or important. For example, investors focused on fulfilling their fiduciary duty may pay limited attention to environmental data points which are not viewed as financially material over their investment time horizon. Likewise, where environmental consciousness is low, consumers may not factor information on the environmental performance of companies into their purchasing decisions (Lee, 2010). In short, we cannot assume that target users necessarily value environmental issues and therefore will seek to incorporate associated disclosures into their decision-making processes.

Another reason why information may not be embedded is that it may not be readily comprehensible or usable to potential users (Weil *et al.*, 2005). These users may not understand how to interpret data, for example, because of inadequate knowledge about the relationship between the volume of specific toxic pollutants and the implied level of environmental risk. Users may also struggle to incorporate information because it is disclosed in a format which is incompatible with existing decision-making criteria and processes. Indeed, if disclosed information requires costly or time-consuming processing to make it user-compatible, it may be ignored by potential users.

Potential users may face constraints on their ability – whether acting individually or collectively, to act effectively on disclosed information, even in situations where this information is useful and usable for their decision-making (Ameli *et al.*, 2019). To give one example: it is unlikely that threats of divestment by smaller shareholders in response to information about inadequate short-term emissions reductions would provide sufficient economic incentives for an oil and gas company to accelerate mitigation efforts. Potential users may find themselves constrained by other factors, such as contractual and legal obligations related to fiduciary duty. Acting on environmental information may also be undermined by uncertainty, for example, about future environmental regulations.

Discloser Embeddedness

Just as with user decision-making, the embeddedness of disclosures in discloser decision-making may also influence their impact on environmental performance (Weil *et al.*, 2005). If companies reporting information do not see environment-related issues and associated disclosures as relevant to organisational goals, these issues are less likely to have a significant impact on decision-making (Weil *et al.*, 2005). Under such conditions, firms may view disclosure as largely a 'compliance' issue, necessary to meet the demands of external stakeholders rather than useful information in and of itself for internal business decision-making. Relatedly, where systems for firm-level disclosure are weakly integrated into operational and strategic management, opportunities for companies to learn from disclosed information may be limited.

In common with users, disclosers can face constraints on their ability to act in relation to new knowledge and insights. They may lack the resources and capabilities, for example, to rectify shortcomings identified through non-financial reporting. Disclosers may also confront hard trade-offs between improving environmental performance and associated disclosures, on the one hand, and maintaining profitability, on the other (Sullivan and Gouldson, 2017). Even if managers would like to act on information, they may be reluctant to do so.

Insights from the Empirical Literature

The relationship between non-financial reporting and corporate environmental performance has been the subject of a growing empirical literature. While instructive, it can be difficult to draw generalisable insights from this work. For a start, the types of disclosures examined in past work vary significantly (Doan and Sassen, 2020). For example, they differ with respect to the environmental topics covered and attributes such as whether the disclosures are mandatory or voluntary. Some studies only use binary measures of disclosure (e.g., whether a company reports using a specific reporting framework), while others seek to capture the 'quality' or 'level' (e.g., with reference to the number of data points or to attributes such as third-party assurance). Different studies use different measures of environmental performance, including ones capturing outputs (e.g., organisational policies and practices), outcomes (e.g., proxies of environmental impact, regulatory compliance) and combinations of these. The samples examined in studies also vary in terms of firm size, sectors, geographies and time. Many studies make use of quantitative techniques (albeit using a range of different statistical designs), some qualitative techniques and still others a mix of quantitative and qualitative (Gehricke *et al.*, 2025; Tang and Demeritt, 2018).

Another reason why it is difficult to draw generalisable insights from the literature is that different studies have different objectives. Some are primarily concerned with investigating whether disclosures – and especially voluntary or mandatory disclosure requirements – are associated with improved environmental performance. Others are primarily concerned with whether higher corporate environmental performance is associated with superior disclosures (i.e., signalling behaviour) or, conversely, whether firms with lower environmental performance disclose more information (i.e., greenwashing behaviour). Complicating any assessment is the idea that the relationship between environmental disclosures and environmental performance is bi-directional: disclosure may impact environmental performance, but environmental performance can also impact disclosures. Unfortunately, comparatively few studies effectively address endogeneity concerns with research designs capable of inferring the direction of causality (Doan and Sassen, 2020).

A third reason why it can be difficult to derive generalised insights is that results from past work are mixed. Studies have found positive, negative and no relationships between disclosure and environmental performance. This is perhaps unsurprising given the diversity of objectives, research designs, disclosures and samples in the literature. Two types of study have nevertheless sought to draw wider conclusions. One is qualitative literature reviews, which have sought to summarise findings from past work. Examples include Velte *et al.* (2020) and Christensen *et al.* (2021), who both examine carbon-related disclosures. Another type of study is quantitative meta-reviews, which use statistical techniques to estimate effects across multiple studies. Doan and Sassen (2020) find a weak negative relationship between corporate environmental performance and disclosures based on 62 primary studies. Conversely, Ali *et al.*'s (2024) meta-analysis of 43 studies finds a positive and statistically significant relationship.

What insights can we draw from the empirical literature? One is that considerable caution needs to be exercised in over-generalising from single studies. Each needs to be understood within the context of its research design, focus and sample. Another insight is that there is compelling evidence that firms may use disclosures to engage in greenwashing. Studies have shown that firms with worse environmental performance have – in certain contexts – disclosed more information (Aragón-Correa *et al.*, 2016; Cong *et al.*, 2020). However, there is nothing inevitable about this, and greenwashing can be mitigated by firm- and country-level factors (Marquis *et al.*, 2016). Indeed, in other studies and contexts, higher disclosures have been shown to be indicative of superior environmental performance (e.g., Mahoney *et al.*, 2013). A further insight is that the central question of this chapter – i.e., do better disclosures lead to superior environmental performance – has only been taken up in a comparatively small number of studies. Many of these examine the effect of mandatory disclosure requirements. A common finding from this work is that firms subject to mandatory disclosures (Aboud *et al.*, 2024; Aluchna *et al.*, 2023; Bauckloh *et al.*, 2022; Doshi *et al.*, 2013; Downar *et al.*, 2021) are more likely to improve on certain measures of environmental performance. The reported gains include reduced emissions (Tomar, 2023), improved carbon efficiency (Bauckloh *et al.*, 2022), increased spending on corporate social responsibility (Fiechter *et al.*, 2022), reduced energy consumption (Krueger *et al.*, 2020) and less environmental pollution (Bonetti *et al.*, 2023).

Data Considerations for Impact

The general argument as to why better non-financial reporting might – or might not – drive or enable better environmental performance is reasonably well understood. This section foregrounds the qualities of data in shaping this relationship. It focuses on five data-related aspects:

- Forward-looking versus backwards-looking data: the balance between historical performance metrics and future commitments affects how disclosure drives action.
- Materiality: whether companies use single or double materiality approaches affects what issues they consider important enough to report and address.
- Investment-grade data: the quality of reported data (accuracy, comparability, timeliness, completeness, external assurance etc.) determines its usefulness for stakeholders.
- Measures of performance: the choice between absolute and relative metrics shapes how performance is assessed and what improvements are prioritised.
- Assurance: whether the quality of disclosed data is independently verified.

Underpinning all these factors is the premise that it is the shape and form of disclosures that drive performance assessments and decision-making. For example, if regulations require companies to report on specific metrics, then management and stakeholder attention is most likely to be focused on those metrics (see, generally, Sullivan (2011)). Similarly, performance benchmarks tend to focus on the data and metrics that are most commonly reported by companies. That is, company management will tend to focus on those issues that are required to be reported (i.e., mandatory requirements) or those that are of strategic importance to the company. For stakeholders, their engagement with the company will inevitably be shaped by the company's disclosures. The absence of disclosure on an issue of concern means that stakeholders will have to focus their attention on obtaining this information, rather than dealing with the substance of the company's performance on the issue. Further, the framing of the issue – i.e., what information is provided, what is the quality and completeness of the information, what is the relevance of the information to the stakeholders in question – will inevitably shape and structure the discussion that the company has with its stakeholders.

Forward-Looking versus Backwards-Looking Data

Companies typically provide information on their environmental performance within a previous reporting period (e.g., the last financial year). This is often referred to as 'backward-looking data'. Taking climate change as an example, this information could include emissions data for the reporting period, trends in these data, the impacts of climate change on the business, descriptions of the actions taken to reduce emissions and performance against climate targets. In addition, companies may provide information on their current performance, e.g., their current policies and performance against benchmarks (see, further, Future of Sustainable Data Alliance (FoSDA), 2021). These are all valuable data and can be used to draw some inferences about likely future performance; for example, a track record of emissions reduction in the past provides insights into likely future performance, and current emissions allow the company's exposure to climate risk to be compared to its industry peers (Sullivan and Gouldson, 2021).

However, backwards-looking data do not necessarily provide insights into future performance. Stakeholders want to know how the company expects its performance to evolve over time (e.g., what are its targets and its commitments) and what actions it will take to manage its risks, opportunities and impacts. These 'forward-looking' data can be used to assess the company's future exposure to risks and opportunities and to assess the company's alignment with long-term sustainability goals. In addition, they enable investors to differentiate between companies that may have the same sustainability performance in the present (such as the same carbon footprint) but may have different potential in terms of their sustainability outlook (FoSDA, 2021).

Materiality

The impact of disclosures is also shaped by what is reported in terms of materiality. An exclusive emphasis on single materiality (see Chapter 3) means reporting on issues that present either a financially material risk or opportunity which could plausibly impact the financial position of the company. The concept of double materiality (again, see Chapter 3) expands the focus of disclosures. Double materiality implies companies reporting both on those issues that could have a significant financial impact on the company (e.g., on its financial performance, on its cost of capital) and on those issues where the company has, or could have, a significant actual or potential, positive or negative, impact on people or the environment over the short-, medium- or long-term.

In the context of this chapter, the focus of reporting – i.e., whether the focus is on managing risk to the company (single materiality) or managing risk to the company and the company's impacts on the environment (double materiality) – defines the decisions that are made on the basis of this reporting. While the case for double materiality (or a more holistic approach to reporting) may be clear to those concerned about wider environmental impacts, double materiality reporting does not dictate the relative importance of risk or impact considerations in decision-making. What issues are seen as being of sufficient importance to report as material (financial or impact), and what data or metrics are provided about these, may be left to the reporting entity to decide (Baumüller and Sopp, 2021). Nevertheless, reporting on double materiality can be valuable for stakeholders – including investors and business customers – concerned with better understanding and seeking to manage social or environmental impacts within value chains.

Investment-Grade Data

The quality of the data reported by companies is also an important determinant of whether they can be used by stakeholders to encourage performance improvements through, for example, peer benchmarking. For data to be used in this sort of way, it needs to be (adapted from London Stock Exchange Group (LSEG) (2024)):

1. Accurate: Data accuracy refers to the extent to which data reflects the real-world conditions that it is intended to represent. The users of these data need to understand how the data has been collected and assured, what assumptions were made, and what uncertainties or limitations apply to the data.
2. Comparable: Data comparability means that company data can be readily assessed against (a) the company's historic performance (i.e., the data should be internally consistent) and (b) against industry peers (i.e., the data should be externally consistent). To allow comparability between peers, companies should use indicators and metrics that are widely used within their sector, gather data in line with common practice and report in a similar manner to sector peers.
3. Timely: Companies should provide sustainability data alongside their annual report and accounts or as soon as possible afterwards.
4. Aligned with company and other reporting boundaries.
5. Complete: Companies should provide absolute and relative data (see below), contextual data and information on the factors that have influenced performance, whether positively or negatively.
6. Balanced: Companies should provide an objective picture of performance, presenting both favourable and unfavourable information clearly and in full to aid the reader's understanding. The issues around greenwashing and greenwashing are discussed in more detail in Chapter 11.

7. Accessible: Companies should make their data publicly available and accessible to their stakeholders.
8. Externally assured (see below for more details).

If reported data do not meet these requirements, the ability of internal and external stakeholders to robustly assess performance and to encourage or enable environmental performance may be reduced. The existence of disclosure alone is less impactful than the existence of high-quality disclosure that investors can readily use for analysis and comparison. Without high-quality data, the potential for disclosures to drive better environmental performance through investor influence is likely to be significantly diminished.

Measures of Performance

Absolute metrics, such as total greenhouse gas emissions, should describe a company's overall environmental impact (Kolk *et al.*, 2016). Such metrics are useful for tracking progress towards specific targets and comparing performance against industry benchmarks or progress, such as achieving net zero greenhouse gas emissions by 2050. However, absolute metrics may not provide a complete picture. For example, they may not account for differences in company size, or they may provide an incomplete picture of performance (e.g., business growth may mean that absolute emissions increase even if business efficiency has improved). Relative metrics, such as emissions intensity per unit of output, account for changes in company size or activity levels. They can be helpful for identifying areas for improvement and for benchmarking company performance against its peers. However, relative metrics may not accurately reflect the company's absolute environmental impact and can mask significant increases in emissions (van den Berg *et al.*, 2015). Both absolute and relative metrics are needed to fully understand and interpret company performance. Providing one without the other risks skewing the decisions made. A focus solely on absolute emissions could, for example, encourage companies simply to sell high-emitting parts of their business even if there are also significant associated benefits (e.g., the manufacturing of energy-efficient equipment). Similarly, a focus on relative emissions may, if business growth runs ahead of efficiency gains, mean that total emissions continue to rise.

Assurance

A further important quality of data concerns whether and how it is assured. Assurance here refers to the process through which an independent party verifies the completeness, accuracy and reliability of disclosed information. This can be undertaken in relation to guidelines and standards within the area of sustainability disclosures. Examples include the AA1000 Assurance Standard, ISSA 5000, ISAE 3000 and ISO 14064-3.

Assurance is important for several reasons. One is that it can help to improve the credibility of disclosed data in the eyes of stakeholders. This may mean that investors and other users are more likely to trust, pay attention to and take steps to integrate information into their decision-making (Quick and Inwinkl, 2020). The issue of addressing concerns over greenwashing (see Chapter 11) is pertinent here. Another closely related reason is that assurance may contribute to better data quality, for instance, in terms of its accuracy, impact materiality and comparability. Assurance can help to identify weaknesses in firm-level processes involved in measuring, collecting, compiling and reporting data, potentially helping companies to improve their reporting over time. Indeed, aware that their disclosures will be subject to external review, disclosers may invest more resources in internal quality control processes. Better data quality, in turn, can improve decision-making by external users. For example, with more accurate data on Scope 3 carbon emissions, investors who value portfolio decarbonisation should be better able to target their stewardship activities.

Yet assurance is not a silver bullet. The academic literature has questioned the integrity of assurance processes on the grounds of, for example, commercial pressures to undertake more superficial verification processes and auditor independence (Boiral *et al.*, 2020; Free *et al.*, 2024). It has also reached mixed conclusions about whether assurance effectively addresses the issue of selective disclosure (García-Sánchez *et al.*, 2022; Roszkowska-Menkes *et al.*, 2024). Such concerns suggest a need to pay attention to the quality of assurance processes, systems and standards themselves. That said, independent, competent and rigorous assurance nevertheless has a role to play in improving the quality and impact of environment-related disclosures.

Closing Reflections

The disclosure of non-financial information has emerged as a central feature of the landscape of contemporary sustainability-related investor governance. This chapter has sought to address the question of whether such disclosures lead to improvements in corporate environmental performance. Although the growing demand for non-financial information has often been driven more by financial concerns, there are nevertheless several ways in which enhanced disclosures could positively contribute to better environmental or sustainability outcomes.

An important theme running through the chapter has been that there is nothing automatic in environment-related disclosures giving rise to improvements in corporate environmental performance. Indeed, past empirical work comes to mixed conclusions about the impact of disclosure, with many studies also failing to adequately resolve questions about the direction of causality (i.e., do better disclosures drive better environmental performance or does better environmental performance drive better disclosures?). Like many other aspects of sustainable finance, the impact of disclosures is dependent on how the disclosure regime is embedded into the decision-making processes of the company's external stakeholders, as well as how the company responds to new information and external pressure.

Mandatory requirements to report on material environmental impacts and how companies are managing them have a role to play in improving the quality, the decision-making value and the impact of environment-related disclosures. Mandatory disclosure requirements cannot, however, address all the issues raised in this chapter. Within this context, the efforts of other actors are necessary to complement, reinforce and enhance mandatory requirements; for example, consistent external scrutiny and pressure can encourage more harmonised reporting that, in turn, can help enhance peer benchmarking (Luo and Tang, 2022; Sullivan and Gouldson, 2012).

While this chapter focuses on disclosure, we also recognise the wider context within which environmental disclosure occurs. In particular, as discussed by various contributors to this book, Disclosure alone is not sufficient to drive performance. It must be part of a broader ecosystem of sustainability governance that includes regulatory oversight, stakeholder engagement and internal corporate commitment to environmental improvement.

Implications for Practitioners

Investors

1. Investors are a key audience for corporate disclosures and should therefore publicly communicate their support for high-quality, decision-useful ('investment grade') data.
2. Investors should encourage companies to report on financially material and environmentally material considerations, to provide data on both absolute and relative performance, and to provide backwards-looking and forward-looking data.
3. Across all the companies in which they invest, investors should encourage the reporting of data and metrics that are:
   - Accurate and reflective of the real-world conditions that they are intended to represent.
   - Comparable and consistent, both in relation to the company's historic performance and against industry peers.
   - Provided in a timely manner.
   - Aligned with company and other reporting boundaries.
   - Complete.
   - Balanced and provide an objective picture of performance.

- ■ Publicly available and accessible to all stakeholders (not just to investors).

4. Investors should ensure that environmental reporting and decision-making are integrated into companies' decision-making processes and structures. This may include ensuring that there is senior management and board oversight of the reporting process, clear responsibilities and accountabilities for environmental performance and an explicit link between environmental performance and executive pay.

Policymakers

1. Policymakers should adopt and effectively implement mandatory measures and encourage voluntary initiatives that support and incentivise better corporate environmental disclosures.
2. In relation to metrics, policymakers should support:
   - Double-materiality reporting frameworks (i.e. reporting on financially material and environmentally material considerations).
   - Encourage reporting on both absolute and relative performance.
   - Encourage the provision of backward-looking and forward-looking data.
3. In relation to data quality, policymakers should encourage the reporting of data and metrics that are:
   - Accurate and reflective of the real-world conditions that they are intended to represent.
   - Comparable and consistent, both in relation to the company's historic performance and against industry peers.
   - Provided in a timely manner.
   - Aligned with company and other reporting boundaries.
   - Complete.
   - Balanced and provide an objective picture of performance.
   - Publicly available and accessible to all stakeholders.
4. Policymakers should support efforts to encourage and enable stakeholder engagement with, and use of, reported information. This could include encouraging the data to be presented in formats that can be used by multiple stakeholder needs, ensuring that the data are accessible and understandable, and ensuring the data are available in a timely manner.

References

Aboud, A., Saleh, A. and Eliwa, Y. (2024), 'Does Mandating ESG Reporting Reduce ESG Decoupling? Evidence from the European Union's Directive 2014/95', *Business Strategy and the Environment,* Vol. 33, No. 2, pp. 1305–1320, https://doi.org/10.1002/bse.3543

Ali, W., Bekiros, S., Hussain, N., Khan, S. and Nguyen, D. (2024), 'Determinants and Consequences of Corporate Social Responsibility Disclosure: A Survey of Extant Literature', *Journal of Economic Surveys,* Vol. 38, pp. 793–822, https://doi.org/10.1111/joes.12556

Aluchna, M., Roszkowska-Menkes, M. and Kamiński, B. (2023), 'From Talk to Action: The Effects of the Non-Financial Reporting Directive on ESG Performance', *Meditari Accountancy Research,* Vol. 31, No. 7, pp. 1–25, https://doi.org/10.1108/MEDAR-12-2021-1530

Ameli, N., Drummond, P., Bisaro, A., Grubb, M. and Chenet, H. (2019), 'Climate Finance and Disclosure for Institutional Investors: Why Transparency Is Not Enough', *Climatic Change,* Vol. 160, No. 4, pp. 565–589, https://doi.org/10.1007/s10584-019-02542-2

Aragón-Correa, J., Marcus, A. and Hurtado-Torres, N. (2016), 'The Natural Environmental Strategies of International Firms: Old Controversies and New Evidence on Performance and Disclosure', *Academy of Management Perspectives,* Vol. 30, No. 1, pp. 24–39, https://doi.org/10.5465/amp.2014.0043

Bauckloh, T., Klein, C., Pioch, T. and Schiemann, F. (2022), 'Under Pressure? The Link between Mandatory Climate Reporting and Firms' Carbon Performance', *Organization & Environment,* Vol. 36, No. 1, pp. 126–149, https://doi.org/10.1177/10860266221083340

Baumüller, J. and Sopp, K. (2021), 'Double Materiality and the Shift from Non-Financial to European Sustainability Reporting: Review, Outlook and Implications', *Journal of Applied Accounting Research,* Vol. 23, No. 1, pp. 8–28, https://doi.org/10.1108/jaar-04-2021-0114

Berger-Schmitz, Z., George, D., Hindal, C., Perkins, R. and Travaille, M. (2023), 'What Explains Firms' Net Zero Adoption, Strategy and Response?', *Business Strategy and the Environment,* Vol. 32, No. 8, pp. 5583–5601, https://doi.org/10.1002/bse.3437

Blowfield, M. and Murray, A. (2019), *Corporate Social Responsibility* (Oxford University Press, Oxford, 4th edition).

Boiral, O., Heras-Saizarbitoria, I. and Brotherton, M. (2020), 'Professionalizing the Assurance of Sustainability Reports: The Auditors' Perspective', *Accounting, Auditing & Accountability Journal,* Vol. 33 No. 2, pp. 309–334, https://doi.org/10.1108/AAAJ-03-2019-3918

Bonetti, P., Leuz, C. and Michelon, G. (2023), *Internalizing Externalities through Public Pressure: Transparency Regulation for Hydraulic Fracturing, Drilling Activity and Water Quality.* Working Paper No. 2023-06 (Becker Friedman Institute for Economics, University of Chicago, Chicago), https://bfi.uchicago.edu/wp-content/uploads/2023/01/BFI_WP_2023-06-2.pdf

Callery, P. (2023), 'The Influence of Strategic Disclosure on Corporate Climate Performance Ratings', *Business & Society,* Vol. 62, No. 5, pp. 950–988, https://doi.org/10.1177/00076503221115715

Cao, J., Liang, H. and Zhan, X. (2019), 'Peer Effects of Corporate Social Responsibility', *Management Science,* Vol. 65, No. 12, pp. 5449–5956, https://doi.org/10.1287/mnsc.2018.3100

CDP (2025), 'CDP Scores and A Lists', www.cdp.net/en/data/scores?cid=9205306762&adgpid=95799580520&itemid=&targid=kwd-870315494791&mt=b&loc=9197923&ntwk=g&dev=c&dmod=&adp=&gad_source=1&gclid=CjwKCAiAmMC6BhA6EiwAdN5iLU6XCk5hqy61aXtOrAfx_R7U3xmWpfKg6nJ9n8bJatxVcdXvUslgJRoCNqgQAvD_BwE (last viewed 14 March 2025).

Christensen, H., Hail, L. and Leuz, C. (2021), 'Mandatory CSR and Sustainability Reporting: Economic Analysis and Literature Review', *Review of Accounting Studies*, Vol. 26. No. 3, pp. 1176–1248, https://doi.org/10.1007/s11142-021-09609-5

Cong, Y., Freedman, M. and Park, J. (2020), 'Mandated Greenhouse Gas Emissions and Required SEC Climate Change Disclosures', *Journal of Cleaner Production*, Vol. 247, p. 119111, https://doi.org/10.1016/j.jclepro.2019.119111

Dhaliwal, D., Li, O., Tsang, A. and Yang, Y. (2011), 'Voluntary Nonfinancial Disclosure and the Cost of Equity Capital: The Initiation of Corporate Social Responsibility Reporting', *The Accounting Review*, Vol. 86, No. 1, pp. 59–100, https://doi.org/10.2308/accr.00000005

Doan, M. and Sassen, R. (2020), 'The Relationship between Environmental Performance and Environmental Disclosure: A Meta-Analysis', *Journal of Industrial Ecology*, Vol. 24, pp. 1140–1157, https://doi.org/10.1111/jiec.13002

Doshi, A., Dowell, G. and Toffel, M. (2013), 'How Firms Respond to Mandatory Information Disclosure', *Strategic Management Journal*, Vol. 34, pp. 1209–1231, https://doi.org/10.1002/smj.2055

Downar, B., Ernstberger, J., Reichelstein, S. and Zaklan, A. (2021), 'The Impact of Carbon Disclosure Mandates on Emissions and Financial Operating Performance', *Review of Accounting Studies*, Vol. 26, pp. 1137–1175, https://doi.org/10.1007/s11142-021-09611-x

European Securities and Markets Authority (ESMA) (2024), *Final Report on Greenwashing, 4th June. ESMA36-287652198-2699* (ESMA, Paris), www.esma.europa.eu/sites/default/files/2024-06/ESMA36-287652198-2699_Final_Report_on_Greenwashing.pdf

Fiechter, P., Hitz, J. and Lehmann, N. (2022), 'Real Effects of a Widespread CSR Reporting Mandate: Evidence from the European Union's CSR Directive', *Journal of Accounting Research*, Vol. 60, No. 4, pp. 1499–1549, https://doi.org/10.1111/1475-679x.12424

Free, C., Jones, S. and Tremblay, M. (2024), 'Greenwashing and Sustainability Assurance: A Review and Call for Future Research", *Journal of Accounting Literature*, https://doi.org/10.1108/JAL-11-2023-0201

Future of Sustainable Data Alliance (FoSDA) (2021), *Forward Looking ESG Data. FoSDA Review 2021*, https://futureofsustainabledata.com/wp-content/uploads/2021/10/FoSDA-Forward-Looking-Data-report-1.pdf

García-Sánchez, I., Hussain, N., Aibar-Guzmán, C. and Aibar-Guzmán, B. (2022), 'Assurance of Corporate Social Responsibility Reports: Does It Reduce Decoupling Practices?', *Business Ethics, the Environment & Responsibility*, Vol. 31, pp. 118–138, https://doi.org/10.1111/beer.12394

Gehricke, S., Leippold, M. and Schimanski, T. (2025, May 8), 'To Disclose, or Not to Disclose: Evaluating the Effectiveness of Mandatory Climate-related Disclosure', *SSRN*, http://dx.doi.org/10.2139/ssrn.5246456

Hahn, R., Reimsbach, D. and Wickert, C. (2023), 'Nonfinancial Reporting and Real Sustainable Change: Relationship Status—It's Complicated', *Organization & Environment*, Vol. 36, No. 1, pp. 3–16, https://doi.org/10.1177/10860266231151

Ilhan, E., Krueger, P., Sautner, Z. and Starks, L. (2023), 'Climate Risk Disclosure and Institutional Investors', *The Review of Financial Studies*, Vol. 36, No. 7, pp. 2617–2650, https://doi.org/10.1093/rfs/hhad002

Kim, E. and Lyon, T. (2011), 'Strategic Environmental Disclosure: Evidence from the DOE's Voluntary Greenhouse Gas Registry,' *Journal of Environmental Economics and Management*, Vol. 61, No. 3, pp. 311–326, https://doi.org/10.1016/j.jeem.2010.11.001

Kolk, A and Van Tulder, R. (2016), *International Business, Corporate Social Responsibility and Global Governance: Models and Cases* (Routledge, London).

Krueger, P., Sautner, Z. and Starks, L. (2020), 'The Importance of Climate Risks for Institutional Investors', *Review of Financial Studies*, Vol. 33, No. 3, pp. 1067–1111, https://econpapers.repec.org/article/ouprfinst/v_3a33_3ay_3a2020_3ai_3a3_3ap_3a1067-1111..htm

La Torre, M., Sabelfeld, S., Blomkvist, M. and Dumay, J. (2020), 'Rebuilding Trust: Sustainability and Non-Financial Reporting and the European Union Regulation', *Meditari Accountancy Research*, Vol. 28, No. 5, pp. 701–725, https://doi.org/10.1108/medar-06-2020-0914

Lee, J., Hsu, L., Han, H. and Kim, Y. (2010), 'Understanding How Consumers View Green Hotels: How a Hotel's Green Image Can Influence Behavioural Intentions', *Journal of Sustainable Tourism*, Vol. 18, No. 7, pp. 901–914, https://doi.org/10.1080/09669581003777747

London Stock Exchange Group (LSEG) (2024), *Your Guide to Sustainability Reporting (LSEG, London)*, www.londonstockexchange.com/raise-finance/sustainable-finance/your-guide-sustainability-reporting

Luo, L. and Tang, Q. (2022), 'The Real Effects of ESG Reporting and GRI Standards on Carbon Mitigation: International Evidence', *Business Strategy and the Environment*, Vol. 32, No. 6, pp. 2985–3000, https://doi.org/10.1002/bse.3281

Mahoney, L., Thorne, L., Cecil, L. and LaGore, W. (2013), 'A Research Note on Standalone Corporate Social Responsibility Reports: Signaling or Greenwashing?', *Critical Perspectives on Accounting*, Vol. 24, No. 4–5, pp. 350–359, https://doi.org/10.1016/j.cpa.2012.09.008

Marquis, C., Toffel, M. and Zhou, Y. (2016), 'Scrutiny, Norms, and Selective Disclosure: A Global Study of Greenwashing,' *Organization Science*, Vol. 27, No. 2, pp. 483–504, https://doi.org/10.1287/orsc.2015.1039

Marti, E., Fuchs, M., DesJardine, M., Slager, R. and Gond, J. (2024), 'The Impact of Sustainable Investing: A Multidisciplinary Review', *Journal of Management Studies*, Vol. 61, pp. 2181–2211, https://doi.org/10.1111/joms.12957

Quick, R. and Inwinkl, P. (2020), 'Assurance on CSR Reports: Impact on the Credibility Perceptions of Non-Financial Information by Bank Directors', *Meditari Accountancy Research*, Vol. 28, No. 5, pp. 833–862, https://doi.org/10.1108/MEDAR-10-2019-0597

Roszkowska-Menkes, M., Aluchna, M. and Kamiński, B. (2024), 'True Transparency or Mere Decoupling? The Study of Selective Disclosure in Sustainability Reporting', *Critical Perspectives on Accounting*, Vol. 98, p. 102700, https://doi.org/10.1016/j.cpa.2023.102700

Sullivan, R. (2011), *Valuing Corporate Responsibility: How Do Investors Really Use Corporate Responsibility Information?* (Greenleaf Publishing, Sheffield).

Sullivan, R. and Gouldson, A. (2012), 'Does Voluntary Carbon Reporting Meet Investors' Needs?', *Journal of Cleaner Production*, Vol. 36, pp. 60–67, https://doi.org/10.1016/j.jclepro.2012.02.020

Sullivan, R. and Gouldson, A. (2017), 'The Governance of Corporate Responses to Climate Change: An International Comparison', *Business Strategy and the Environment*, Vol. 26, No. 4, pp. 413–425, https://doi.org/10.1002/bse.1925

Sullivan, R and Gouldson, A. (2021), *Climate Change and the Governance of Corporations: Lessons from the Retail Sector* (Routledge, London).

Tang, S. and Demeritt, D. (2018), 'Climate Change and Mandatory Carbon Reporting: Impacts on Business Process and Performance', *Business Strategy and the Environment*, Vol. 27, No. 4, pp. 437–455, https://doi.org/10.1002/bse.1985

Tomar, S. (2023), 'Greenhouse Gas Disclosure and Emissions Benchmarking', *Journal of Accounting Research*, Vol. 61, No. 2, pp. 451–492, https://doi.org/10.1111/1475-679x.12473

van den Berg, M., Hof, A., van Vliet, J. and van Vuuren, D. (2015). 'Impact of the Choice of Emission Metric on Greenhouse Gas Abatement and Costs', *Environmental Research Letters*, Vol. 10, No. 2, p. 024001. https://doi.org/10.1088/1748-9326/10/2/024001

Velte, P., Stawinoga, M. and Lueg, R. (2020), 'Carbon Performance and Disclosure: A Systematic Review of Governance-related Determinants and Financial Consequences', *Journal of Cleaner Production*, Vol. 254, p. 120063, https://doi.org/10.1016/j.jclepro.2020.120063

Weil, D., Fung, A., Graham, M. and Fagotto, E. (2005), 'The Effectiveness of Regulatory Disclosure Policies', *Journal of Policy Analysis and Management*, Vol. 25, No. 1, pp. 155–181, https://doi.org/10.1002/pam.20160

Chapter 10

What Is the Value of Collective Action in Sustainable Investment?

Tristan Gilet, Krishnapriya J,
Himanshu Pabreja and Valeria Piani

Introduction

Stewardship (or active ownership) involves investors using their formal rights (e.g. to vote shares) and their informal influence to encourage companies and other actors to take action to better manage sustainability-related risks and impacts. Investors can undertake these activities on their own or together with other investors. The core argument for collaboration is that, by pooling or combining their ownership stakes, investors can significantly increase their leverage or influence in relation to the issue in question.

As can be seen in Table 10.1, collaborative initiatives are a long-standing feature of the responsible investment and sustainable finance landscape. The membership of these initiatives usually comprises asset managers, pension funds, insurers, endowments and foundations. The members or supporters may also include non-governmental organisations (NGOs), other financial institutions,

 DOI: 10.4324/9781003467632-10

policymakers and other stakeholder groups. While the specific goals differ, the overarching aim of these initiatives is to achieve common objectives of reducing financial risks and/or managing social and environmental impacts, through collaboration, advocacy and knowledge-sharing.

This chapter analyses the role that collective investor action (such as those listed in Table 10.1) can play in supporting and delivering better sustainability outcomes. Its focus is on the key concepts and general principles that shape why and how such initiatives are established and run, rather than a detailed analysis of specific initiatives. The chapter starts by discussing the reasons why investors join and participate in collective initiatives. It then describes how collaborations might support their members in achieving sustainability objectives, the mechanisms through which collaborations deliver their desired outcomes, and the practical challenges that determine whether these outcomes are achieved. The final section of the chapter offers some wider reflections on collaborations and on the factors that practitioners should consider when establishing or joining such initiatives.

Why Are Collaborative Initiatives Established and Why Do Investors Join Them?

The stated goals of sustainable finance-related collaborative initiatives generally divide into those relating to financial performance (e.g. reducing portfolio risks from particular social or environmental challenges, creating long-term investment value), those relating to wider economic performance (e.g. managing systemic risks), and those relating to social or environmental impacts (e.g. supporting the transition to a greener and resilient economy) (Danilov, 2022). In practice, however, these initiatives also serve investors' interests in other ways. For example, they can build member capacity and knowledge (McDonnell *et al.*, 2022), address information asymmetries between members and their stakeholders (e.g. encouraging better disclosure by companies, defining reporting expectations for investors), enable the sharing of views on responsible investment (e.g. the members' views on good practice) (Louche, 2004), and set out members' positions on how specific risks might be managed by policymakers (e.g. on policy frameworks for the transition to net zero) (Schoenmaker, 2017: 60–70; Yamahaki, 2019). These initiatives may also allow investors to promote voluntary or self-regulatory approaches through developing their own standards and presenting alternatives to mandatory regulation (McDonnell *et al.*, 2022; Yamahaki, 2019). In addition, through reinforcing expectations of performance and transparency, they may help protect the collective reputation and social licence to operate of the investment industry as a whole (McDonnell *et al.*, 2022; Yamahaki, 2019).

Table 10.1 Examples of Investor Collaborative Initiatives

Initiative Name	*Year Established*	*Approximate Number of Members (as of 31 July 2024)*	*Approximate Member Assets under Management (as of 31 July 2024)*
Interfaith Center on Corporate Responsibility (ICCR)	1971	300	US$4 trillion
Ceres	1989	220	US$44 trillion
UK Sustainable Investment and Finance Association (UKSIF)	1991	300	US$25 trillion
United Nations Environment Programme Finance Initiative (UNEP FI)	1992	500	US$170 trillion
International Corporate Governance Network (ICGN)	1995	870	US$70 trillion
Asian Corporate Governance Association (ACGA)	1999	100	US$40 trillion
CDP (previously Carbon Disclosure Project)	2000	680	US$130 trillion
Institutional Investors Group on Climate Change (IIGCC)	2001	400	US35 trillion
Principles for Responsible Investment (PRI)	2006	5000	US$100 trillion
Global Impact Investing Network (GIIN)	2009	450	……
Eurosif	2010	400	……
Net Zero Asset Owner Alliance (NZAOA)	2019	89	US$9.5 trillion
Focusing Capital on the Long Term Global (FCLT Global)	2013	70	US$564 billion
Investor Forum	2014	55	……
Farm Animal Investment Risk and Return Initiative (FAIRR)	2015	370	US$70 trillion
Asia Investor Group on Climate Change (AIGCC)	2016	71	US$35 trillion
Climate Action 100+	2017	700	US$60 trillion
Nature Action 100	2022	200	US$28 trillion

Source: Authors, based on information published on the initiatives' websites as at 31 July 2024

From a member or signatory perspective, Schoenmaker and Schramade (2019: 102–116) identify six reasons why investors may choose to join a collaborative initiative:

1. Peer pressure, where the size and influence of the coalition and the participation of key competitors or key clients create pressure on others to join. In this situation, participation is often driven by the fear of being at a competitive disadvantage if the investor remains outside the alliance. As more significant industry players decide to participate in an initiative, the perceived risks of non-participation grow, prompting others to align themselves to maintain their market position and avoid falling behind.
2. Outside (or external) pressure, where consumers and NGOs encourage (or even compel) an investment organisation to join and align its objectives with those of a particular coalition.
3. Reputation, where an investment organisation chooses to join a coalition in order to position itself as a pioneer in sustainability or to improve its image, where membership of the coalition serves as a signal of their values and ethical priorities. A related motivation could be to establish credibility with stakeholders who value sustainable or ethical practices.
4. Risk avoidance, where participation provides the investor with information and insights that enable it to better understand and manage the financial and other implications of particular social or environmental challenges. As investors typically seek to minimise uncertainty as much as possible, being part of these coalitions could be a way of being informed and being prepared for sustainability-related risks that may materialise in the short-, medium-, or long-term.
5. Collective advocacy, where being part of the collective action allows the investor to have greater influence on policy decisions.
6. Collective engagement, where being part of the initiative can boost the effectiveness of the investor's own stewardship activities (e.g. through being able to engage with more companies, through being able to engage more intensively, through providing access to better research about companies' practices and performance).

How Do Collective Initiatives Drive Change?

To deliver the changes that they seek, collective initiatives use a range of strategies. This section focuses on the three that are most commonly identified by the organisers or coordinators of collective investor initiatives, namely standard-setting, advocacy and knowledge-sharing. Some or all of these are central to the theory of change used by the initiatives listed in Table 10.1.

Standard-Setting

The establishment of industry standards and market norms can play a critical role in harmonising expectations and practices across an industry sector. In the case of sustainable finance, such standards and norms have been used to define what qualifies as sustainable investments, provide transparency, enable accountability and reduce the risk of greenwashing. Examples include the Green Bond Principles – a standard-setting initiative involving organisations in the green bond market (investors, issuers, underwriters) and coordinated by the International Capital Market Association (ICMA) (2024) – and the net-zero investment framework established by the Institutional Investors Group on Climate Change (IIGCC) (2024). Credible standards help investors manage reputational risks, align with international sustainability practices, and mitigate financial risks associated with environmental and social factors (Conley and Williams, 2011).

Standards and norms enable progress through several mechanisms. They provide a consistent message, ensuring that companies and investors are clear on expectations in terms of practice and reporting. They reduce transaction costs by limiting competing obligations, allowing companies to align their reporting requirements and investors to avoid developing independent criteria. When recognised as credible and backed by well-established organisations, standards foster market trust. They help align investments with sustainability objectives by specifying investment criteria to meet specific sustainability goals, good management practices, and positive environmental and social due diligence processes (Contreras *et al.*, 2019; Macve and Chen, 2010).

One such example is the Global Standard on Responsible Corporate Climate Lobbying (2022), developed by AP7, BNP Paribas Asset Management, the Church of England Pensions Board and Chronos Sustainability, with support from investor networks such as IIGCC and the Principles for Responsible Investment (PRI). The Global Standard aims to define responsible corporate climate lobbying based on alignment with the goals of the Paris Agreement. It calls on companies to make formal commitments to responsible climate lobbying, disclose funding and other support to trade associations involved in climate-related lobbying, and take action if lobbying activity conflicts with the Paris Agreement's goals. The Global Standard consolidated previous investor statements and expectations on climate lobbying and has formed the basis for the Climate Action 100+ (CA100+) expectations on climate lobbying (Climate Action 100+ (CA100+), 2024a).

Another role of voluntary standards is to build communities of practice by creating peer pressure and providing benefits to organisations that support them (Conley and Williams, 2011). For example, the support provided by organisations such as PRI to initiatives like the Task Force on Climate-related Financial Disclosures (TCFD) and the UN Guiding Principles on Business and Human Rights (UNGPs) has reinforced expectations for companies and investors regarding practices and performance (Principles for Responsible Investment

(PRI), 2018, 2023). Aggregated, standards and norms can increase demand for sustainable investments, encouraging more entities to issue and invest in green and sustainable projects (Macve and Chen, 2010).

Two important factors are particularly important in determining the effectiveness of sustainability standards and frameworks. First, the level of ambition underpinning a framework determines the level of ambition in its outcomes. This also affects credibility with stakeholders and their willingness to support the framework. However, an overly ambitious standard may deter investor support, creating a tension between ambition and market acceptance. Second, robust review and enforcement mechanisms are crucial to ensuring that commitments made by participating organisations are upheld (Bauckloh *et al.*, 2023). Many standards rely on self-reporting or voluntary disclosures, often without formal review processes, which raises concerns about transparency and accountability.

Advocacy/Influence

By forming coalitions (and demonstrating that there is a critical mass of investor support for a particular set of actions or interventions), investors can encourage corporations and policymakers to enact practices, regulations, and policies that support sustainable finance. They can do so through direct engagement with the companies or governments in question, where they explain their proposals and the case for action. Such engagement can provide tangible evidence of the willingness of the participating investors to commit time to the issue in question. Investors may also seek to exert influence indirectly through, for example, running press campaigns, building alliances with other investors or stakeholders, and issuing reports and other materials supporting the calls that they are making (Kawabata, 2023). Beyond the direct changes that are the objective of the investor collaboration, these efforts might increase awareness among investors or other stakeholders about the benefits and necessity of sustainability practices (McDonnell *et al.*, 2022), create public support for policy changes (Kawabata, 2023) and foster the voluntary adoption of more sustainable practices by businesses and investors (McDonnell *et al.*, 2022).

An example of collaborative engagement by investors focused on companies is CA100+. CA100+ is an investor-led initiative to ensure the world's largest corporate greenhouse gas emitters take appropriate action on climate change to mitigate financial risk and maximise the long-term value of assets. CA100+ engages with major greenhouse gas emitters to push for board oversight, emissions reductions, and enhanced disclosure – the three original objectives of the initiative – by leveraging the collective influence of its members who collectively manage substantial assets (Climate Action 100+ (CA100+), 2025; Kawabata, 2023). Focus companies are evaluated against the initiative's Net Zero Benchmark criteria, which include emissions reduction targets, governance, capital allocation, and disclosure related to net zero transition plans. CA100+ reports annually on progress, presenting case studies of investor action, case studies of corporate action, and an assessment of company performance against the Net Zero Benchmark criteria. The 2024 annual report shows consistent increases in the number of companies making net zero commitments and setting short- and medium-term net zero-aligned goals, but more progress is needed in terms of the number of companies setting long-term net zero-aligned goals (Climate Action 100+ (CA100+), 2025).

The Investor Agenda is an illustration of a collaborative engagement targeting government. The Investor Agenda coordinates investors to advocate for regulations supporting a sustainable financial system. For example, the Investor Agenda's 2024 Global Investor Statement to Governments on the Climate Crisis – supported by investors representing over US$30 trillion in assets under management (AUM) – provides policy recommendations for all governments, including the adoption and implementation of nationally determined contributions (NDCs) (Investor Agenda, 2024).

There are factors that determine whether the stated goals of collaborative investor initiatives will be met. First, if the goals are relatively unambitious, it is more likely that they will be achieved, but they may not deliver substantial change. It is also important to acknowledge that there may be a trade-off between the level of support for a particular advocacy agenda and its level of ambition, with investors being potentially reluctant to support overly ambitious demands. Second, the level of support – as measured by the number of investors and their total AUM – for a particular policy or corporate agenda may influence how seriously that agenda is taken by policymakers and other decision-makers (Gifford, 2010; Majoch *et al.*, 2017). This is particularly the case for companies, for whom investors are key stakeholders, and investor support for a particular issue adds to the perceived legitimacy and importance of that agenda. Third, the degree of alignment with existing government policies (for public policy advocacy) and the company's understanding of the business case for action (for corporate advocacy) are important determinants of whether advocacy calls are listened to and acted on (Gifford, 2010; McDonnell *et al.*, 2022). Finally, the views of other stakeholders matter. If policy advocacy calls are supported by companies and the public, if there is a sense of urgency or if there is significant media coverage, there is a greater likelihood that companies or policymakers will respond positively (Kawabata, 2023; McDonnell *et al.*, 2022).

Knowledge-Sharing

Knowledge-sharing and awareness-raising about sustainable finance practices, both among members and other stakeholders, are often key objectives of collaborative initiatives. The rationale is that by facilitating the exchange of information and best practices, significant behavioural changes may occur. For example, high-quality information about the investment benefits of analysing specific sustainability-related issues may make investors more likely to integrate them into their investment research and decision-making processes (Wagemans *et al.*, 2013). Knowledge-sharing processes may allow participants to learn from each other's experiences, enhance their understanding of effective integration and engagement strategies, and, in turn, improve their own investment processes (Gond and Piani, 2013). These processes may also help establish trust among the participants, which, in turn, offers the potential for better dialogue and information-sharing (Wagemans *et al.*, 2013).

What Are the Limitations to Collaborative Approaches?

Collective initiatives face a range of challenges from inception (where they need to find sufficient members with motivation and willingness to invest time and resources to get the initiative established), recruitment (where they need to offer sufficient incentives for actors to join and participate), and delivery (where they need to progress on their objectives and provide sufficient incentives/support to members to comply with membership requirements) (Potoski and Prakash, 2013). While these are common issues for all collective initiatives, there are three specific aspects that are of particular importance to the effectiveness of collective initiatives in sustainable finance: free-riding, external pressure, and legitimacy. These have been touched on above, but each is discussed in more detail here.

Free-Riding

For investors, the decision to join or not to join a collective initiative will be driven by their analysis of the costs and benefits of joining. In most cases, the costs are relatively straightforward to determine; they will include membership fees or other financial support, plus the time and resources required for organising and coordinating participants to agree on engagement objectives, monitoring the initiative's progress and performance, engaging with companies and other entities, and dealing with resistance from corporations, regulators, or other actors. In contrast, the benefits (in financial terms) are often more difficult to quantify or describe. Many of the collective initiatives in sustainable finance are focused on public goods (e.g. climate change), where the benefits of success accrue to all regardless of individual contributions (Clark and Hebb, 2004). In a seminal piece on collective action, Olson (1965) argued that such initiatives often face free-riding risks, particularly those focused on public goods (i.e. where the costs are borne by the participants but the benefits accrue more widely). In these situations, there is a strong incentive for individual organisations to allow others to bear the costs and to free-ride on the benefits generated (Sandler, 2015). Therefore, collaborative initiatives need to consider how to encourage others to join or contribute, or how to provide participating organisations with incentives that are not available to non-participants (e.g. economic or social status, recognition, or rewards). For example, Ostrom's (1990) collaborative arrangement principle seeks to address free-riding by building institutions that facilitate communication among actors to build cooperation, mutual understanding, and reciprocity towards common objectives.

A related issue is that there is often limited commercial reward for investment managers to participate in collaborative engagement initiatives. Bebchuk *et al.* (2017) highlight this concern for institutional investors like index funds, which frequently receive limited direct incentives – as their investment fees are generally expressed as a percentage of their AUM – for engaging in stewardship activities for governance and value improvement in corporations. Some argue that engagement could improve index fund managers' reputations and attract more clients, resulting in higher AUM and fee revenues. However, in a price-sensitive commercial environment, if such funds increase fees to support engagement activities, it may shift clients to rival funds who enjoy the same benefits (due to improvement in the overall index performance as a result of the collective engagement) without incurring additional costs (Krouse *et al.*, 2016).

External Pressure

Withdrawal from collaborative initiatives is generally not an attractive solution for large institutional investors, as they typically join in anticipation of benefits such as addressing particular risks, building knowledge and capacity, and expanding networks. In addition, since membership is generally not time-limited, withdrawal may raise questions about an organisation's commitment to sustainable finance and damage relationships with other participating entities.

These factors suggest that once investors join a collective initiative, they face strong incentives to remain. However, this assumption has been challenged in 2024 and 2025, with large institutions such as State Street Global Advisors, JP Morgan Asset Management, PIMCO and Vanguard withdrawing from initiatives like CA100+, the Net Zero Asset Managers Initiative and the Net Zero Insurers Alliance (Climate Action 100+ (CA100+), 2024b; Masters and Temple-West, 2024; Wilkes, 2023a). These departures can be attributed to several factors, including perceptions that the initiatives were becoming more ambitious (i.e. moving from climate-related disclosures to the implementation of transition plans), enhanced monitoring and reporting requirements, legal risks related to anti-trust laws and fiduciary duties, misalignment with internal sustainability goals, and potential constraints on autonomy (Baker, 2024; Jessop and Kerber, 2024; Masters and Temple-West, 2024). In relation to anti-trust, it is relevant to note that all of the initiatives have stressed that their members do not collude on voting decisions, engage in anti-competitive behaviour, or have to follow the initiatives' recommendations when exercising investor rights (Wilkes, 2023b).

The withdrawal of high-profile organisations, especially those with high stakeholder salience, can undermine the effectiveness of collaborative shareholder engagement (Eesley and Lenox, 2006) and reduce the legitimacy of these initiatives. These pressures highlight the trade-off between increasing ambition and maintaining a broad membership base (Couto, 2023). As noted by Barrett and Toman (2010), maintaining a broad membership can enhance cost-effectiveness, reduce free-riding, and increase legitimacy. However, it may also limit the ambition of the initiative. Ultimately, collective initiatives must balance their overall goals with the need to attract and retain members.

Legitimacy

Legitimacy refers to whether an initiative's actions are considered desirable or acceptable within relevant corporate norms, systems or beliefs (Suchman, 1995). The ability of collaborative initiatives to influence corporate behaviour depends, at least in part, on their acceptance by the finance sector, companies and stakeholders (Gond and Piani, 2013). Assessments of legitimacy are based on factors such as the initiative's value in relation to sustainable finance, the sustainability issues it addresses, and its capacity to initiate and maintain collective action (Gond and Piani, 2013). The results of such assessments shape stakeholder confidence and influence the initiative's long-term viability.

One issue with collective investor initiatives, particularly in climate change, is that their objectives and targets are often contingent on external actions. For example, the Net Zero Asset Managers Initiative committed to supporting net zero greenhouse gas emissions by 2050, consistent with fiduciary duty to clients and beneficiaries (Net Zero Asset Managers Initiative, 2025). Gosling and MacNeil (2023) criticised these commitments, arguing that they were conditional on client mandates, fiduciary duty interpretations, regulatory environments, and government policies. They contended that these caveats allowed members to meet official objectives without making substantial real-world impacts, while also providing justification for maintaining business-as-usual investment practices.

Membership of collective initiatives is often heterogeneous in terms of sustainability objectives, organisational requirements, engagement methods, and overall views on sustainability (Gond and Piani, 2013). As a consequence, members may not act in a consistent manner. Some initiatives address this through information-sharing, knowledge transfer, training, and awareness raising (Bauckloh *et al.*, 2023), as well as highlighting key sustainability-related decisions for members' reference. However, analysis by Schoenmaker and Schramade (2019) suggests that many initiatives fail to provide adequate guidance, enforce monitoring and compliance, or resolve conflicts among members. McDonnell *et al.* (2022) raised similar concerns about sustainability reporting, emissions disclosure, transparency and accountability.

Free-riding concerns also affect legitimacy, particularly in ensuring that all members take meaningful action, contribute to engagement efforts, support strategy development, and disclose necessary information. Gond and Piani

(2013) highlighted disparities in member efforts, uneven workload distribution, and weaknesses in coordination within PRI-coordinated engagement strategies. In addition, most initiatives rely on self-reporting, which can allow members to withhold information, undermining credibility and legitimacy.

Enforcement

Effective enforcement mechanisms – such as membership rules, monitoring processes, sanctions for non-compliance, and dispute resolution (Ostrom, 1990; Tosun and Schoenefeld, 2017) – are often necessary to ensure adherence to initiatives' objectives and to reduce free-riding (Potoski and Prakash, 2013). Schoenmaker (2017) noted that the non-enforceability of commitments affects both the functionality and credibility of collaborative initiatives. Without effective enforcement, members may join initiatives to signal commitment to sustainability without fully adhering to their objectives (Bauckloh *et al.*, 2023). For example, Majoch *et al.* (2017) expressed concerns about discrepancies between the commitments made by PRI signatories and their actual policies and practices.

Consistency versus Flexibility

An important practical consideration for investor-backed initiatives is the diversity among participating organisations in terms of size, asset mix, engagement strategies, and influence (Bundy *et al.*, 2013). This heterogeneity affects collective initiatives, requiring tailored, context-specific engagement strategies to avoid fragmentation and maintain credibility (Slager *et al.*, 2023). These engagement strategies must consider sector-specific attributes, financial standing, environmental, social and governance (ESG) performance, and companies' receptivity to investor demands.

Case-Study: The Principles for Responsible Investment

The PRI initiative is one of the well-recognised, largest, and oldest collaborative investor initiatives. Launched in 2006, it provides a framework for investors to incorporate sustainability and ESG considerations into their investment strategies and practices (Gond and Piani, 2013). Among other activities, PRI facilitates collaborative engagement between investors and corporations, promotes long-term investing, and works with policymakers to encourage the adoption of policy measures that support and enable sustainable finance (Bauckloh *et al.*, 2023; PRI, 2024). At the end of March 2024, the PRI had more than 5,000 signatories representing over US$120 trillion in AUM (PRI, 2024). The signatories to

PRI are required to self-report annually on their performance against the PRI's principles.

Since 2018, several studies have examined the connection between PRI membership and the sustainable investment practices of its members. The context for some of these studies is that, due to the relatively low requirements for membership, some organisations may choose to become signatories even if they have not committed to meaningful sustainability efforts. Kim and Yoon (2021) analysed the ESG investments of US mutual funds after they signed up to the PRI. While they observed that these managers widely advertised their PRI affiliation on their websites and were able to attract substantial fund inflows, they did not note an increase in either fund-level ESG scores or fund returns. In contrast, Bauckloh *et al.* (2023) demonstrated a relationship between being a PRI signatory and undertaking sustainable engagement activities, suggesting that PRI signatories had integrated ESG criteria significantly more than non-signatories. They also observed that early signatories made stronger commitments compared to those who signed later, suggesting that later signatories were more driven by the brand and reputation benefits of signing. These findings echo those presented in earlier work by Delmas and Montes-Sancho (2010), who found that in environmental voluntary agreements, late signatories tended to join symbolically, whereas early joiners cooperated substantively.

In sum, has the PRI initiative contributed to advancing sustainable finance? Despite the relatively modest expectations of signatories, there are reasons to suggest that the PRI has made an important contribution. Bauckloh *et al.* (2019) noted the growth and success of responsible investment since the PRI was established in 2006. Bauckloh et al. (2023) suggested that PRI has provided a platform for financial actors to share, engage, and educate themselves on sustainable investments, has pushed issues such as climate change to the forefront of investment practice, and has served as a model for the development of other collective initiatives such as the Principles for Responsible Banking. Finally, Dimson *et al.* (2023) suggested that PRI-coordinated collaborative engagements have been correlated with positive financial returns.

Concluding Comments

Collective action initiatives play a significant role for investors seeking to deliver on their commitments to responsible investment and sustainable finance. Their growth reflects the services they offer in terms of allowing investors to work efficiently and effectively together to address systemic issues, as well as other benefits, such as enhanced reputation, access to networks, and reduced transaction costs, which accrue to their participants. It is likely that these initiatives will remain central to sustainable finance, but their success, credibility, and effectiveness will depend on how participants manage challenges linked to free-riding, the balance between consistency and flexibility, the desire for ambition versus the desire for broad membership, and legitimacy.

Implications for Practitioners

1. Collective investor initiatives have helped investors to deliver their net zero objectives, to address socio-environmental impacts, to improve corporate disclosures and governance structure, to mobilise private finance, and to increase investor awareness about sustainability-related issues.
2. Collective investor initiatives have been particularly valuable when dealing with systemic issues such as climate change which need a clear and coordinated voice from the investment community. Collective initiatives have also been beneficial when transaction costs (e.g. research and engagement) are high and when investors are fragmented or dispersed (e.g. in the share registers of large companies).
3. Collective investor initiatives face challenges due to free-riding, external pressures to retreat from the stated ambitions of the initiatives, a lack of legitimacy and credibility with stakeholders, and a limited ability to enforce objectives.
4. When deciding to establish or join a collective investor initiative, investors should be clear on:

   - The goals of the initiative, and whether these goals align with the investor's motivations, goals, and ambitions.
   - Whether the advantages of collaborating outweigh the advantages of acting alone.
   - Their capacity to substantially contribute to the delivery of the initiative's objectives.
   - The costs of participation, in terms of membership fees and in terms of the time and other resources required for participation.
   - How the initiative intends to deliver the changes that it seeks and whether these strategies and actions are likely to deliver the changes that are being sought.
5. The coordinators of collective initiatives should have clear strategies for:
   - Attracting members.
   - Retaining members.
   - Addressing free-riding (and ensuring that members make a substantial contribution to the goals of the initiative).
   - Setting objectives, including the ratcheting up of ambitions over time.
   - Enforcing participation through incentives and sanctions.
   - Ensuring the credibility and legitimacy of the initiative.

References

Baker, S. (2024, March 27), 'Investors Lament Climate Initiative Departures; Managers Offer Rationales', *Pensions & Investments*, www.pionline.com/esg/investors-lament-climate-initiative-departures-and-managers-outline-rationales

Barrett, S. and Toman, M. (2010), 'Contrasting Future Paths for an Evolving Global Climate Regime', *Global Policy*, Vol. 1, No. 1, pp. 64–74, https://doi.org/10.1111/j.1758-5899.2009.00010.x

Bauckloh, T., Schaltegger, S., Utz, S., Zeile, S. and Zwergel, B. (2023), 'Active First Movers vs. Late Free-riders? An Empirical Analysis of UN PRI Signatories' Commitment', *Journal of Business Ethics*, Vol. 182, No. 3, pp. 747–781, https://doi.org/10.1007/s10551-021-04992-0

Bauckloh, T., Utz, S., Zeile, S. and Zwergel, B. (2019, May 10), 'UN PRI Signatories' Ethics: Walk the Talk or Talk the Talk? Serious Ethical First Movers vs. Late Free Riders', https://papers.ssrn.com/sol3/papers.cfm?abstract_id=3386095

Bebchuk, L., Cohen, A. and Hirst, S. (2017), 'The Agency Problems of Institutional Investors', *Journal of Economic Perspectives*, Vol. 31, No. 3, pp. 89–102, https://doi.org/10.1257/jep.31.3.89

Bundy, J., Shropshire, C. and Buchholtz, A. (2013), 'Strategic Cognition and Issue Salience: Toward an Explanation of Firm Responsiveness to Stakeholder Concerns', *The Academy of Management Review*, Vol. 38, No. 3, pp. 352–376, www.jstor.org/stable/43700495

Clark, G. and Hebb, T. (2004), 'Pension Fund Corporate Engagement: The Fifth Stage of Capitalism', *Industrial Relations*, Vol. 59, No. 1, pp. 142–171, https://doi.org/10.7202/009130ar

Climate Action 100+ (CA100+) (2024a, July 24), 'How Climate Action 100+ Supports Making Corporate Lobbying a Force for Good', www.climateaction100.org/news/how-climate-action-100-supports-making-corporate-lobbying-a-force-for-good/

Climate Action 100+ (CA100+) (2024b, February 26), 'Climate Action 100+: Reaction to Recent Departures', www.climateaction100.org/news/climate-action-100-reaction-to-recent-departures/

Climate Action 100+ (CA100+) (2025), *Progress Report 2024*, www.climateaction100.org/wp-content/uploads/2025/02/Climate-Action-100-Progress-Update-2024.pdf

Conley, J. and Williams, C. (2011), 'Global Banks as Global Sustainability Regulators? The Equator Principles', *Law & Policy*, Vol. 33, No. 4, pp. 542–575, https://doi.org/10.1111/j.1467-9930.2011.00348.x

Contreras, G., Bos, J. and Kleimeier, S. (2019), 'Self-Regulation in Sustainable Finance: The Adoption of the Equator Principles', *World Development*, Vol. 122, pp. 306–324, https://doi.org/10.1016/j.worlddev.2019.05.030

Couto, L. (2023), *How to Boost International Private Climate Finance: The Role of Central Banks, Financial Regulators and Sectoral Coalitions* (Chatham House, London), www.chathamhouse.org/2023/04/how-boost-international-private-climate-finance/04-industry-initiatives-greening-financial

Danilov, Y. (2022), 'Coalitions for Sustainable Finance and Sustainable Development', *Herald of the Russian Academy of Sciences*, Vol. 92, pp. S91–S99, https://doi.org/10.1134/S1019331622080032

Delmas, M. and Montes-Sancho, M. (2010), 'Voluntary Agreements to Improve Environmental Quality: Symbolic and Substantive Cooperation', *Strategic*

Management Journal, Vol. 31, No. 6, pp. 575–601, https://doi.org/10.1002/smj.826

Dimson, E., Karakaş, O. and Ki, X. (2023), *Coordinated Engagements. European Corporate Governance Institute – Finance Working Paper No. 721/2021*, https://papers.ssrn.com/sol3/papers.cfm?abstract_id=3386095

Eesley, C. and Lenox, M. (2006), 'Firm Responses to Secondary Stakeholder Action', *Strategic Management Journal*, Vol. 27, No. 8, pp. 765–781, https://doi.org/10.1002/smj.536

Gifford, E. (2010), 'Effective Shareholder Engagement: The Factors that Contribute to Shareholder Salience', *Journal of Business Ethics*, Vol. 92, pp. 79–97, https://doi.org/10.1007/s10551-010-0635-6

Global Standard on Responsible Corporate Climate Lobbying (2022), 'The 14 Indicators of Responsible Climate Lobbying', https://climate-lobbying.com/wp-content/uploads/2022/03/2022_global-standard-responsible-climate-lobbying_APPENDIX.pdf

Gond, J. and Piani, V. (2013), 'Organizing the Collective Action of Institutional Investors: Three Case Studies from the Principles for Responsible Investment Initiative', in *Institutional Investors' Power to Change Corporate Behavior: International Perspectives (Critical Studies on Corporate Responsibility, Governance and Sustainability)*, Vol. 5 (Emerald Group Publishing Limited, Leeds), pp. 19–59, https://doi.org/10.1108/S2043-9059(2013)0000005010

Gosling, T. and MacNeil, I. (2023), 'Can Investors Save the Planet? NZAMI and Fiduciary Duty', *Capital Markets Law Journal*, Vol. 18, No. 2, pp. 172–193, https://doi.org/10.1093/cmlj/kmad002

Institutional Investors Group on Climate Change (IIGCC) (2024), *Net Zero Investment Framework 2.0. June 2024* (IIGCC, London), www.iigcc.org/hubfs/NZIF%202.0%20Report%20PDF.pdf

International Capital Market Association (ICMA) (2024), *Guidance Handbook. November 2024* (ICMA, Paris), www.icmagroup.org/assets/documents/Sustainable-finance/2024-updates/The-Principles-Guidance-Handbook-November-2024-041124.pdf

Investor Agenda (2024), '2024 Global Investor Statement to Governments on the Climate Crisis', https://theinvestoragenda.org/wp-content/uploads/2024/08/2024-Global-Investor-Statement-to-Governments-on-the-Climate-Crisis.pdf

Jessop, S. and Kerber, R. (2024, February 15), 'JPMorgan, State Street Quit Climate Group, BlackRock Steps Back', *Reuters*, www.reuters.com/sustainability/sustainable-finance-reporting/jpmorgan-fund-arm-quits-climate-action-100-investor-group-2024-02-15/

Kawabata, T. (2023), 'Climate Finance Governance through Transnational Networks', *Journal of Sustainable Finance & Investment*, Vol. 13, No. 4, pp. 1624–1643, https://doi.org/10.1080/20430795.2021.1925522

Kim, S. and Yoon, A. (2021), 'Analyzing Active Fund Managers' Commitment to ESG: Evidence from the United Nations Principles for Responsible Investment', *Management Science*, Vol. 69, No. 2, pp. 741–758, https://doi.org/10.1287/mnsc.2022.4394

Krouse, S., Benoit, D., McGinty, T. and Benoit, D. (2016, October 24), 'Meet the New Corporate Power Brokers: Passive Investors', *Wall Street Journal*, www.wsj.com/articles/the-new-corporate-power-brokers-passive-investors-1477320101

Louche, C. (2004), *Ethical Investment: Processes and Mechanisms of Institutionalisation in the Netherlands. PhD Dissertation* (Erasmus University Rotterdam), https://repub.eur.nl/pub/1430/ESM-dissertation-003.pdf

Macve, R. and Chen, X. (2010), 'The "Equator Principles": A Success for Voluntary Codes?', *Accounting, Auditing & Accountability Journal*, Vol. 23, No. 7, pp. 890–919, https://doi.org/10.1108/09513571011080171

Majoch, A., Hoepner, A. and Hebb, T. (2017), 'Sources of Stakeholder Salience in the Responsible Investment Movement: Why Do Investors Sign the Principles for Responsible Investment?', *Journal of Business Ethics*, Vol. 140, No. 4, pp. 723–741, https://doi.org/10.1007/s10551-016-3057-2

Masters, B. and Temple-West, P. (2024, February 15), 'JPMorgan and State Street Quit Climate Group as BlackRock Scales Back', *Financial Times*, www.ft.com/content/3ce06a6f-f0e3-4f70-a078-82a6c265ddc2

McDonnell, C., Rempel, A. and Gupta, J. (2022), 'Climate Action or Distraction? Exploring Investor Initiatives and Implications for Unextractable Fossil Fuels', *Energy Research & Social Science*, Vol. 92, p. 102769, https://doi.org/10.1016/j.erss.2022.102769

Net Zero Asset Managers Initiative (2025), 'Net Zero Asset Managers Initiative', www.netzeroassetmanagers.org/ (last viewed 18 February 2025).

Olson, M. (1965), *The Logic of Collective Action: Public Goods and the Theory of Groups* (Harvard University Press, Cambridge).

Ostrom, E. (1990), *Governing the Commons: The Evolution of Institutions for Collective Action* (Cambridge University Press, Cambridge), https://doi.org/10.1017/CBO9781316423936

Potoski, M. and Prakash, A. (2013), 'Green Clubs: Collective Action and Voluntary Environmental Programs', *Annual Review of Political Science*, Vol. 16, pp. 399–419, https://doi.org/10.1146/annurev-polisci-032211-211224

Principles for Responsible Investment (PRI) (2018), *Implementing the Task Force on Climate-Related Financial Disclosures (TCFD) Recommendations: A Guide for Asset Owners* (PRI, London), www.unpri.org/download?ac=4652

Principles for Responsible Investment (PRI) (2023), *PRI Reporting Guidance on Human Rights* (PRI, London), https://dwtyzx6upklss.cloudfront.net/Uploads/z/f/v/pri_reporting_guidance_on_human_rights_may_2023_920336.pdf

Principles for Responsible Investment (PRI) (2024), *Annual Report 2024* (PRI, London), www.unpri.org/download?ac=21536

Sandler, T. (2015), 'Collective Action: Fifty Years Later', *Public Choice*, Vol. 164, No. 3/4, pp. 195–216, www.jstor.org/stable/24768825

Schoenmaker, D. (2017), *Investing for the Common Good: A Sustainable Finance Framework* (Bruegel, Brussels), www.bruegel.org/system/files/wp_attachments/From-traditional-to-sustainable-finance_ONLINE.pdf

Schoenmaker, D. and Schramade, W. (2019), *Principles of Sustainable Finance* (Oxford University Press, Oxford).

Slager, R., Chuah, K., Gond, J., Furnari, S. and Homanen, M. (2023), 'Tailor-to-Target: Configuring Collaborative Shareholder Engagements on Climate Change', *Management Science*, Vol. 69, No. 12, pp. 7693–7718, https://doi.org/10.1287/mnsc.2023.4806

Suchman, M. (1995), 'Managing Legitimacy: Strategic and Institutional Approaches', *The Academy of Management Review*, Vol. 20, No. 3, pp. 571–610, https://doi.org/10.2307/258788

Tosun, J. and Schoenefeld, J. (2017), 'Collective Climate Action and Networked Climate Governance', *WIREs Climate Change*, Vol. 8, No. 1, https://doi.org/10.1002/wcc.440

Wagemans, F., van Koppen, C. and Mol, A. (2013), 'The Effectiveness of Socially Responsible Investment: A Review', *Journal of Integrative Environmental Sciences*, Vol. 10, No. 3–4, pp. 235–252, https://doi.org/10.1080/1943815X.2013.844169

Wilkes, T. (2023a, May 30), 'Insurers' Climate Alliance Loses Nearly Half its Members after More Quit', *Reuters*, www.reuters.com/business/insurers-climate-alliance-loses-nearly-half-its-members-after-more-quit-2023-05-30/

Wilkes, T. (2023b, June 8), 'Big Investor Group Urges Action, Not Words, to Meet Climate Goals', *Reuters*, www.reuters.com/sustainability/big-investor-group-urges-action-not-words-meet-climate-goals-2023-06-08/

Yamahaki, C. (2019), 'Responsible Investment and the Institutional Works of Investor Associations', *Journal of Sustainable Finance & Investment*, Vol. 9, No. 2, pp. 162–181, https://doi.org/10.1080/20430795.2018.1558029

Chapter 11

Can the Finance Sector Be Trusted?

Greenwashing, Greenhushing and Greenwishing

Noga Natanson, Hilary Lai, Sumira Bothé and Johan Florén

Introduction

Amid growing efforts to redirect financial flows towards building a low-carbon economy with positive environmental and social outcomes, greenwashing – providing false or selective information to create an overly optimistic impression of a firm or a product's environmental performance – has emerged as a central point of debate and contention. The concern is that greenwashing can significantly affect the credibility, efficiency, and profitability of sustainable finance products and activities (Dempere *et al.*, 2024).

This chapter offers a practical framework for analysing greenwashing and the related phenomena of greenhushing and greenwishing. It begins by describing the characteristics of greenwashing, greenhushing and greenwishing and by examining the main reasons why organisations might engage in these activities. The chapter then discusses the implications of greenwashing and reflects on how policymakers and other stakeholders might respond. It concludes by offering

DOI: 10.4324/9781003467632-11

practical suggestions for investors on how they might identify and respond to greenwashing, both in company disclosures and in their own reporting.

Understanding Greenwashing

Greenwashing and Social-Washing

Greenwashing refers to the provision of false information or the selective disclosure of positive information about a firm or a product's environmental performance to create an overly optimistic impression (Lyon and Maxwell, 2011). Greenwashing can be intentional or unintentional, can occur at various levels (e.g., entity, product, and advice), and can happen at different stages of the business cycle (e.g., manufacturing, marketing, and sales) or the sustainable finance value chain (European Securities and Markets Authority (ESMA), 2024).

Despite this general understanding of the term, there is no globally standardised definition to guide regulations and practices. For the purposes of this chapter, we follow the definition produced by the European Securities and Markets Authority (ESMA) to help guide supervisory activities and internal monitoring in the financial sector. ESMA defines greenwashing as 'sustainability-related statements, declarations, actions, or communications that do not clearly and fairly reflect the underlying sustainability profile of an entity, a financial product, or financial services' (ESMA, 2024: 2).

While greenwashing is generally understood as relating to environmental matters, similar issues are also prevalent in social and other ethical domains (see Box 11.1).

Box 11.1 Social-Washing

Social-washing involves creating a deceptive impression of social responsibility and positive impact, which does not align with the organisation's actions.

Social-washing can be categorised into various 'colours'. For example, blue-washing – the blue refers to the blue colour of the United Nations's (UN) logo – refers to organisations that claim to but actually do not align with various principles proposed by the UN, such as those outlined in the UN Global Compact or the UN Sustainable Development Goals (SDGs). Similarly, pink-washing points out inconsistent claims and actions towards LGBT+ inclusiveness goals.

(Adapted from Garnelo-Gomez, 2022)

Greenhushing

In contrast to greenwashing (which is essentially the creation of an overly positive impression of a company or a product's environmental performance), greenhushing involves suppressing information about a company or a product's environmental performance, because of concerns that this information may be misrepresented or that the reporting entity may be accused of greenwashing. Greenhushing is reportedly rising as companies keep climate plans from public scrutiny (Ayoade, 2023). For example, in 2022, climate solutions provider South Pole surveyed over 1,200 global sustainability executives from 12 regions; a quarter of the respondents confirmed that their organisation had greenhushed at least some of their environmental performance information (South Pole, 2022). These greenhushing actions included choosing not to publicise climate goals, and deliberately reducing external communications around environmental strategies. Greenhushing occurs for various reasons, such as avoiding political backlash, appealing to investors who worry that green investments yield lower returns, or reducing the risk criticism from stakeholders who might view the company's sustainability efforts as inadequate and accuse it of greenwashing (Fisher *et al.*, 2023).

Greenhushing has several potentially negative implications for companies and for investors. It may damage investor confidence in a company, as investors may assume that the company is not managing its environmental issues and impacts effectively, or they may assume that the company is hiding other information from investors. It may result in governments and regulators increasing their focus on environmental disclosures and exposes companies to unpredictable regulatory swings (ESMA, 2023). It may create share price volatility when information surfaces unexpectedly. Finally, organisations that greenhush may not receive constructive feedback from others and, as a result, may not develop the tools or capacity to effectively manage their environmental issues.

Greenwishing

The growth in demand for green sustainable products has also spurred organisations to 'greenwish', which essentially involves setting unrealistic targets in hopes of their company becoming 'greener'. Even if the underlying motivation is to improve environmental performance and even if serious efforts have been made to achieve these targets, a failure to deliver on commitments or to meet targets can undermine a company's credibility and broader corporate sustainability commitments (Winkler *et al.*, 2020).

Greenwishing typically occurs when an organisation promotes ambitious yet justifiable projects without necessarily having enough capacity, expertise, or understanding of the practical challenges to achieve the desired corporate objectives (Winkler *et al.*, 2020). For example, companies that rely on unproven and overly optimistic assumptions about technology to achieve their green transition goals may invest in ventures that fail to deliver either the expected financial returns or the desired environmental outcomes. Therefore, similar to greenhushing, greenwishing also has important implications for sustainable finance outcomes because it can lead to asset mispricing and the misallocation of capital.

One particularly important issue in this regard is that commitments and targets are often based on assumptions around public policy, regulations, and incentives. Relying heavily on institutional factors such as government subsidies can result in greenwishing when unexpected regulatory changes occur (Delmas and Burbano, 2011; Greiner and Kim, 2021). If anticipated incentives for sustainable practices fail to materialise (e.g. due to shifts in government policies, changes in political leadership, changes in economic conditions), companies may no longer be able to meet their sustainability targets. Changes in public policy are just one scenario that could result in greenwishing. Another scenario is that market pressures or changes in consumer preferences may force companies to alter their strategies and pull back from their environmental goals (Huang *et al.*, 2016; Zameer *et al.*, 2020).

Why Do Organisations Greenwash?

Corporate Legitimacy

Prevailing norms within financial markets dictate that firms must incorporate sustainability considerations into their activities or risk damaging their organisational legitimacy – i.e. views on their trustworthiness, credibility, and honesty – and their financial standing (Akyildirim *et al.*, 2024; Bauckloh *et al.*, 2023; Delmas and Montes-Sancho, 2010 Lyon and Montgomery, 2013). Being seen as trustworthy, as credible, and as reputable can help organisations to secure resources, to forge and expand business relationships, to attract and maintain a robust workforce, and to build a positive reputation (Clarkson *et al.*, 2008; Seele and Gatti, 2017). Conversely, damage to a firm's legitimacy can severely harm all these benefits and, if severe enough, may even threaten the financial feasibility and survival of the firm (Bauckloh *et al.*, 2023).

The rise of these norms has been driven by three factors. First, the sharp decline in public trust in the finance sector following the 2008 financial crisis and a series of subsequent corporate scandals have prompted growing demands for greater scrutiny and accountability within the finance sector (Sustainalytics, 2023). Second, the climate crisis has generated both internal and external pressure on private actors to actively contribute to addressing environmental challenges (Sustainalytics, 2023). Third, there has been increased political momentum in certain regions and states to embed sustainability within financial systems. For example, the UK's 2021 roadmap to align its financial system with net-zero goals and the EU's 2018 Sustainable Finance Action Plan have both sent strong signals to the corporate world regarding the importance of aligning business practices with sustainability objectives (Bauckloh *et al.*, 2023).

These norms are not uniform; they vary across regions, countries, industries and political contexts, as well as in relation to the presence or absence of regulation. Furthermore, that the actions required to protect and enhance corporate legitimacy may at times involve short-term costs. That is, there may be a tension between firms' interest in building and retaining legitimacy, and the potentially significant costs of effective environmental actions. In that context, greenwashing can be understood as a strategy to improve corporate legitimacy but not implementing unprofitable or costly environmental initiatives.

Market Competition

Heightened attention on environmental considerations in both the public and private sectors has ushered in a slew of new financial opportunities. As has been discussed through this book, there has been a rapid growth in the number of investors including sustainability-related considerations in their investment decisions, and in the number of sustainability-related funds, bonds and other investment products. Companies have seen that being able to label themselves, their products and their services as sustainable may enable them to attract eco-conscious investors and consumers. However, the reality is that genuine environmental transformation is often costly and complex. As a result, some firms may attempt to capitalise on the sustainability trend by greenwashing but without incurring the financial and operational burdens of implementing meaningful environmental change (Parguel *et al.*, 2011).

A widely publicised example of how market-driven incentives can lead to greenwashing is the case of DWS, the asset management arm of Deutsche Bank. In 2022, its former head of sustainability accused the firm of falsely claiming that US$475.76 billion in assets were 'ESG-integrated' when, in fact, only a considerably smaller share met the criteria (Storbeck, 2023). Following these allegations, DWS agreed to pay $25 million to settle charges brought by the US Securities and Exchange Commission (SEC) (Prentice, 2023).

Regulatory Frameworks and Stakeholder Expectations

Geography appears to significantly influence firms' propensity to greenwash, due to differences in regulatory environments, enforcement capacities, societal norms and the degree of scrutiny from non-governmental organisations (NGOs) and the media.

Research indicates that firms in jurisdictions with stricter regulations – either focused on climate issues or focused on greenwashing – are less likely to engage in misleading environmental practices (Delmas and Burbano, 2011; Mateo-Márquez *et al.*, 2022; Tashman *et al.*, 2019). The reason appears to be that firms operating under more stringent regulatory conditions typically have greater certainty about enforcement and face heightened risks of penalties, both of which discourage greenwashing (Lyon and Montgomery, 2015; Delmas and Burbano,

2011; Delmas and Montes Sancho, 2010). According to Delmas and Burbano (2011), the absence of mandatory environmental disclosures and weak regulatory enforcement exacerbate information asymmetries, undermining accountability mechanisms. A study by Mateo-Márquez *et al.* (2022) illustrates this geographical variation by highlighting Australia, where the proportion of firms engaged in greenwashing was twice that of those not engaged in greenwashing, primarily due to uncertainties around regulatory enforcement. In contrast, jurisdictions like the UK and France, which were found to possess clearer and more robust regulatory frameworks, experienced comparatively lower levels of greenwashing (Mateo-Márquez *et al.*, 2022).

Societal values and levels of environmental awareness play a significant role in shaping geographical variations in greenwashing behaviour. In regions where public environmental consciousness is high, firms are subject to greater scrutiny – substantially raising the likelihood of greenwashing being identified and penalised (Akyildirim *et al.*, 2024). For instance, research by the European Banking Authority (EBA) noted an elevated number of greenwashing accusations against EU-based firms, suggesting that the EU's heightened attention on sustainability and environmental issues was resulting in more rigorous monitoring (European Banking Authority (EBA), 2023). It is important to emphasise that this is not necessarily reflective of higher rates of greenwashing but of higher levels of scrutiny and attention to greenwashing.

Moreover, societal environmental values can shape regulatory environments directly. Regions where consumers demand greater transparency and credible environmental information typically have more robust regulatory frameworks (Akyildirim *et al.*, 2024; Parguel *et al.*, 2011). The European Union again illustrates this dynamic, with high societal environmental awareness being a key driver for regulations such as the Sustainable Finance Disclosure Regulation (SFDR), EU taxonomy, and Corporate Sustainability Reporting Directive (CSRD) (ClientEarth and Asia Investor Group on Climate Change (AIGCC), 2023).

Honest Mistakes

Greenwashing does not necessarily involve deliberate deception; often, it arises unintentionally. This may occur when market participants rely on incomplete or inconsistent information, face knowledge gaps or interpretive errors, or hold differing views on what constitutes greenwashing or sustainability (Eurofi, 2023; ESMA, 2024).

Market participants frequently base their green claims on information derived from company disclosures and third-party data, ratings and index providers such as S&P, Bloomberg, ISS and RepRisk (Berg *et al.*, 2022; see also Chapter 12). If the underlying data are incomplete, inconsistent or flawed, sustainability-related claims, even if made in good faith, may nonetheless be unintentionally misleading and constitute greenwashing (EBA, 2024).

A common example relates to greenhouse gas emissions data. These data are an essential input for sustainable finance assessments and for setting and measuring net zero targets but are frequently the focus of greenwashing allegations against investors (Fraser and Fiedler, 2023). Emissions data are often self-reported, and firms are often free to choose from a range of methodologies and guidelines to calculate their emissions (InfluenceMap, 2022). This flexibility hampers the ability to compare emissions accurately and reliably across firms (Lashitew, 2021; Network for Greening the Financial System (NGFS), 2024; Sullivan and Gouldson, 2012). Although emerging mandatory frameworks such as the EU's CSRD aim to improve the consistency and comparability of emissions data, firms continue to retain some discretion over how they calculate and report their emissions (EBA, 2024; ESMA, 2024). These issues are compounded by the frequent absence of independent third-party verification (Dorfleitner and Utz, 2023; Marquis *et al.*, 2016). Another important issue in greenhouse gas emissions reporting is the frequent exclusion of the indirect greenhouse gas emissions across a company's value chain (often referred to as Scope 3 emissions). For many firms, Scope 3 emissions represent the largest share of their total carbon footprint, and an understanding of these emissions is often essential to robustly assess a company's actual carbon performance and transition risk exposure (Montgomery *et al.*, 2024).

The challenges associated with carbon emissions data are indicative of broader issues affecting the sustainability-related information relied upon by market participants, and the tools and products (e.g. ratings, indices, scores) that are developed based on these data. Sustainability or ESG ratings, for example, often vary significantly depending on the number and type of factors assessed, the specific indicators used to measure those factors, and the weighting assigned to each indicator (Berg *et al.*, 2022; Fichtner *et al.*, 2024; Lashitew, 2021). For example, one agency may consider corporate lobbying for net-zero policies as a relevant factor, while another may omit it entirely or apply different metrics to evaluate its significance. Taken together, these issues create a landscape in which investors and market participants may base their strategies, their products, or their disclosures on flawed or incomplete information, potentially resulting in sustainability claims that mislead or misrepresent actual performance.

Accidental greenwashing can also occur when market participants lack sufficient knowledge and awareness of climate and sustainability issues (Montgomery *et al.*, 2024; Nemes *et al.*, 2022). Without a strong understanding of these topics, investors may struggle to critically assess the quality of the data they rely on or to distinguish between superficial commitments and genuine sustainability performance (Montgomery *et al.*, 2024; Nemes *et al.*, 2022). This, in turn, increases the risk of the users of this information unintentionally endorsing misleading claims (Leung *et al.*, 2023). The absence of globally agreed definitions only exacerbates this issue; the sustainable investment landscape remains filled with vague or ambiguous terminology and assessing the true credibility of 'green' claims often requires knowing which questions to ask and where to probe (Eurofi, 2023).

A further practical issue is the quality of internal communication within organisations (Delmas and Burbano, 2011). In cases where communication between departments is ineffective or fragmented, accidental greenwashing may arise. For example, Delmas and Burbano (2011) describe how poor coordination between a public relations team and departments with technical sustainability knowledge can result in overstated or inaccurate environmental claims. This risk applies not only to corporate issuers but also to investment firms and their portfolio companies, where alignment between sustainability and communications functions is crucial.

As with any form of communication, how greenwashing is interpreted – by both the communicator and the recipient of the information – is shaped by individual perspectives and assumptions (Lyon and Montgomery, 2015). In sustainable investment, this challenge is further compounded by the absence of globally agreed definitions of greenwashing or of sustainability (ESMA, 2023). This has allowed different actors to develop their own frameworks, assumptions, and definitions of greenwashing (Leung *et al.*, 2023). This is particularly evident in debates around transition finance, which refers to capital flows that support the shift from high-emission economic activities to a low-carbon economy (EBA, 2024). For example, some asset managers may argue that transition finance should be reserved for companies with clearly defined and measurable net-zero targets. Others might take a broader view, considering companies with stated commitments to reduce emissions, even if these commitments are not accompanied by specific or quantifiable targets, as legitimate recipients of transition funding. These divergent interpretations, even when underpinned by good faith, can give rise to conflicting assessments and accusations of greenwashing.

This problem is further exacerbated by the rapid evolution of environmental regulations, frameworks, and disclosure requirements. The dynamic and fragmented nature of these developments adds to the lack of clarity surrounding key sustainability definitions (EBA, 2023, 2024). As a result, firms and investors may struggle to stay abreast of shifting expectations, increasing the risk of unintentional non-compliance or the publication of sustainability targets, strategies, or claims that could later be viewed as misleading (Eurofi, 2023).

Classifying Greenwashing Strategies

Siano *et al.* (2017) classify greenwashing into three core strategies: (a) decoupling, (b) attention deflection, and (c) deceptive manipulation. We discus each of these below but we note that these strategies are not mutually exclusive; for example, a company's annual sustainability report might simultaneously exhibit both decoupling and attention deflection, such as by pairing minimal action with highly curated, yet misleading, imagery.

Decoupling

Decoupling refers to organisations that claim to meet stakeholders' expectations but do not make any actual changes to their practices (i.e. they 'fail to walk the talk') (Bromley and Powell, 2012; Meyer and Rowan, 1977; Siano *et al.*, 2017). For example, organisations may claim to be committed to climate actions but in reality, lobby against certain proposed climate regulations, or even support policies that would significantly increase greenhouse gas emissions. Other examples include organisations joining green alliances or standard schemes that signal a commitment to sustainability but that do not require substantive action (Callery, 2023) or organisations exaggerating their sustainability performance in external reports (Delmas and Burbano, 2011).

Attention Deflection

Another form of greenwashing is using symbolic actions to deflect stakeholders' attention. This approach views greenwashing as an asymmetric communication strategy that aims to present an overly optimistic corporate image (Siano *et al.*, 2017).

Selective disclosure is one form of attention deflection, where a company reports its environmental successes while concealing poor commitments or negative behaviours (Aragón-Correa *et al.*, 2016; Lyon and Maxwell, 2011; Patten, 2002). Selective disclosure creates a 'halo effect', where consumers attribute positive qualities to a company, product, or service based on one claimed quality (Crilly *et al.*, 2016; Lyon and Montgomery, 2015).

Attention deflection can also involve vague, unsubstantiated, and unproven claims that lack credible evidence. For example, terms like 'green', 'sustainable', or 'eco-friendly' give the impression of environmental consciousness without specifying the reason, or without the support of in-depth information and reliable certifications, granted by third parties (TerraChoice, 2010).

Besides misleading text, attention deflection can also involve the use of visual imagery to communicate a firm or product's 'sustainability' credentials (Parguel *et al.*, 2015). For example, the use of nature-evoking elements – e.g., images of nature landscapes (e.g., forests, oceans), endangered animal species (e.g., pandas, tigers), colours (e.g., green, blue), and sounds (e.g., mountain streams, bird calls) – in advertisements can give a misleading impression of a brand or product's ecological image (Parguel *et al.*, 2015; for a specific case-study involving an oil company's use of images of children and their parents playing next to a wind turbine under a clear sky, see ClientEarth (2020)).

Deceptive Manipulation

Deceptive manipulation involves altering organisational practices maliciously to support inaccurate or false sustainability statements (Siano *et al.*, 2017). Unlike decoupling and attention deflection, deceptive manipulation results not only from 'omissions' but also from outright 'lies' in false green reporting, deliberately portraying an inaccurate image of a company's environmental behaviour (Seele and Gatti, 2017).

One of the most high-profile examples of deceptive manipulation has involved the German carmaker Volkswagen and the Dieselgate Scandal. In 2015, Volkswagen ran a marketing campaign trumpeting its diesel cars' low emissions in 2015. However, the US Environmental Protection Agency (USEPA) discovered that many Volkswagen vehicles were equipped with defeat device software to manipulate emissions control (US Environmental Protection Agency (USEPA), 2024). This software could detect when the vehicle was being tested and adjust the emissions accordingly. In reality, the nitrogen oxide emissions from these vehicles were up to 40 times above the legal limit. Volkswagen later admitted that around 11 million cars worldwide, including 8 million in Europe, had this defeat device installed. It cost Volkswagen over US$34 billion to settle the scandal (Taylor, 2020).

The Challenges of Adjudicating on Greenwashing Claims

Assessments of greenwashing often depend on the perspective of the observer and are often highly context dependent. It is important to acknowledge these interpretive dimensions, as organisations may face accusations of greenwashing even when intent or wrongdoing is not immediately clear.

One major source of difficulty (as discussed above) is the absence of a standardised, globally agreed-upon definition of greenwashing across different markets, sectors, and geographies (ClientEarth and AIGCC, 2023). This means that it is difficult to construct a comprehensive and indisputable shared language across countries, sectors, disciplines, and even within organisations (Eccles *et al.*, 2019). The consequence is that competing claims lack a definitive framework through which they can be judged. While some allegations of greenwashing are more straightforward to detect (an example could be whether a company meets its emission reduction claims), others allow for more debate on what can be categorised as misleading communication. For example, the use of nature-related images or a green colour scheme does not contain any explicit sustainability or environmental promises but can be seen as implying a certain kind of green conduct. In the absence of consensus around whether such uses are or are not trying to deflect attention, different actors will inevitably draw different conclusions about the validity of greenwashing allegations relating to these uses.

Another important aspect of adjudicating greenwashing is the centrality of perception and identification. How stakeholders, both financial market participants and the public, perceive green communications and what they choose to do about it is fundamental to how accusations of greenwashing, or lack thereof, play out in practice (ClientEarth and AIGCC, 2023; Seele and Gatti, 2017). Regardless of the actual extent of misleading communications, the practice often only comes to light and gains recognition when third-party actors such as media outlets, NGOs, or other stakeholders call it out and name it as greenwashing (Seele and Gatti, 2017). Therefore, stakeholders' perceptions of what constitutes 'green', their willingness to challenge perceived greenwashing, and their capacity to voice such claims – shaped by their resources and reputational standing – are key drivers of greenwashing accusations. These factors influence not only the consequences of greenwashing but also whether an accusation arises at all.

Of course, the motives and interests of those making claims of greenwashing need to be understood (Dorfleitner and Utz, 2023; Seele and Gatti 2017). Just as firms can profit from engaging in greenwashing, organisations can also benefit from making greenwashing accusations; these benefits could include media attention and increases in followers, members, and funding (Akyildirim *et al.*, 2024).

Greenwashing: The Implications

Reputational Risks

The reputational risks associated with accusations of greenwashing, whether or not the claims are valid, are among the most significant issues linked to this phenomenon (see, for example, the views expressed in EBA, 2023). Allegations of greenwashing may undermine public, client, and investor trust in the organisation, in turn increasing the risk of financial setbacks as customers may choose to step away from the firm (ESMA, 2023). These allegations can often be difficult to control once they become public (Pears *et al.*, 2023), and rebuilding trust can be a costly and uncertain process, with no guaranteed returns.

Concern about these impacts has grown as media outlets, activist groups, and NGOs have challenged financial market participants about greenwashing (Delmas and Burbano, 2011; ESMA, 2023). The informal monitoring role of stakeholders has been significantly enhanced by social media platforms, which has made it easier and cheaper to disseminate and to amplify claims around greenwashing activities (Akyildirim *et al.*, 2024; Lyon and Montgomery, 2013). An example of the sort of concerns that have been raised is the NGO Rainforest Action Network (RAN) which, in 2020, identified the investment bank JP Morgan Chase as being the world's leading financier of fossil fuels; RAN argued that JP Morgan Chase had provided over \$268 billion in financing to fossil fuel companies since the 2015 Paris Agreement, which directly contradicted its claims of being a leader in sustainable finance (Dempere *et al.*, 2024).

Investors can, depending on how seriously they view claims about greenwashing and the consequence of such claims, take a range of actions. They can investigate the claims. They can reduce their holdings in companies that are the subject of such claims or that have suffered reputational damage as a result of such claims (EBA, 2023; ESMA, 2023). They can demand that the organisation provides robust evidence of its sustainability practices and performance, such as through independent audits or third-party assurance (EBA, 2023); for example, the EY Global Institutional Investor Survey 2024 found that nearly two-thirds of investment decision-makers advocate for independent audits of sustainability disclosures under frameworks such as the International Sustainability Standards Board (ISSB) and the CSRD (Ernst & Young Global Limited, 2024).

Finally, the effects of greenwashing are not just confined to an individual organisation; the spillover effects can be significant. For example, after the Dieselgate Scandal (discussed above), a wave of investigations was launched into other car manufacturers like BMW, Renault, Nissan, and Ford (De Prez, 2021; Hotten, 2015). This sort of contagion, where organisations experience what Pek *et al.* (2017) call a 'common reputational fate' with other firms within their sector, is not uncommon (EBA, 2023). Poor practices by one organisation can erode trust in entire sectors or broader industry segments (Akyildirim *et al.*, 2024; Pek *et al.*, 2017).

Regulatory and Litigation Risks

Greenwashing can also create regulatory and litigation risks. For example, the Dieselgate scandal opened the door for litigation and liability risks for Volkswagen and for other car manufacturers. Such risks can disrupt company operations, incur financial penalties and losses, and, if severe enough, even compromise the financial stability of the firms involved (EBA, 2023; Pears *et al.*, 2023).

The legal grounds for greenwash-based litigation are often rooted in existing laws, such as consumer and investor protection laws like the EU's Unfair Commercial Practices Directive, which protects consumers from misleading business practices (ClientEarth and AIGCC, 2023; European Banking Authority (EBA), 2024). These cases often involve adjudicating against false representations, omissions, deceptive evidence, and incorrect labelling related to organisations' claims about product characteristics, corporate and governmental commitments, and the disclosure of financial risks, climate investments, and the damage caused by companies (Pears *et al.*, 2023). A good example is provided by the case brought by the Australian Securities and Investments Commission (ASIC) against Mercer Superannuation for making misleading representations about the characteristics of their 'Sustainable Plus Options' and failing to implement a monitoring system to ensure investments excluded companies related to fossil fuels, gambling, or alcohol (Federal Court of Australia, 2024). The case was brought under the Australian Securities and Investments Commission Act 2001 (Cth), a law regulating financial markets in Australia, which rules against many types of misleading statements, not exclusive to greenwashing. The

Australian Federal Court found Mercer guilty and ordered them to pay a fine of AU$11.3 million and publish a notice on their sustainable investments page (Federal Court of Australia, 2024).

The increased attention being paid to greenwashing has accelerated the implementation of policies and regulations directed at improving the quality of information provided by companies (Fichter *et al.*, 2024) and at protecting investors and consumers from misleading green claims (ClientEarth and AIGCC, 2023). These have included the following:

- Measures to ban deceptive and false advertising. These often take the form of guidelines which support the enforcement of consumer protection laws (Ford, 2023; Rotman *et al.*, 2020). The guidelines generally require that green claims (a) are clear, unambiguous, and specific, (b) are truthful and accurate, (c) do not omit or hide important information, (d) are substantiated, (e) are supported by a plan when relating to future goals, and (f) use the same methodology when making comparisons (Ford, 2023). Similar measures are being seen to reduce greenwashing in relation to sustainable investment-related services and products. Examples include the EU's SFDR (discussed below), the UK's anti-greenwashing law (Financial Conduct Authority (FCA), 2024), and public statements from the Japanese Financial Services Agency that it will clamp down on greenwashing (ClientEarth and AIGCC, 2023).
- Eco-labels (which indicate whether products have met certain criteria) and eco-scores (which rate the environmental impact of particular products, allowing their sustainability performance to be directly compared). These labels and scores can focus on a specific aspect of performance (e.g. whether a product has been produced organically) or can aim to cover a range of issues (Darnall and Aragón-Correa, 2014). Examples from the sustainable investment field include the European Union's regulations on benchmarks (European Parliament and Council of the European Union, 2019a) and on green bonds (European Parliament and Council of the European Union, 2023).
- Sustainability reporting/disclosure requirements that specify the information that companies and other actors need to report, and that may include guidance on how data are to be calculated and presented. For example, the European CSRD (European Parliament and Council of the European Union, 2022) requires large companies to disclose their contributions to sustainability, their sustainability risks, and their sustainability-related targets and plans. In the area of sustainable investment, the European SFDR (European Parliament and Council of the European Union, 2019b) requires medium- and large-sized financial organisations to publicly report on how they integrate sustainability-related risks into their decision-making and on how their activities affect the environment. In addition, financial

products, which claim to be sustainable, must demonstrate why this is the case, including the methodology used for their assessment.

- Taxonomies. These are classification systems that define whether activities can be considered environmentally sustainable (Sullivan *et al.*, 2022). For example, the EU taxonomy defines sustainability across six dimensions: the sustainable use and protection of water and marine resources, the circular economy, pollution prevention, the protection of biodiversity and ecosystems, climate mitigation, and climate change adaptation (European Parliament and Council of the European Union, 2020). To be taxonomy-aligned, a company's activity must support at least one of these six sustainability dimensions without causing harm to any of the others.

These measures have all been helpful in addressing greenwashing. However, they also raise other issues. First, single issue frameworks and labels could distract attention from other environmental considerations, e.g. an investment portfolio with a significant number of technology companies could have low greenhouse gas emissions but have significant concerns around human rights or privacy issues. Second, this is a crowded area. There has been a significant growth in the number of voluntary and mandatory frameworks, with these frameworks often having significant differences in scope, content and ambition (Berg *et al.*, 2022; Kolling and Busch, 2025; Marx *et al.*, 2022). The overall effect could be to create confusion rather than to provide clarity (Darnall and Aragón-Correa, 2014).

Concluding Comments

From an investment perspective, greenwashing, greenhushing, and greenwishing all result in unreliable information being provided to investors. This limits investors' ability to make informed decisions and may result in capital being diverted from sustainable options towards more harmful alternatives (Lashitew, 2021). Greenwashing may also undermine some of the important mechanisms of sustainable investment – such as the ability to compare firms' sustainability progress, the ability to hold companies to account, the ability to support good performers – are compromised (Leung *et al.*, 2023). If greenwashing is a systemic market practice, it may divert time, effort, and finance away from the development and improvement of genuine sustainable finance products and solutions (Ayoade, 2023; Bauckloh *et al.*, 2023; Nemes *et al.*, 2022) and may undermine trust in sustainable investment as a whole (ClientEarth and AIGCC, 2023; ESMA, 2023; Leung *et al.*, 2023).

While the implications of greenwashing are clear, there is much that investors can do to manage these risks. As the Box below indicates, investors can – and should – inform themselves about greenwashing, they can identify and challenge greenwashing in the information provided by companies and other entities that they invest in, and they can minimise the likelihood that they will be accused of greenwashing.

Implications for Practitioners

1. The landscape of greenwashing, greenhushing, and greenwishing is complex and rapidly evolving. Investors need to understand both the formal legal requirements that apply to their reporting, and how their reporting might be interpreted (and misinterpreted) by different stakeholders.
2. Investors need to develop the skills to critically analyse the sustainability-related disclosures provided by the companies and other entities that they invest in. They need to pay particular attention to:
    a. Decoupling, which is when organisations claim to meet stakeholders' expectations but do not make any substantive changes to their practices.
    b. Attention deflection, which is when companies present an overly optimistic corporate image through selective disclosures, through vague or unproven claims, and through the use of visual imagery to communicate a firm or product's 'sustainability' credentials.
    c. Deceptive manipulation, which is when companies lie about their practices and performance.
3. Investors need to ensure that statements they make about their practices and their products can be backed up by data and by evidence. They also need to be prepared to respond to questions and challenges about their sustainability performance. This means that they need to:

    a. Critically review the data and information that underpin their reporting, so that they can be confident that it is an actual reflection of performance and impact.
    b. Be able to explain how their data and commitments (a) align with relevant regulatory requirements (e.g. taxonomy definitions) and (b) align with relevant environmental goals such as planetary boundaries or 1.5 degree warming benchmarks.
    c. Be able to demonstrate that they have considered the full range of relevant impacts, including as relevant wider life-cycle impacts.
    d. Be able to explain how they will meet their commitments and targets, including discussion of the factors that may influence whether or not these are met.
    e. Provide details of the data and methodologies that underpin their reporting.

References

Akyildirim, E., Corbet, S., Ongena, S. and Oxley, L. (2024), 'Greenwashing: Do Investors, Markets and Boards Really Care?', *SSRN Electronic Journal*, https://doi.org/10.2139/ssrn.4598145

Aragón-Correa, J.A., Marcus, A. and Hurtado-Torres, N. (2016), 'The Natural Environmental Strategies of International Firms: Old Controversies and New Evidence on Performance and Disclosure', *Academy of Management Perspectives*, Vol. 30, No. 1, pp. 24–39, www.jstor.org/stable/43822135

Ayoade, A. (2023), 'What Is Greenhushing and Is It Worse Than Greenwashing?' *Futerra*, www.wearefuterra.com/blog/what-is-greenhushing-and-is-it-worse-than-greenwashing

Bauckloh, T., Schaltegger, S., Utz, S., Zeile, S. and Zwergel, B. (2023), 'Active First Movers vs. Late Free-Riders? An Empirical Analysis of UN PRI Signatories' Commitment', *Journal of Business Ethics*, Vol. 182, pp. 747–781, https://doi.org/10.1007/s10551-021-04992-0

Berg, F., Kölbel, J. and Rigobon, R. (2022), 'Aggregate Confusion: The Divergence of ESG Ratings', *Review of Finance*, Vol. 26, No. 6, pp. 1315–1344, https://doi.org/10.1093/rof/rfac033

Bromley, P. and Powell, W. (2012), From Smoke and Mirrors to Walking the Talk: Decoupling in the Contemporary World', *Academy of Management Annuals*, Vol. 6, No. 1, pp. 483–530, https://doi.org/10.1080/19416520.2012.684462

Callery, P. (2023), 'The Influence of Strategic Disclosure on Corporate Climate Performance Ratings', *Business and Society*, Vol. 62, No. 5, pp. 950–988, https://doi.org/10.1177/00076503221115715

Clarkson, P., Li, Y., Richardson, G. and Vasvari, F. (2008), 'Revisiting the Relation Between Environmental Performance and Environmental Disclosure: An Empirical Analysis', *Accounting, Organizations and Society*, Vol. 33, No. 4, pp. 303–327, https://doi.org/10.1016/j.aos.2007.05.003

ClientEarth (2020). 'BP Greenwashing Complaint Sets Precedent for Action on Misleading Ad Campaigns', www.clientearth.org/latest/news/bp-greenwashing-complaint-sets-precedent-for-action-on-misleading-ad-campaigns/

ClientEarth, and Asia Investor Group on Climate Change (AIGCC) (2023), *Greenwashing and How to Avoid It: An Introductory Guide for Asia's Finance Industry*, www.aigcc.net/wp-content/uploads/2023/04/Greenwashing-and-how-to-avoid-it-An-introductory-guide-for-Asias-Finance-Industry-AIGCC-ClientEarth.pdf

Crilly, D., Hansen, M. and Zollo, M. (2016), 'The Grammar of Decoupling: A Cognitive-linguistic Perspective on Firms' Sustainability Claims and Stakeholders' Interpretation', *Academy of Management Journal*, Vol. 59, No. 2, pp. 705–729, www.jstor.org/stable/24758308

Darnall, N. and Aragón-Correa, J. (2014), 'Can Ecolabels Influence Firms' Sustainability Strategy and Stakeholder Behavior?', *Organization & Environment*, Vol. 27, pp. 319–327, https://doi.org/10.1177/1086026614562963

De Prez, M. (2021, March 5), 'All Manufacturers Accused of Cheating on Diesel Emissions Tests', *Fleet News*, www.fleetnews.co.uk/news/manufacturer-news/2021/03/05/all-manufacturers-accused-of-cheating-on-diesel-emissions-tests

Delmas, M. and Burbano, V. (2011), 'The Drivers of Greenwashing', *California Management Review*, Vol. 54, No. 1, pp. 64–87, https://doi.org/10.1525/cmr.2011.54.1.64

Delmas, M.A. and Montes-Sancho, M.J. (2010), 'Voluntary Agreements to Improve Environmental Quality: Symbolic and Substantive Cooperation', *Strategic Management Journal*, Vol. 31, No. 6, pp. 575–601, https://doi.org/10.1002/smj.826

Dempere, J., Alamash, E. and Mattos, P. (2024), 'Unveiling the Truth: Greenwashing in Sustainable Finance', *Frontiers in Sustainability*, Vol. 5, https://doi.org/10.3389/frsus.2024.1362051

Dorfleitner, G. and Utz, S. (2023), 'Green, Green, It's Green they Say: A Conceptual Framework for Measuring Greenwashing on Firm Level', *Review of Managerial Science*, Vol. 18, No. 12, pp. 3463–3486, https://doi.org/10.1007/s11846-023-00718-w

Eccles, R., Lee, L. and Stroehle, J. (2019), 'The Social Origins of ESG: An Analysis of Innovest and KLD', *Organization and Environment*, Vol. 33, No. 4, pp. 575–596, www.jstor.org/stable/27001597

Ernst & Young Global Limited (2024), *How Can Investors Balance Short-Term Demands with Long-Term Sustainability? EY Institutional Investor Survey*, www.ey.com/en_gl/insights/climate-change-sustainability-services/institutional-investor-survey

Eurofi (2023), *Avoiding Greenwashing in the Financial Sector*, www.eurofi.net/wp-content/uploads/2023/07/the-eurofi-high-level-seminar_stockholm_avoiding-greenwashing-in-the-financial-sector_summary_april-2023.pdf

European Banking Authority (EBA) (2023), *EBA Progress Report on Greenwashing Monitoring and Supervision.* EBA/REP/2023/16 (EBA, Paris), www.eba.europa.eu/sites/default/files/document_library/Publications/Reports/2023/1055934/EBA%20progress%20report%20on%20greewnwashing.pdf

European Banking Authority (EBA) (2024), *Greenwashing Monitoring and Supervision.* Final Report. EBA/REP/2024/09 (EBA, Paris), www.eba.europa.eu/sites/default/files/2024-05/a12e5087-8fd2-451f-8005-6d45dc838ffd/Report%20on%20greenwashing%20monitoring%20and%20supervision.pdf

European Parliament and Council of the European Union (2019a), 'Regulation (EU) 2019/2089 of the European Parliament and of the Council of 27 November 2019 Amending Regulation (EU) 2016/1011 as Regards EU Climate Transition Benchmarks, EU Paris-Aligned Benchmarks and Sustainability-Related Disclosures for Benchmarks', https://eur-lex.europa.eu/legal-content/EN/ALL/?uri=CELEX:32019R2089

European Parliament and Council of the European Union (2019b), 'Council Regulation (EU) 2019/2088 of 27 November 2019 on Sustainability-Related Disclosures in the Financial Services Sector', https://eur-lex.europa.eu/eli/reg/2019/2088/oj/eng

European Parliament and Council of the European Union (2020), 'Council Regulation (EU) 2020/852 of the 18 June 2020 on the Establishment of a Framework to Facilitate Sustainable Investment, and Amending Regulation (EU) 2019/2088', https://eur-lex.europa.eu/eli/reg/2020/852/oj/eng

European Parliament and Council of the European Union (2022), 'Council Directive (EU) 2022/2464 of 14 December 2022 Amending Regulation (EU) No 537/2014, Directive 2004/109/EC, Directive 2006/43/EC and Directive 2013/34/EU, as Regards Corporate Sustainability Reporting', https://eur-lex.europa.eu/eli/dir/2022/2464/oj/eng

European Parliament and Council of the European Union (2023), 'Council Regulation (EU) 2023/2631 of 22 November 2023 on European Green Bonds and Optional

Disclosures for Bonds Marketed as Environmentally Sustainable and for Sustainability-linked Bonds', https://eur-lex.europa.eu/eli/reg/2023/2631/oj/eng

European Securities and Markets Authority (ESMA) (2023), *The Financial Impact of Greenwashing Controversies*, www.esma.europa.eu/sites/default/files/2023-12/ESMA50-524821-3072_TRV_Article_The_financial_impact_of_greenwashing_controversies.pdf

European Securities and Markets Authority (ESMA) (2024), *Final Report on Greenwashing Response to the European Commission's Request for Input on "Greenwashing Risks and the Supervision of Sustainable Finance Policies"*, www.esma.europa.eu/sites/default/files/2024-06/ESMA36-287652198-2699_Final_Report_on_Greenwashing.pdf.

Federal Court of Australia (FCA) (2024), 'Australian Securities and Investments Commission v Mercer Superannuation (Australia) Limited 2024 [FCA] 850', https://download.asic.gov.au/media/bq0nxstc/24-173mr-asic-v-mercer-superannuation-australia-limited-judgment-2-aug-2024.pdf

Fichtner, J., Jaspert, R. and Petry, J. (2024), 'Mind the ESG Capital Allocation Gap: The Role of Index Providers, Standard-setting, and "Green" Indices for the Creation of Sustainability Impact', *Regulation & Governance*, Vol. 18, No. 2, pp. 479–498, https://doi.org/10.1111/rego.12530

Financial Conduct Authority (FCA) (2024), *Finalised Non-Handbook Guidance on the Anti-Greenwashing Rule*, www.fca.org.uk/publication/finalised-guidance/fg24-3.pdf

Fisher, R., Hodge, M. and Beals., B. (2023, June 21), 'Greenwashing, Greenhushing and Greenwishing: Don't Fall Victim to these ESG Reporting Traps', *ESG Today*, www.esgtoday.com/guest-post-greenwashing-greenhushing-and-greenwishing-dont-fall-victim-to-these-esg-reporting-traps/

Ford, E. (2023), *Tackling Greenwashing from a Governance Perspective* (Chartered Governance Institute, UK & Ireland), https://cgiglobal.org/media/me3h3qjs/tackling-greenwashing-from-a-governance-perspective-04-2023.pdf

Fraser, A. and Fiedler, T. (2023), 'Net-Zero Targets for Investment Portfolios: An Analysis of Financed Emissions Metrics', *Energy Economics*, Vol. 126, p. 106917, https://doi.org/10.1016/j.eneco.2023.106917

Garnelo-Gomez, I. (2022, March 18), 'Green to Pink to Blue: Companies' Dirty Washing', *Henley Business School*, www.henley.ac.uk/news/2022/green-to-pink-to-blue-companies-dirty-washing

Greiner, M. and Kim, J. (2021), 'Corporate Political Activity and Greenwashing: Can CPA Clarify Which Firm Communications on Social and Environmental Events Are Genuine?', *Corporate Social Responsibility and Environmental Management*, Vol. 28, No. 1, pp. 1–10, https://doi.org/10.1002/csr.2026

Hotten, R. (2015, December 10), 'Volkswagen: The Scandal Explained', *BBC News*, www.bbc.com/news/business-34324772

Huang, X., Hu, Z., Liu, C., Yu, D. and Yu, L. (2016), 'The Relationships between Regulatory and Customer Pressure, Green Organizational Responses, and Green Innovation Performance', *Journal of Cleaner Production*, Vol. 112, No. 4, pp. 3423–3433, https://doi.org/10.1016/j.jclepro.2015.10.106

InfluenceMap (2022), *Finance and Climate Change: A Comprehensive Climate Assessment of the World's Largest Financial Institutions*, https://influencemap.org/report/Finance-and-Climate-Change-17639

Kolling, C. and Busch, T. (2025), 'Sustainability Labels Matter', *Finance Research Letters*, Vol. 73, p. 106609, https://doi.org/10.1016/j.frl.2024.106609

Lashitew, A. (2021), Corporate Uptake of the Sustainable Development Goals: Mere Greenwashing or an Advent of Institutional Change?', *Journal of International Business Policy*, Vol. 4, No. 1, pp. 184–200, http://dx.doi.org/10.2139/ssrn.3789574

Leung, P., Wan, W. and Wong, J. (2023), *The Shade of Green: Greenwashing in the Corporate Green Bond Markets* (Hong Kong Institute for Monetary and Financial Research), https://doi.org/10.2139/ssrn.4326216

Lyon, T. and Maxwell, J. (2011), 'Greenwash: Corporate Environmental Disclosure Under Threat of Audit', *Journal of Economics and Management Strategy*, Vol. 20, No. 1, pp. 3–41, https://doi.org/10.1111/j.1530-9134.2010.00282.x

Lyon, T. and Montgomery, A. (2013), 'Tweetjacked: The Impact of Social Media on Corporate Greenwash', *Journal of Business Ethics*, Vol. 118, No. 4, pp. 747–757, https://doi.org/10.1007/s10551-013-1958-x

Lyon, T. and Montgomery, A. (2015), 'The Means and End of Greenwash', *Organization and Environment*, Vol. 28, No. 2, pp. 223–249, https://doi.org/10.1177/10860 26615575332

Marquis, C., Toffel, M. and Zhou, Y. (2016), 'Scrutiny, Norms, and Selective Disclosure: A Global Study of Greenwashing', *Organization Science*, Vol. 27, No. 2, pp. 483–504, https://doi.org/10.1287/orsc.2015.1039

Marx, A., Depoorter, C. and Vanhaecht, R. (2022), 'Voluntary Sustainability Standards: State of the Art and Future Research', *Standards*, Vol. 2, No. 1, pp. 14–31, https://doi.org/10.3390/standards2010002

Mateo-Márquez, A., González-González, J. and Zamora-Ramírez, C. (2022), 'An International Empirical Study of Greenwashing and Voluntary Carbon Disclosure', *Journal of Cleaner Production*, Vol. 363, p. 132567, https://doi.org/10.1016/j.jcle pro.2022.132567

Meyer, J. and Rowan, B. (1977), 'Institutionalized Organizations: Formal Structure as Myth and Ceremony', *American Journal of Sociology*, Vol. 83, No. 2, pp. 340–363.

Montgomery, A., Lyon, T. and Barg, J. (2024), 'No End in Sight? A Greenwash Review and Research Agenda', *Organization & Environment*, Vol. 37, No. 2, pp. 221–256, https://doi.org/10.1177/10860266231168905

Nemes, N., Scanlan, S.J., Smith, P., Smith, T., Aronczyk, M., Hill, S., Lewis, S.L., Montgomery, A., Tubiello, F. and Stabinsky, D. (2022). 'An Integrated Framework to Assess Greenwashing', *Sustainability*, Vol. 14, No. 8, p. 4431, https://doi.org/10.3390/su14084431

Network for Greening the Financial System (NGFS) (2024), *Improving Greenhouse Gas Emissions Data: Information Note*, www.ngfs.net/system/files/import/ngfs/medias/documents/ngfs_information_note_on_improving_ghg_emission_data.pdf

Parguel, B., Benoît-Moreau, F. and Larceneux, F. (2011), 'How Sustainability Ratings Might Deter 'Greenwashing': A Closer Look at Ethical Corporate Communication', *Journal of Business Ethics*, Vol. 102, No. 1, pp. 15–28, https://doi.org/10.1007/s10 551-011-0901-2

Parguel, B., Benoit-Moreau, F. and Russell, C. (2015), 'Can Evoking Nature in Advertising Mislead Consumers? The Power of 'Executional Greenwashing'', *International Journal of Advertising*, Vol. 34, No. 1, pp. 107–134, https://doi.org/10.1080/02650 487.2014.996116

Patten, D. (2002), 'The Relation between Environmental Performance and Environmental Disclosure: A Research Note', *Accounting, Organizations and Society*, Vol. 27, No. 8, pp.763–773, https://doi.org/10.1016/S0361-3682(02)00028-4

Pears, P., Baines, T., Williams, O. and Brown, M. (2023, July 24), 'Greenwashing: Navigating the Risk', *The Harvard Law School Forum on Corporate Governance*, https://corpgov.law.harvard.edu/2023/07/24/greenwashing-navigating-the-risk/

Pek, S., Oh, C. and Rivera, J. (2017), 'MNC Foreign Investment and Industrial Disasters: The Moderating Role of Technological, Safety Management, and Philanthropic Capabilities', *Strategic Management Journal*, Vol. 39, No. 2, pp. 502–526, https://doi.org/10.1002/smj.2737

Prentice, C. (2023, September 25), 'DWS to Pay $25 Million to End US Probe into Greenwashing, Other Issues', *Reuters*, www.reuters.com/legal/dws-pay-25-mln-over-us-charges-over-esg-misstatements-other-violations-2023-09-25/

Rotman, R., Gossett, C. and Goldman, H. (2020), 'Greenwashing No More: The Case for Stronger Regulation of Environmental Marketing', *Administrative Law Review*, Vol. 72, No. 3, pp. 417–443, www.jstor.org/stable/27177113

Seele, P. and Gatti, L. (2017), 'Greenwashing Revisited: In Search of a Typology and Accusation-Based Definition Incorporating Legitimacy Strategies', *Business Strategy and the Environment*, Vol. 26, No. 2, pp. 239–252, https://doi.org/10.1002/bse.1912

Siano, A., Vollero, A., Conte, F. and Amabile, S. (2017), '"More Than Words": Expanding the Taxonomy of Greenwashing After the Volkswagen Scandal', *Journal of Business Research*, Vol. 71, pp. 27–37, https://doi.org/10.1016/j.jbusres.2016.11.002

South Pole (2022), *Net Zero and Beyond: A Deep-Dive on Climate Leaders and What's Driving Them*, / www.southpole.com/publications/net-zero-and-beyond

Storbeck, O. (2023, July 26), 'DWS Closes in on Settlement Over Greenwashing Scandal', *Financial Times*, www.ft.com/content/38be4231-21cf-46e3-8b6a-88a4e923f01c

Sullivan, R., Black, R., Pirovska, M. and Stewart, F. (2022), *How Policymakers Can Implement Reforms for a Sustainable Finance System. Part II: Implementation Guide for Sustainable Investment Policy and Regulation Tools – Taxonomies of Sustainable Economic Activities* (Principles for Responsible Investment, World Bank Group and Chronos Sustainability), www.unpri.org/download?ac=16315

Sullivan, R. and Gouldson, A. (2012), 'Does Voluntary Carbon Reporting Meet Investors' Needs?', *Journal of Cleaner Production*, Vol. 36, pp. 60–67, https://doi.org/10.1016/j.jclepro.2012.02.020

Sustainalytics (2023), *Seeing Through the Green: A Guide to Greenwashing Risks for Asset Managers*, https://connect.sustainalytics.com/inv-ebook-guide-to-greenwashing-risks-for-asset-managers

Tashman, P., Marano, V. and Kostova, T. (2019), 'Walking the Walk or Talking the Talk? Corporate Social Responsibility Decoupling in Emerging Market Multinationals', *Journal of International Business Studies*, Vol. 50, pp. 153–171, https://doi.org/10.1057/s41267-018-0171-7

Taylor, E. (2020, March 17), 'Volkswagen Says Diesel Scandal has Cost it 31.3 Billion Euros', *Reuters*, www.reuters.com/article/business/volkswagen-says-diesel-scandal-has-cost-it-313-billion-euros-idUSKBN2141JA/

TerraChoice (2010), *The Sins of Greenwashing: Home and Family Edition*, www.sinsofgreenwashing.org

US Environmental Protection Agency (USEPA) (2024), 'Learn About Volkswagen Violations', www.epa.gov/vw/learn-about-volkswagen-violations (last viewed, 4 May 2025).

Winkler, P., Etter, M. and Castelló, I. (2020), 'Vicious and Virtuous Circles of Aspirational Talk: From Self-Persuasive to Agonistic CSR Rhetoric', *Business and Society*, Vol. 59, No. 1, pp. 98–128, https://doi.org/10.1177/0007650319825758

Zameer, H., Wang, Y. and Yasmeen, H. (2020), 'Reinforcing Green Competitive Advantage through Green Production, Creativity and Green Brand Image: Implications for Cleaner Production in China', *Journal of Cleaner Production*, Vol. 247, p. 119119, https://doi.org/10.1016/j.jclepro.2019.119119

Chapter 12

Can the Information Provided by Data and Ratings Providers Be Relied Upon?

Claudio Cichi, Áine O'Dea, Duo Xu and Valentin Jahn

Introduction

The growth in sustainable finance has led to significant growth in investor demand for more and better-quality sustainability-related data. Many institutional investors now rely heavily on third-party sustainability data and ratings providers to provide data and assessments of the sustainability performance of the companies and other entities that they invest in (Berg *et al.*, 2022; ERM, 2023). The consequence is that the data that these third-party organisations provide and the views that these organisations hold on sustainability-related issues have potentially profound implications for investment decision-making.

This chapter describes why investors have turned to third-party sustainability data and ratings providers, and the roles that these providers now play in sustainable finance. It then discusses the data and assessments provided by

 DOI: 10.4324/9781003467632-12

these organisations, and the implications for investment decision-making and sustainable finance more generally. The chapter concludes with some practical suggestions for investment practitioners on what they should think about and look for when using sustainability ratings and scores in their decision-making.

A Description of the Sustainability Data and Information Ecosystem

Who Are the Key Actors?

In very broad terms, the relationships between companies, data providers and investors presented can be summarised as follows (adapted from Abramskiehn *et al.* (2025); Boffo and Patalano (2020)):

- Companies and other entities disclose sustainability-related information through mandatory (e.g. 10-K filings) and voluntary channels (e.g. sustainability reports, responses to questionnaires from data and information providers).
- Sustainability data and ratings organisations aggregate, process and contextualise this and other information (e.g. media analysis, non-governmental organisation (NGO) reports) so that it can be used in investment analysis and as inputs to ratings, scores, investment products and tools.
- Investors use sustainability-related data and information to assess company and portfolio performance and to make investment decisions. The inputs to investor decision-making include data provided directly by companies and other reporting entities, data and information provided by sustainability data and research organisations, and data and information from other sources.

The Need for Sustainability-Related Data

The reasons for investor interest in and demand for high-quality sustainability data are discussed in more detail elsewhere in this book. There are three broad reasons. First, sustainability-related issues are drivers of investment performance. The higher the quality and accuracy of sustainability data, the more likely it is that financial actors will be able to make informed decisions. Second, there is increasing legislative and regulatory focus on how investors consider and take account of the sustainability characteristics of potential investments. There has also been a significant growth in mandatory and voluntary reporting requirements. Third, there is increased demand for green and socially responsible investment products.

Investors use sustainability-related data in a variety of ways (see, generally, International Organization of Securities Commissions (IOSCO) (2021: 24–25)). They can, among other applications, use these data to:

- Identify and assess sustainability-related risks and opportunities at the asset and the portfolio level.
- Assess the financial significance of these risks and opportunities.
- Screen out (exclude) or screen in (include) companies or other entities from their investment portfolios.
- Systematically integrate sustainability-related issues into their investment processes (e.g. through weighting companies according to their sustainability performance, through preferentially investing in better performing entities).
- Inform their dialogue with companies and other entities (e.g. to identify entities who could improve their sustainability-related disclosures, management processes and performance).
- Develop sustainable products such as investment funds based on sustainability themes.
- Support their regulatory reporting and their reporting to clients and to other stakeholders.

What Are Sustainability Data and Where Do the Data Come From?

Sustainability data refer to the metrics and other information used to understand a company's (or other entity's) environmental, social and economic impacts and its governance of these and other issues. This data covers a wide range of areas (Larcker, 2022). Environmental data could relate to aspects such as energy use, water consumption, pollution, waste management, greenhouse gas emissions and raw material consumptions. Social data could relate to issues such as human capital, employee engagement, community impacts, stakeholder relationships, human rights, health and safety and labour practices. Economic data could relate to the capital and operating costs and benefits of sustainability-related initiatives, and to the overall financial performance of an entity. Finally, governance data could relate to issues such as executive remuneration, ownership structures, business ethics, board composition, transparency and accounting and auditing practices.

The sustainability-related data used by investors can come from a variety of sources. It can be provided by companies or other entities that are being invested in. For example, many now report on the social and environmental characteristics of their supply chains, their products and their activities and operations. Intergovernmental organisations, sovereigns, government agencies and sub-sovereign entities (e.g. state-owned enterprises, municipalities) also provide information; examples include economic data, state of the environment reporting, greenhouse gas inventories and local environmental, social and economic information. This information can be used both to inform investment decisions related to these entities (e.g. whether to purchase their bonds) and wider investment decisions (e.g. on whether to invest in companies operating in a particular country or region).

Investors also use a range of other data sources in their investment decision-making. Examples include NGO reports and benchmarks, news reports and social media coverage, consumer sentiment surveys and other analyses of brand, reputation and customer loyalty, records of regulatory fines and penalties, and satellite and geo-location data.

Why Use Third-Party Data and Information Providers?

Portfolio investors need sustainability data that are accurate, consistent, timely, complete and balanced (see further Chapter 9 and London Stock Exchange Group (LSEG) (2024)). However, sustainability is just one of the issues that they need to pay attention to in their investment processes. Investors' ability to focus on specific sustainability issues is also shaped by the reality that they often have hundreds of companies in their portfolios, that they often need to analyse performance over multiple years and that there are multiple sustainability issues they could look at. In relation to this latter point, Larcker (2022: 4) notes that the number of input variables involved in assessing an individual company or entity is extremely large, with the major sustainability data providers claiming to use between 300 and 1,000 data points when analysing companies (Larcker, 2022: 4).

Ultimately, for sustainability data to be decision-useful to investors, these data must be collected, processed and delivered in formats that are useful in decision-making. This involves collecting data from a large number of entities (e.g. the many hundreds of companies in a typical investment portfolio) and ensuring the quality and accuracy of these data. These data then need to be put into formats (e.g. databases) that allow them to be readily processed. These activities all require specialised knowledge and expertise. Furthermore, the analysis of these data also requires knowledge of sustainability issues, the ability to create actionable insights from the available sustainability data and the ability to integrate these insights into investment decision-making.

For most institutional investors, building these capabilities in-house would demand significant resources and expertise. Starting from scratch, they would probably need years of investment to build and refine the required processes and systems. It is, therefore, unsurprising that many investors have turned to sustainability data and information providers to support them in their analysis and decision-making. Using third-party providers allows investors to benefit from the economies of scale and data collection efficiencies offered by these providers. It also allows investors to gain access to technical expertise in areas such as data analysis and data modelling. Third-party providers also often have access to third-party data sources, allowing them to fill gaps and enhance the comprehensiveness of sustainability data.

There are currently around 10–15 major sustainability data and information providers (ERM, 2023; Mazzacurati, 2021). The major players include MSCI, ISS, Morningstar Sustainalytics London Stock Exchange Group (LSEG), S&P Global, Moody's and Bloomberg. While the industry has experienced significant consolidation in recent years, there are also many hundreds, if not thousands, of smaller data and ratings agencies currently in existence (International Organization of Securities Commissions (IOSCO), 2021: 6–9; Mazzacurati, 2021: 107).

Sustainability Data and Ratings Providers

In broad terms, sustainability data and ratings providers enable the flow of sustainability data and information from the producers of information to the end-users of that information (Larcker *et al.*, 2022). They do so by collating data and information from companies – from public disclosure or through questionnaires – and from a range of other sources. They then review and quality assure these data and present these data in structured, standardised formats (Boffo and Patalano, 2020; International Organization of Securities Commissions (IOSCO), 2021: 8–11; Larcker *et al.*, 2022).

The review and quality assurance of data may include removing duplicates, addressing inconsistencies and errors, presenting data in standardised units, comparing reported data to third-party data sources, proxies and industry benchmarks and engaging directly with reporting entities to check the accuracy and trustworthiness of reported data. Data providers may fill data gaps through data (estimation) models that use proxy measures, economic data and previously reported data to develop new data points. They may also provide supplementary data (e.g. from alternative data sources and third-party data sets) and combine sustainability-related data with relevant financial information (e.g. turnover), thereby putting these data into context (e.g. green expenditure as a portion of total capital expenditure).

Finally, once data have been processed, they can be provided to end-users (i.e. investors). Data providers may provide raw data (i.e. data as collected from entities) and/or cleaned and quality-assured data. They generally provide these in accessible, usable formats (e.g. as Excel or CSV files) so that the data can be readily analysed and integrated into clients' own data warehouses and data management systems. Data providers generally provide contextual data (e.g. data and information that enables peer comparisons and benchmarking, insights into year-on-year trends, insights into drivers of changes in sustainability performance) and tools that allow complex data to be transformed into charts, graphs and dashboards.

Sustainability data and ratings providers also provide a range of tools and products. These include sustainability-related indices that enable investors to track the performance of companies with strong sustainability practices and benchmarks that align portfolios with sustainability goals (e.g. by overweighting companies with high sustainability scores and under-weighting companies with lower scores). Other products include, depending on the provider, corporate and country sustainability-related assessments and scores, risk assessment tools, assessments of companies' exposure to and management of sustainability-related controversies such as conflict or controversial weapons, and assessments of companies' involvement in sectors and products such as alcohol, intensive farming, gambling, pornography and tobacco.

Specific Issues

The sustainability data and ratings industry has emerged to meet the particular needs of investors. However, this growth has not been without controversy. Two issues that recur in the literature are the quality of the data provided by these organisations, and the scores and ratings that they produce.

Data

There are two major issues with the sustainability-related data provided by companies and other entities. The first relates to the data coverage. There are significant gaps in the data provided by companies and reporting entities. Large companies are more likely to report than smaller companies (Dobrick *et al.*, 2023), publicly listed companies are more likely to report than private companies, entities operating in sophisticated or developed financial markets with robust disclosure requirements tend to provide more disclosures (IOSCO, 2021: 11–12).

The second issue relates to the quality of the information provided (BNP Paribas, 2023; ERM, 2023). The scope of reporting is often unclear, e.g. it is often difficult to tell whether the reported data cover all aspects of the reporting entity, and whether subsidiaries and outsourced activities are included or excluded. There are often questions around the quality and credibility of the data provided. In practice, reporting entities tend to rely heavily on estimation techniques (e.g. emission factors for calculating emissions to air, water and land, proxy measures where direct measures of impact are not available). These estimation techniques are often applied to contexts and activities that are not relevant; a common example is the use of default greenhouse gas emission factors from a different country to calculate the emissions associated with a company's electricity consumption (see, generally, Sullivan (2011)). There are also issues, despite frameworks such as those from the Global Reporting Initiative (GRI), around the lack of standardisation in how sustainability-related indicators are defined and measured (Amel-Zadeh and Serafeim, 2018; Berg *et al.*, 2022: 1319; Governance & Accountability Institute, 2024: 22).

The sustainability data and ratings providers are acutely aware of the issues with the data and information provided by companies and other entities, and they take various actions to address these issues. Some send curated assessment questionnaires to firms to check reported data and to request supplementary information, some use other public data and indirect sources to cross-check the reported data and some use AI and other tools to check the collected data (IOSCO, 2021; IRIS Carbon, 2023; Jonsdottir and SigurJonsson, 2022). The data providers, depending on their approach, may also clean the data by correcting errors and standardising the units in which data are reported.

Beyond the issues with the data provided by companies and other entities, there are also weaknesses in the data and information provided by sustainability data and ratings agencies. From a coverage perspective, while some providers do cover private companies, there is a heavier coverage of publicly listed companies, and there is more coverage of larger companies relative to smaller companies (IOSCO, 2021: 11–12). From a data quality perspective, there are issues around completeness of data, standardisation and consistency (Larcker *et al.*, 2022).

In relation to completeness, different sustainability data and ratings agencies make different decisions about how to handle missing data. One approach is to simply omit the data point, but this penalises companies that do report. Another approach is to make assumptions about what the data might be e.g. through assuming that the company's performance is the industry average, through assuming that the company's performance is the worst in the sector, through making estimates using various statistical techniques (Larcker *et al.*, 2022). Perhaps paradoxically, the use of industry averages may create an incentive for poor performers not to report their information.

In relation to standardisation, companies often report information using scales that are not directly comparable. For example, workplace safety information may be described using raw numbers (number of incidents, number of deaths or injuries, amount of time lost), using a time scale (injuries per unit of time worked) or a percentage scale (lost-time frequency). These inconsistencies mean that the sustainability data and ratings agencies need to make decisions on which metrics to use, on how to convert metrics from one form to another and on how to meaningfully compare performance (IOSCO, 2021: 16).

Finally, in relation to consistency, data providers might adjust historic data, e.g. if new data become available, if new estimation techniques emerge, if the core business activities have changed. Such changes may limit users' ability to track or to understand changes in performance over time (see, for example, Berg *et al.* (2021)) and may mean that the data providers' numbers are different to those provided by the company or reporting entity.

Ratings and Scores

Many investors rely heavily on the sustainability ratings and scores produced by sustainability data providers (Boffo and Patalano, 2020: 21; Larcker *et al.*, 2022). In fact, one survey cited by Larcker *et al.* (2022) suggested that 88% of investment professionals used third-party sustainability ratings as a part of their investment process, and that 92% expected to do so in the future.

Sustainability ratings and scores aim to reduce the sustainability-related issues and impacts associated with a company or other entity to a single measure or score that describes or characterises performance. Essentially, they aim to aggregate performance across ESG aspects (Mazzacurati, 2021: 108).

There is no formal difference between ratings and scores. The Future of Sustainable Data Alliance (FoSDA) defines sustainability (or ESG) ratings as products that are marketed as providing an opinion regarding the environmental, social or governance performance of an entity, a financial instrument or a product, a company's sustainability profile or characteristics or exposure to sustainability, climatic or environmental risks or impact on society and the environment issued (Future of Sustainable Data Alliance (FoSDA), 2023; see also (IOSCO, 2021). FoSDA also notes that these products tend to use defined ranking systems of rating categories; these could be letter grades such as AAA or CCC, or numeric bands such as 1–5. In contrast, sustainability (or ESG) scores are a measure of the environmental, social or governance performance of an entity, a financial instrument or a product, a company's sustainability profile or characteristics or exposure to sustainability, climatic or environmental risks or impact on society and the environment (FoSDA, 2023; IOSCO, 2021). These are commonly presented as a numerical score (e.g. 45 out of 100).

Ratings and scores are constructed in different ways by different sustainability data providers. The specific approaches adopted reflect the objectives of the rating or score (Larcker *et al.*, 2022; Mazzacurati, 2021). Reflecting the discussion of single (financial) and double (financial and impact) materiality in Chapter 3, scores and ratings can be designed to (amongst others): (a) assess the financial significance of social and environmental factors to the company or entity; (b) assess how well the company is managing the commercial or financial implications of social or environmental issues (e.g. through strategic planning, through risk management processes, through operational controls); (c) assess the impact the company has on employees, suppliers, customers, the local community and/or the environment; (d) assess how well the company is managing its impacts (e.g. through adopting policies, through taking action to reduce its negative social and environmental impacts). Unsurprisingly, given the potential range of uses, ratings and scores also differ widely in terms of the issues they focus on. For example, an assessment of environmental performance could assess one, some or all of water use, greenhouse gas emissions, energy efficiency and biodiversity impacts, to name just a few. ESG ratings and scores inevitably, also differ widely in terms of the data and metrics they use (and don't use), how different metrics are weighted, whether forward-looking and/or backward-looking data are used and how different sectors and industries are assessed (Boffo and Patalano, 2020: 21; Mazzacurati, 2021: 19–20).

The consequence is that the scores and ratings from different providers are not consistent with each other; for example, Boffo and Patalano (2020) highlight that some companies, ranked top by one provider, have much lower scores from other providers. Furthermore, various authors have suggested that the scores and ratings, individually or in aggregate, do not appear to be consistently linked to the performance outcomes (e.g. financial risk, investment performance, impact management) that the scores and ratings are trying to measure (Berg *et al.*, 2022; Boffo and Patalano, 2020: 27; Larcker *et al.*, 2022; Mazzacurati, 2021).

There have been efforts to understand the factors that drive differences in ratings and scores. Berg *et al.* (2022) analysed the ratings from five prominent data providers, and found that ESG ratings were only 60% correlated, compared with 99% for credit ratings from the largest credit ratings agencies. They suggested that differences in measurement (i.e. the metrics and indicators used to assess performance) contributed 56% of the divergence, differences in scope (i.e. the attributes or topics used to assess performance) contributed 38% and differences in weight (i.e. how the indicators are combined) contributed 6%. Another analysis (conducted for the Organisation for Economic Co-operation and Development (OECD)) suggested that the range of factors that could contribute to differences in ratings included the metrics used, the treatment of controversies (i.e. how they are identified and how they are assessed), the use of subjective assessments (in ratings), the weighting of indicators and the specific rules used for high impact sectors (Boffo and Patalano, 2020).

Mirroring the discussion about data above, there are notable patterns in ESG ratings and scores. First, ratings and scores that include controversy assessments tend to penalise larger companies as these tend to be more exposed to public scrutiny and more likely to receive press coverage (Mazzacurati, 2021). Second, large companies tend to receive higher average ratings than smaller companies; this might be due to the more significant resources large firms are able to invest in sustainability-related initiatives, or it might be due to large companies often providing greater disclosure of sustainability data (Larcker *et al.*, 2022; Mazzacurati, 2021). Third, industry ratings affect scoring. If ratings and scores are not adjusted, certain industries may perform better than others. For example, Larcker *et al.* (2022) suggest that banks and wireless communications may perform better than tobacco and gaming. Fourth, geography is important. Larcker *et al.* (2022) suggest that European companies have higher average scores than US companies, and that firms in emerging markets have lower ratings than firms in more developed economies. These differences may reflect political and regulatory differences between countries and regions.

As a final reflection, the importance of variations in ratings and scores depends on how they are used in investment decisions. Such variations are perhaps more important in situations where the ratings and scores are used to construct investment portfolios that have a tilt toward higher scores or ratings. In these situations, the question is whether the higher scores or ratings are good measures of the outcomes being sought (e.g. do they measure better risk management, do they measure better environmental performance). This question is of direct importance to the end-investors in these investment products as it raises the question of whether they can be assured that the investment product provides enhanced investment returns or delivers the promised social or environmental performance outcomes (Boffo and Patalano, 2020: 28; Larcker *et al.*, 2022). This divergence is also important to other stakeholders as it makes it difficult to evaluate (or to differentiate) the sustainability performance of companies, funds and portfolios, which, ultimately, is a key function of sustainability-related ratings and scores (Berg *et al.*, 2022).

The wider context to this discussion is that a lack of trust in sustainability ratings and scores may undermine confidence both in the investment products that use these ratings and scores and in sustainable finance more generally. For example, Boffo and Patalano (2020: 6) suggested that most corporates and investors only had moderate trust that ESG ratings accurately reflected sustainability performance. A more recent survey presented similar findings suggesting that, of the investors that responded to the survey, 59% had moderate trust in sustainability ratings and 38% had high to very high trust (ERM, 2023: 34–35). The ERM study stressed that when investors incorporate sustainability data and ratings into their investment decisions, they must be able to trust the information. It also noted that the use of unreliable or unsupportable data could result in regulatory actions and lawsuits, as well as reputational damage (ERM, 2023).

Conclusions

Sustainability-related ratings and scores are important in the field of sustainable finance. They provide an external opinion on the sustainability credentials of companies and countries. They can enable structured assessments and comparisons based on consistent methodologies. These ratings and scores are used to inform investment decisions, to build investment products and can shape investors', and other stakeholders', views of the performance of individual companies or other entities.

The fact that ratings and scores diverge presents issues for sustainable finance. The absence of common definitions and approaches can lead to confusion. The existence of different methodologies and approaches limits the comparability of these ratings. Ultimately, these issues may mean that end-investors cannot be certain that the investment products that they invest in will meet their financial or sustainability-related objectives. This divergence can also be used to criticise sustainability data, ratings and scores and even the wider sustainable finance industry for a lack of rigour and a lack of credibility.

There are practical actions that can be taken to respond to some of these challenges. Sustainability data and ratings agencies can be transparent – and many already are – about their sources of data, about how they address data gaps and about how they construct their ratings and scores. These organisations can also advise on the extent to which their ratings and scores deliver, or are likely to deliver on, the goals they have set for these. For example, does a 'high climate score' mean that a company has robust carbon management practices and processes, lower greenhouse gas emissions than its peers stronger emission reduction targets or a lower financial risk? Similar points apply to the organisations that use these ratings and scores in their investment products. Are they clear about how the scores are produced, what the scores mean and how the scores relate to the overarching goals (e.g. reduced emissions, lower financial risk) of the investment product?

The final comment we would like to make is that we are not calling for the regulation of ratings or scores, nor are we suggesting that all ratings and scores should converge. We recognise that effective markets rely on differences of opinion. In that context, we see differences in sustainability ratings and scores as reflecting legitimate differences of opinion around the sustainability issues that are relevant to an individual company or entity, around how these might be assessed and how these relate to the outcomes that are sought (see, also, Edmans (2022)).

Implications for Practitioners

1. There are significant weaknesses in the sustainability-related data provided by companies and other entities, both in relation to the completeness of these data and the accuracy of the reported data. Sustainability data and ratings providers often rely on estimates to fill these gaps. However, the assumptions that they make may create a misleading impression about the actual performance of individual companies and entities, and the way they process data may limit users' ability to track or to understand changes in performance over time.
2. Sustainability ratings and scores are widely used in investment decision-making, and in the design of investment products. As a consequence of the wide range of rating and scoring practices, the scores and ratings from different providers tend not to be consistent with each other and are often not consistently linked to the performance outcomes (e.g. financial risk, investment performance, impact management) that the scores and ratings are trying to measure.
3. Investors using sustainability ratings and data should

- Understand how the ratings and scores have been constructed. Specifically, they should understand (a) what factors have been included in the score or rating (and what factors have been excluded) and the reasons for these inclusions and exclusions; (b) what metrics have been used to construct the score or rating; (c) how these metrics have been weighted or combined.
- Understand what the score or rating actually tells the user about the issue of concern. For example, is it measuring processes or performance? Is it measuring financial impact or social or environmental impact? Is it measuring the impacts that are of greatest concern (e.g. for a climate find, are supply chain-related emissions included in the assessment)?
- Understand how investment products have been constructed and how the specific ratings and scores used in the product will shape the outcomes the investment product will deliver.

References

Abramskiehn, D., Wang, D. and Buchner, B. (2015), 'The Landscape of Climate Exposure for Investors (Climate Policy, Initiative)', www.climatepolicyinitiative.org/wp-content/uploads/2015/08/The-Landscape-of-Climate-Exposure-for-Investors_full-report.pdf

Amel-Zadeh, A. and Serafeim, G. (2018), 'Why and How Investors Use ESG Information: Evidence from a Global Survey', *Financial Analysts Journal*, Vol. 74, No. 3, pp. 87–103, https://doi.org/10.2469/faj.v74.n3.2

Berg, F., Fabisik, K. and Sautner, Z. (2021), *Is History Repeating Itself? The (Un)predictable Past of ESG Ratings*. Finance Working Paper No. 708/2020 (European Corporate Governance Institute), www.ecgi.global/sites/default/files/working_papers/documents/bergfabisiksautnerfinal_3.pdf

Berg, F., Kolbel, J. and Rigobon, R. (2022), 'Aggregate Confusion: The Divergence of ESG Ratings', *Review of Finance*, Vol. 26, No. 6, pp. 1315–1344, https://doi.org/10.1093/rof/rfac033

BNP Paribas (2023), *ESG Global Survey 2023: Data and Reporting* (BNP Paribas, Paris), https://securities.cib.bnpparibas/app/uploads/sites/3/2023/09/esg-global-survey-report1-data-challenge-vf.pdf

Boffo, R. and Patalano, R. (2020), *ESG Investing: Practices, Progress and Challenges* (OECD, Paris), www.oecd.org/finance/ESG-Investing-Practices-Progress-and-Challenges.pdf

Dobrick, J., Klein, C. and Zwergel, B. (2023), 'Size Bias in Refinitiv ESG Data', *Finance Research Letters*, Vol. 55, No. Part B, p. 104014, https://doi.org/10.1016/j.frl.2023.104014

Edmans, A. (2022), 'The End of ESG', *Financial Management*, Vol. 52, No. 1, pp. 3–17, https://doi.org/10.1111/fima.12413

ERM (2023), *Rate the Raters 2023: ESG Ratings at a Crossroads*, www.erm.com/globalassets/sustainability.com/thinking/pdfs/2023/rate-the-raters-report-april-2023.pdf

Future of Sustainable Data Alliance (FoSDA) (2023), 'FoSDA Position Paper on ESG Ratings, Scores and Data Products', https://futureofsustainabledata.com/wp-content/uploads/2023/10/FOSDA-Position-on-ESG-ratings-and-scores-policy-initiatives.pdf

Governance & Accountability Institute (2024), *Sustainability Reporting in Focus 2024* (Governance & Accountability Institute, New York), www.ga-institute.com/research/research/sustainability-reporting-trends/2024-sustainability-reporting-in-focus/

International Organization of Securities Commissions (IOSCO) (2021), *Environmental, Social and Governance (ESG) Ratings and Data Products Providers*. Final Report (IOSCO), www.iosco.org/library/pubdocs/pdf/IOSCOPD690.pdf

IRIS Carbon (2023, January 23), 'A Beginner's Guide to ESG Rating Agencies and Methodologies', www.iriscarbon.com/a-beginners-guide-to-esg-rating-agencies-and-methodologies/

Jonsdottir, B., Sigurjonsson, T., Johannsdottir, L. and Wendt, S. (2022), 'Barriers to Using ESG Data for Investment Decisions', *Sustainability*, Vol. 14, No. 9, p. 5157, https://doi.org/10.3390/su14095157

Larcker, D., Tayan, B., Pomorski, L. and Watts, E. (2022), *ESG Ratings: A Compass without Direction* (The Hoover Institution, Stanford University), www.hoover.org/sites/default/files/research/docs/cgri-closer-look-97-esg-ratings_0.pdf

London Stock Exchange Group (LSEG) (2024), *Sustainability Reporting Guide* (LSEG, London), www.londonstockexchange.com/raise-finance/sustainable-finance/your-guide-sustainability-reporting

Mazzacurati, J. (2021), *ESG Ratings: Status and Key Issues Ahead* (ESMA (European Securities and Markets Authority), Paris), www.esma.europa.eu/sites/default/files/trv_2021_1-esg_ratings_status_and_key_issues_ahead.pdf

Sullivan, R. (2011), *Valuing Corporate Responsibility: How Do Investors Really Use Corporate Responsibility Information?* (Greenleaf Publishing, Sheffield).

Chapter 13

Assessing the Effectiveness of Sustainable Investment in the Global South

Gaps, Contestations and Ways Forward

Abi Perriman, Dido Gompertz and Jisoo You

Introduction

Sustainable investment is at the forefront of efforts to address global sustainability challenges, particularly in the Global South, where financial needs for development are acute. As climate change accelerates amid demand for equitable economic growth in varied and complex settings, sustainable investment is often seen as a key mechanism to bridge critical financing gaps.

While sustainable investment has gained significant traction, its effectiveness in meeting the specific and diverse needs of the Global South remains contested.

DOI: 10.4324/9781003467632-13

This chapter critically examines this issue, offering practical insights into the debates, challenges and opportunities that shape its impact. It aims to ensure that industry professionals are:

1. Aware of the issues and understand core debates, contradictions and limitations in sustainable investment as it pertains to investment in the Global South.
2. Attuned to complexity and able to recognise the governance, transparency, capacity and other issues that influence the success of sustainable investment.
3. Equipped for action and able to apply these insights in their investment processes to drive more effective, just and context-sensitive financial flows.

The chapter begins by introducing and interrogating the notion of the 'Global South', a term that both unites marginalised countries under a common framework but that also risks oversimplification. We explore how development needs are defined, who holds the power to shape these narratives and the implications of these definitions for financing priorities. Understanding how needs are framed is crucial for aligning investments with genuine development priorities rather than external agendas.

We then move to assessing whether sustainable investment is effectively addressing the needs of the Global South. We examine not only the volume and quality of finance needed, but also the importance of governance systems, risk environments and institutional capacity of the Global South that are the keys to effective investment. In addition, we explore how factors such as high debt burdens, elevated risk premiums and equity concerns affect investment outcomes.

Finally, we offer policy and practice recommendations for enhancing the effectiveness of sustainable investment in the Global South. We discuss potential ways to reform financial governance, to rethink investment strategies and to decolonise sustainable investment to ensure it serves the interests of the communities it aims to support.

By engaging with these discussions, we hope that practitioners will gain a nuanced understanding of sustainable investment in the Global South and of how investment can support sustainable development without reinforcing existing inequalities. The aim is to enable practitioners to transcend traditional sustainability approaches and adopt investment strategies that are more context-sensitive and justice-oriented, thereby genuinely reflecting the priorities of the Global South.

The Needs of the Global South

Defining the 'Global South'

The 'Global South' is commonly used to describe countries – typically in Africa, Asia, Latin America and Oceania – that are less prosperous than their wealthier industrialised counterparts (Atapattu and Gonzalez, 2015). With the gradual abandonment of the term 'Third World' (and its 'pejorative connotations of otherness and backwardness'), the 'Global South' has been adopted as a useful term that broadly describes regions outside of Europe and North America (Randall, 2004: 41; Patrick and Huggins, 2023). The term has gained traction since the 1970s, serving as an umbrella term that encompasses countries that are politically or economically marginalised in different continents (Atapattu and Gonzalez, 2015). However, in the absence of an agreed definition, the 'Global South' has, in practice, been used as a catch-all term that lumps emerging economies, developing countries and the least developed countries (LDCs) together (see Box 13.1).

Box 13.1 Key Terms in Global Development

While the following terms do not have a single agreed-upon definition, they are commonly used in the global development landscape and financial world.

- 'Emerging economies', often referred to as emerging markets, are characterised by several attributes, such as sustained market access, increasing integration into the global market and rapid economic growth with strong potential for market investment (Duttagupta and Pazarbasioglu, 2021).
- 'Developing countries' are considered as countries with relatively lower development indicators in comparison to those classified as developed countries or advanced economies. Although widely used in political discourse, the term is controversial due to the dichotomous division between 'developed' and 'developing' and the dynamic nature of development (Farias, 2024).
- 'Least developed countries (LDCs)' are defined as 'low-income countries confronting severe structural impediments to sustainable development' that are extremely vulnerable to economic and environmental crisis by the United Nations (UN) (2005). Forty-four countries are currently classified as LDCs, but the list of LDCs is subject to change and is reassessed every three years by the Committee for Development (United Nations (UN), 2005).

The term 'Global South' dates to 1969 when Carl Oglesby described the Vietnamese War as a culmination of US 'dominance over the Global South' (Di Nicola, 2020: 21). It was after the 1980s that the term gained popularity, especially after the Brandt report separated the developing Global South from the developed Global North by drawing a line around a latitude of 30 degrees in the Northern Hemisphere. Since then, this simplified demarcation line has been regarded as an effective tool for visualising a geographical division between the rich North and the poor South (Lees, 2020).

The 'Global South' is not merely an indicator of political or economic development. The countries that form the Global South have been shaped by multiple layers of histories of colonialism, imperialism and neo-colonial practices (Lopez and Quintana-Vallejo, 2024). These countries share a colonial history that is closely linked to structured exploitation by powerful and wealthy nations, sustained poverty and lack of industrialisation (Gordon, 2019; Hogan and Patrick, 2024). As such, the term Global South can be used as a broad metaphor for poverty, oppression and suffering, which encourages and advances an understanding of knowledge rooted in the experiences of the Global South (Levander and Mignolo, 2011: 9).

While the term 'Global South' is often criticised for perpetuating unwarranted generalisations and not capturing the nuances of each nation, many countries have adopted the term as a useful framework for describing collective action promoting 'South-South' collaboration. For example, the Group of 77 (G77), consisting of postcolonial and developing countries, represents the Global South under the objective of 'providing the means for the countries to articulate and promote their collective economic interests and enhance their joint negotiating capacity on all major international economic issues within the UN system and promote South-South cooperation for development' (Group of 77 (G77), 2005). The G77 is one of the largest coalitions in contemporary international negotiations, with 134 member countries comprising two-thirds of the entire UN membership (G77, 2005). This alliance under the name of 'Global South' has amplified the voice and representation of coalition countries in global politics, overcoming the structural disadvantages of a lack of negotiation resources (Vihma *et al.*, 2011).

The G77 is not, however, a uniform entity but is better understood as a constellation of a wide range of developing countries, including emerging powers, the LDCs and the alliance of small island states (AOSIS), all of which have different interests and needs (Kasa *et al.*, 2008). Some of these countries – for example, Brazil, South Africa, India and China – have made significant progress in reducing extreme poverty and establishing industrial foundations to facilitate economic growth (Hallding *et al.*, 2011). In contrast, others continue to need significant financial resources to deliver basic needs such as food, water, shelter, health, education and transportation (Hallding *et al.*, 2011; Wale-Oshinowo *et al.*, 2022). As another example of the differences in needs and interests, within the LDCs, small island developing states (SIDS) have consistently called for immediate action to address mitigation and adaptation to climate change, given that these countries are faced by existential threats resulting from rising sea levels and frequent weather events (Schwebel, 2018).

In summary, classifying countries into a single group of 'South' has the potential to oversimplify the diverse contexts of each country, and thus, hinder the identification of their challenges, such as poverty, unemployment, corruption, conflict and climate vulnerability. Capturing the specific needs and opportunities of the Global South countries is crucial to addressing their challenges with tailored developmental solutions. That is, while the term 'Global South' has helped to create a cohesive alliance of marginalised countries, these countries cannot and should not be seen as a monolithic or homogenous entity.

Defining the Needs of the Global South

Global Goals and National and Local Priorities: How Development Needs are Determined

As the 'Global South' consists of a variety of developing countries under unique circumstances and contexts, the needs and priorities of these countries also vary significantly. Economic conditions, social structures, political systems, geographic features and historical legacies all shape the development challenges faced by different nations. Despite this diversity, intergovernmental bodies and international organisations have often sought to define development needs and development objectives that can be applied to all countries.

Perhaps the most significant are the Sustainable Development Goals (SDGs), which set universal targets to guide development efforts (see Box 13.2). Established by the UN in 2015, the SDGs are the result of an extensive consensus-building process involving governments, international institutions and civil society actors. This approach has led to widespread alignment of international and national policies with the 17 goals (United Nations (UN), 2024). However, the SDGs have been criticised for not fully capturing the specific and evolving needs of developing countries. For example, contradictions among the three pillars of sustainable development (i.e. economic growth, social inclusion and environmental protection) can lead to trade-offs, with financial actors prioritising certain goals over others based on their own criteria and standards (Hickel, 2019; Spangenberg, 2016). Given that domestic public financing is often insufficient, this raises fundamental questions about whether and how private finance and private investment prioritise competing needs.

Box 13.2 The Sustainable Development Goals (SDGs)

In 2015, all United Nations Member States adopted the 2030 Agenda for Sustainable Development, which includes 17 Sustainable Development Goals (SDGs) and 169 targets. While recognising the eradication of all forms of poverty as the greatest global challenge that has to be addressed for sustainable development, the SDGs seek to balance economic, social and environmental development (UN General Assembly, 2015). Despite their roles as a global framework for tackling urgent economic, social and environmental challenges across different geographies and disciplines, the SDGs have been criticised for their universal template founded on the ideology of the Global North (see, for example, Arora-Jonsson (2023)). For instance, their ambiguous language obscures the fundamental tension between poverty alleviation, environmental sustainability and economic growth, presuming that sustainable development can be achieved by prioritising economic growth (Arora-Jonsson, 2023).

In contrast to the SDGs, Nationally Determined Contributions (NDCs) under the Paris Agreement on Climate Change follow a bottom-up approach, where each country is allowed to define its own climate targets and strategies within an international framework. Unlike the SDGs, NDCs can reflect country-specific priorities and can take into account the varied capacities, vulnerabilities and policy landscapes of individual countries. This approach provides greater national ownership and flexibility and allows governments to set targets that align with their development realities. However, while NDCs may be more responsive to national priorities, they also depend heavily on the ambition and political will of individual governments. The lack of binding commitments and variability in implementation capacity can lead to fragmentation, with some countries setting weaker targets due to financial or political constraints.

Both the top-down approach of the SDGs and the more bottom-up approach of NDCs have strengths and weaknesses in defining and addressing the needs of the Global South. The SDGs provide a common vision and facilitate coordinated action but may overlook context-specific challenges. NDCs, by contrast, allow countries to articulate their own priorities but may result in uneven ambition and limited accountability.

The Influence of Global and Local Actors in Defining Development Needs

Who defines the needs of the Global South influences what needs are prioritised. The consequence is that priorities (and, in turn, capital flows) are strongly influenced by the interests of those with power and influence. In the international arena, bilateral and multilateral financial institutions have significant influence in defining the needs of the Global South. These institutions act as leaders in promoting sustainable development and channel considerable funding to developing countries. Multilateral development banks (MDBs), for example, play a critical role in setting agendas, norms and practices of sustainable finance within the international finance and investment regime (Mendez and Houghton, 2020). The World Bank and the International Monetary Fund (IMF) provide loans with conditionality clauses; these clauses often stipulate that borrowing countries must privatise public sectors, liberalise trade and deregulate their labour markets (Rogerson, 2016). These measures may foster economic growth and improved governance, but they may also exacerbate inequalities and result in uneven development (Konadu-Agyemang, 2004).

The flow of bilateral aid or official development assistance also shapes the needs of the Global South (OECD, 2025), with more powerful nations driving agendas of global influence. For example, in 2017, the Trump Administration insisted the United States would withdraw from the Paris Climate Agreement, raising concerns that multilateral climate governance would be weakened and that climate efforts in the Global South would be downsized (Zhang *et al.*, 2017). Even though the Biden Administration rejoined the Paris Agreement in 2020, the executive orders signed by the re-elected Trump Administration in 2025 to withdraw from the World Health Organization and the Paris Agreement, followed by the dismantling of the United States Agency of International Development (USAID), signalled that there would be a substantial reduction in US official development assistance and in US funding for climate-related mitigation and adaptation (Swain *et al.*, 2025). Given that the United States was one of the largest contributors, with an official development assistance totalling US$65 billion in 2023, the decisions made by the Trump Administration may result in significant reductions in aid and a significant scaling back of development initiatives worldwide (Focus 2030, 2025).

Concerns over the scale and dependability of donor funding are leading to growing significance and influence of alternative funders in the Global South. For instance, more than US$180 billion in Chinese loans flowed into Africa, mostly for large-scale infrastructure projects, such as dams, roads, railways and ports (Boston University, 2024). This infrastructural development has the potential to stimulate economic growth and facilitate access to essential services based on mutually beneficial South–South cooperation. However, these loans have been criticised for steering low-income countries into debt traps, exacerbating their indebtedness (Mlambo, 2022). It is also important to acknowledge that, despite the growing influence of Chinese aid (which is generally not reported as official development assistance), relatively little is known about the terms and conditions of this aid (see Box 13.3). A paper by Gelpern *et al.* (2023) analysed 100 contracts between Chinese state-owned entities and government borrowers in 24 developing countries in Africa, Asia, Eastern Europe, Latin America and

Oceania. They noted that these Chinese contracts contain strong confidentiality clauses that bar borrowers from revealing the terms or even the existence of the debt, that Chinese lenders seek advantage over other creditors and that cancellation, acceleration and stabilisation clauses in Chinese contracts potentially allow these lenders to influence debtors' domestic and foreign policies.

Box 13.3 China in AfricaSino-Africa Optimists vs Pessimists

Narratives on China in Africa have, in very broad terms, been dominated by two opposing perspectives. The Sino-Africa Optimists treat China as an exceptional development partner and financier given its recent development experience and South–South solidarity (Cheru and Oqubay, 2019; Doi, 2024). According to these optimists, Chinese capital brings knowledge and development expertise, increases the policy space and is underpinned by a cooperative relationship between China and African states.

In contrast, the Sino-Africa Pessimists present a narrative of China as the new coloniser, pursuing its own self-interest in capitalist expansion whilst driving African nations into unsustainable debt and creating unhealthy dependencies due to a misalignment between Africa's development needs and the nature of Chinese capital (Carmody and Wainwright, 2022).

Both these perspectives are limited in that they ignore the nature of the global economy, and they downplay the agency of African countries to define their needs and to develop and implement industrial policies and developmental regulations that ensure that foreign capital has a positive impact on long-term development (Brautigam and Xiaoyang, 2011). In addition, China is not a monolith investor, and many Chinese firms invest in Africa, driven by incentives, support and diplomacy from the Chinese government.

Multilateral and bilateral donors and their economic and political conditionalities have both supported liberalisation and democratisation in Global South countries, but also limited national sovereignty in ways that are detrimental to establishing statehood and true democracy. Thandika Mkandawire, a scholar on African development, has argued that such financial relations lead to 'choiceless democracies' as policies built upon donor pressures narrows down the policy options to address domestic needs and challenges (Mkandawire, 1998). In many African countries, the legacies of authoritarian regimes and the realities of immature democracies deter the type of bottom-up decision-making process essential to democracy. These counties frequently rely on a few technocrats who often have closer relationships with international financial institutions than with domestic constituencies (Mkandawire, 1998).

A further issue is that economic and political elites often define domestic and local needs by responding to specific pressures from influential domestic constituencies (Hoelscher *et al.*, 2023). For example, politicians and entrepreneurs in the Global South can justify policies that enable urban expansion as a response to the priorities of local residents (Hoelscher *et al.*, 2023). Urban expansion can provide benefits such as increased access to adequate, safe and affordable housing, improved basic services and economic revitalisation. However, it may also involve dispossessions and land grabs, it may promote speculation and may concentrating land ownership in the hands of elites who already have access to capital (Gutierrez, 2023).

Finally, the interests of private investors can result in financial resources being allocated to certain sectors and activities and not to others. For instance, as discussed in Chapter 8, private climate finance flows to emerging markets have been concentrated in the energy sector. The OECD (2023) estimates that in the period 2016–2021, US$7 billion of private finance flowed annually into the energy sector, while less than US$1 billion was mobilised for each of transport, investment and forestry, and water supply and sanitation. This uneven allocation of private finance into sectors with the greatest return on investment and least risk (from an investment perspective) limits the availability of capital for other pressing needs, such as improving climate-resilient agricultural practices and ecosystem restoration.

In conclusion, capital flows to the Global South are not only driven by the development needs of these countries or by actors or decision-makers within these countries. In practice, these flows are shaped by the way in which international bodies understand development, by the terms and conditions under which investments are made, by the financial and strategic interests of the organisations making these investments, and by the ability of local stakeholders and communities to have their needs and interests integrated into investment decision-making.

Assessing Finance Flows Against the Needs of the Global South

So far, this chapter has identified that the Global South has a wide range of development needs, and that these needs vary between countries and depending on who is defining the needs, be it international development institutions, bilateral donors, national governments or local elites. Nonetheless, beyond the complexities of defining the specific needs, it is clear that the Global South requires significant investment into sectors such as energy, infrastructure, agriculture, health and education to address the SDGs and to deliver on the climate goals set out in NDCs.

This section explores finance flows against the needs of the Global South by first looking at the scale of investment needed. We then look at the features of that investment to understand whether and under what conditions 'decolonial' approaches to investment (see Box 13.4 and Ghosh *et al.* (2025) for a more detailed review) may be better and to challenge investment practitioners to think more deeply about what sustainable investment could and should mean in the Global South.

Box 13.4 Comparing Neo-Liberal and Decolonial Approaches to Finance

In broad terms, neo-liberal approaches to finance (and public policy more generally) emphasise free markets, deregulation and reduced government involvement in the finance sector. These measures are justified by the contribution they make to economic growth, efficiency and the establishment of effective market-based solutions. Neoliberal approaches have been criticised for contributing to increased inequality, financial instability and the erosion of social safety nets.

In contrast, decolonial approaches to finance aim to address the ongoing effects of colonialism on financial systems and policies, particularly in the Global South. This generally involves challenging existing structures and power dynamics within international financial institutions, advocating for greater autonomy and equitable distribution of resources and promoting equitable, democratic and inclusive financial systems.

Climate and development finance have been criticised because they are predominantly controlled by the Global North, because they have not raised sufficient funds to meet the needs of the Global South, and because funds have not been distributed to those in the greatest need. Calls to decolonise climate and development finance aim to properly integrate the Global South (including indigenous peoples and marginalised communities) in decision-making around matters such as provide this finance, how is this finance distributed, who accesses or receives this finance and what projects and initiatives are financed.

Scale: Does the Amount of Capital Meet the Needs of the Global South?

The Finance Gap

Achieving global sustainability goals requires vast financial resources. Estimating financial needs is complicated by the inconsistency in methodologies, variations in economic assumptions and the volatility of global markets (Schmidt-Traub, 2015). The unique developmental contexts and priorities of different countries further exacerbate the challenge of aligning financial estimates with actual needs, making accurate financing predictions difficult (Schmidt-Traub, 2025).

Notwithstanding these issues, it is widely agreed the scale of global funding required for sustainable development far exceeds current investments (Schoenmaker and Schramade, 2019). For example, current global investments in sustainable projects fall well below the US$5–7 trillion annually estimated to be required to achieve the SDGs by 2030 (Schoenmaker and Schramade, 2019; United Nations Conference on Trade and Development (UNCTAD), 2022).

Furthermore, the investments that are being made are highly sensitive to economic fluctuations and geopolitical events. For example, United Nations Conference on Trade and Development (UNCTAD) (2024) reported that, in 2023, global foreign direct investment dropped for a second consecutive year, decreasing by 2% to US$1.3 trillion. The decline was more severe in developing countries, where investment fell by 7%, with the declines particularly affecting agrifood systems, water and sanitation (UNCTAD, 2024). On the other hand, demand for investment is likely to increase as climate change accelerates and intensifies the economic impact of natural disasters, resource shortages and forced migration. The UN Environment Programme (UNEP) estimates that annual adaptation financing needs were US$187–359 billion in 2023, yet finance flows to developing countries for adaptation were just US$28 billion, i.e. about one-tenth of what is required (UN Environment Programme (UNEP), 2024). Most of the adaptation finance is almost entirely public, the private sector preferring to invest in mitigation, in particular in energy and transport (Climate Policy Initiative (CPI), 2024).

Financing Critical Sectors for Development

Development finance encompasses a broad range of objectives, including economic growth, social development and environmental sustainability (Mawdsley, 2018). Energy, infrastructure, food, healthcare and education are widely seen as critical for achieving these objectives for sustainable development. While finance has begun addressing these sectors, there remain significant gaps in scale and targeting, and sectors and regions receive uneven attention.

Sustainable energy projects are driven by both environmental and economic incentives, and the falling costs of renewable technologies (International Renewable Energy Agency (IRENA), 2024) have made energy a prime target for sustainable finance. It is argued that, with support, developing countries can 'leapfrog' the energy ladder climbed by historical emitters and transition to directly to clean energy sources, bypassing the need to invest in new coal, oil or gas due to modern technology; this has been seen to some extent in China and India, where adopting new, more efficient technologies has helped electricity consumption take hold (Elias and Victor, 2005).

Investments in renewable energy projects, particularly solar and wind, have grown substantially as part of the global push towards decarbonisation. For example, foreign investment in clean energy is accelerating sustainability in Africa, notably through global greenfield megaprojects, the largest in 2023 being a green hydrogen project in Mauritania, expected to attract US$34 billion (UNCTAD, 2024). In total, over US$10 billion was invested in African wind and solar projects in 2023, with major initiatives in Egypt, South Africa and Zimbabwe.

To reach urban communities, grid expansion provides stable power supply to those who can be connected to existing infrastructure. For rural communities, who comprise 80% of those without electrification, decentralised solutions such as Kenya's M-KOPA off-grid solar systems are an important complement to centralised power generation facilities (Alstone *et al.*, 2015). The IEA has estimated that, in 2022, solar home systems and small-scale solar lighting provided electricity access to 2.5 million more households (International Energy Agency (IEA), 2023a), and The World Bank reported that off-grid solar solutions served around 490 million people in 2022, targeting hard-to-reach and previously unconnected areas (World Health Organisation, 2023). Despite the progress, a lack of affordable financing has held back the growth of solar power in Africa (Rangelova, 2024). There are various reasons, including relatively high upfront costs and private investors' preference for large projects (e.g. wind farms, hydropower) over distributed, modular sources such as rooftop solar or biogas (IEA, 2023b).

While infrastructure also attracts considerable funding, particularly in urban areas, this funding is often unevenly distributed. The rapid urbanisation of recent decades – over 50% of the world's population now live in cities, with this proportion expected to increase to 70% by 2050 (World Bank Group, 2025) – means that investment in urban infrastructure is crucial to meet the rising need for housing, transport systems and other services and to manage urban sprawl. However, the adoption of effective solutions can be hampered by gaps in financing and capacity. For example, Kenya's government-led Affordable Housing Finance Project, supported by World Bank financing, aimed to increase housing stock by 250,000 per year from 2018 to 2022 alongside financial incentives, including tenant purchasing schemes (World Bank Group, 2023). The project was criticised for inadequate financing and delayed timelines, meaning less than 10% of the target housing stock was delivered by 2022 (Kenya Institute for Public Policy Research and Analysis 2024). The need for infrastructure investment is not confined to urban areas. While an estimated 80% of the world's poor live in rural areas, rural infrastructure projects, particularly those focused on transport, water and sanitation, are often overlooked, leading to persistent gaps in underserved regions (Global Commission on the Economy and Climate, 2016).

Despite its critical role in food security and livelihoods, especially in the Global South, agriculture also receives less attention and less funding than energy or infrastructure. Food provision is highly exposed to economic shocks, conflicts and climate impacts, and global hunger and food insecurity rose in 2020 and 2021, respectively, with 828 million people impacted (Food and Agriculture Organization (FAO), 2022). At the same time, there are notable ongoing projects in this sector (e.g. agroecology initiatives in Latin America (Altieri and Nicholls, 2017), initiatives to improve agricultural workers' rights (Raynolds, 2016), the sector struggles to secure adequate investment. Smallholder farmers and rural communities face particular challenges in this regard (FAO, 2022; Pretty *et al.*, 2018).

Finally, social sectors, in particular education and healthcare, face significant financing gaps. Investments in these areas are crucial for improving cross-generational development outcomes and for catering to growing populations. The World Bank (2018) has highlighted the persistent gaps in access to quality education and healthcare, which are exacerbated by poverty and conflict in many regions. While the case for investment is clear, in practice, these sectors often lose out to sectors that offer clearer and more immediate financial returns.

Beyond Scale: Does the Quality of Finance Flows Meet the Needs of the Global South?

The level of funding available to the Global South is only part of the picture. It is also important to look at the features of that investment. For the purposes of this discussion, we focus on four attributes – governance, financial risk management processes, transparency and accountability and domestic capacity. These attributes (acknowledging that there are others we could also have looked at) allow us to describe how investment actors manage their investments, to describe the implications – positive and negative – for the countries receiving that investment and to discuss how these implications may be managed. In turn, they provide important insights into whether and how investment flows align with local development priorities and address the root causes of underdevelopment and inequality (Kothari, 2006). This analysis also allows us to explore whether financial flows directed towards climate and sustainability-related goals also contribute to job creation, technology transfer and economic diversification, fostering resilient, stable and self-reliant economies (Fletcher, 2021; Sachs, 2015).

Governance

Financial governance structures and mechanisms determine who decides and how decisions are made regarding financial flows to the Global South. The current global financial system provides the inescapable backdrop to today's (sustainable) financial markets. Global power imbalances – which are mirrored in the dynamics of global financial markets – have direct implications for the autonomy of Global South countries. While no single actor can change these power imbalances, an awareness of this context is crucial for sustainable finance professionals seeking to mitigate some of its negative effects and to address the needs of the Global South.

We start by looking at the architecture and governance of international development finance. The international development finance architecture has become increasingly decentralised – large public financing gaps have led to increased reliance on non-state actors and donors such as China and Brazil have become increasingly important – which has led the sustainable finance ecosystem to become more decentralised and more diversified.

Climate finance architecture – which has been described as polycentric, multi-scalar and dispersed (Bracking and Leffel, 2021) – illustrates this shift. Various types of funding institutions exist and are organised around international institutions such as the United Nations Framework Convention on Climate Change (UNFCCC) and the Convention on Biological Diversity (CBD). The organisations involved in (or proximate to) these institutions include development finance institutions (DFIs), climate-specific funds, green bond issuers and private transnational standard-setters. In addition, networked transnational non-state actors, such as environmental and business non-governmental organisations (NGOs), are playing a growing role in addressing environmental governance gaps (Nasiritousi *et al.*, 2016).

Although it has not always been the case, many climate finance institutions are now aligned with neoliberal governance norms, emphasising voluntary disclosure, self-labelling and reporting standards as key elements of the policy response (Bracking and Leffel, 2021). This shift has enabled the climate finance system to engage a broad set of sub- and non-state actors more directly, enhancing its scalability and efficiency. At the same time, it has shifted significant decision-making power to market actors such as international brands and financial fund managers, diminishing transparency and accountability in the governance of environmental standards and financial products.

There are different perspectives on the appropriate balance between market- and state-centred governance of national and international financial markets. While a core argument in favour of neoliberal approaches to 'green finance' (e.g. the greater involvement of the private sector, the use of market-based mechanisms that internalise environmental costs) is that these approaches are more likely to get political support than alternative approaches (Jager and Schmidt, 2020), neoliberal approaches have been criticised for prioritising profit over environmental or social outcomes, for relying on voluntary standards that show limited evidence of achieving substantial environmental benefits and for avoiding stricter government regulations that could negatively impact market profits. At the other end of the spectrum, the advocates of 'progressive green finance' (e.g. the Degrowth movement) (Hickel, 2019), Global South-led post-development movements (Escobar, 2015) challenge the compatibility of capitalist principles with environmental sustainability. They argue for a radical rethinking of both national and international financial regulation, with strict controls on cross-border financial flows and governance systems driven by democratic decision-making (Hickel and Kallis, 2020). Somewhere in the middle, agencies such as UNCTAD have advocated for a more prominent role for domestic public finance, increased state intervention, stricter regulation and the greater involvement of central banks and public DFIs in the governance of green finance.

Another important aspect of governance relates to the structure and operation of the policy space and the power dynamics within this space. When external forces have excessive influence over policy decisions, citizens as voters (and democratic processes more generally) are overshadowed, and the long-term effectiveness of government is compromised (Peinhardt *et al.*, 2019).

The distribution of capital for sustainable development occurs within a historical context marked by inequality and exploitation (Ciplet, 2015). Global South countries face significant power imbalances that affect their influence over investment decisions, affecting state sovereignty and self-governance objectives. The structure of the policy space, therefore, has a critical influence on the extent to which countries in the Global South can overcome dependency and pursue development on their own terms (Ciplet, 2015).

However, the degree of influence (or control) over the policy space available to Global South governments varies depending on the type of finance actors and mechanisms at play. For example, major ESG indices, dominated by private firms in the Global North, have significant sway over the criteria for sustainable investment by determining ratings, shareholder engagement and, ultimately, capital allocation (Fichtner *et al.*, 2024). As these indices have been developed by firms in the Global North, they may not reflect local realities in the Global South; the consequence is that they may marginalise local knowledge and development priorities, effectively sidelining local communities in decision-making processes. These indices have been criticised because they do not properly account for the potential impact mechanisms (Fichtner *et al.*, 2024), increasing the risk that projects will be ineffective or fail to address the specific social and environmental needs of the region. Another example relates to MDBs. MDBs often impose conditions when providing development finance to Global South countries. While these conditionalities form part of the MDBs' risk management processes, they also limit the ability of developing nations to influence the policy space. For example, requirements to privatise certain state services could require governments to prioritise foreign capital interests over their national development goals (Fukuyama, 2004; Kohli, 2004), in turn potentially compromising the state's role in development and weakening the policy autonomy necessary for self-governance. Box 13.5 discusses the specific case of the Green Climate Fund (GCF).

Box 13.5 The Limits of the Green Climate Fund's Transformative Agenda

The Green Climate Fund (GCF) was created to promote country ownership and representation, thereby addressing power imbalances in climate finance. However, its transformative agenda faces significant limitations due to its foundation in neoliberal principles, which prioritise private sector engagement, market-based mechanisms and low-carbon development pathways, without challenging the market-oriented system driven by production and consumption that reinforces patterns of environmental degradation.

Despite rhetoric about 'transformational potential', the GCF primarily selects investments based on economic efficiency, technology and market mechanisms (Kuhl *et al.*, 2024). Bracking (2015) also argues that its institutional design fails to deliver the paradigm shift it promises, focusing more on replicating and scaling up established project models rather than catalysing transformative system change.

In addition, the GCF's emphasis on private sector mobilisation often conflicts with its goals of country ownership and transparency (Kalinowski, 2024). This tension can undermine civil society participation and limit the empowerment of recipient countries. Furthermore, Garschagen and Doshi (2022) point out that the GCF has not yet succeeded in ensuring equitable access to project funding for many of the countries that are most vulnerable to climate change – particularly Least Developed Countries (LDCs) in Africa and conflict-affected states. Most of these countries still struggle to access funding independently through their national entities, while depending heavily on other international entities that are accredited by the Fund to draw on GCF resources.

In summary, while the GCF aims for transformation, its neoliberal framework and focus on market-based solutions have hindered its ability to enact real change, limiting its effectiveness in addressing climate vulnerability. This case of the GCF illustrates how even when financial institutions aim to address historic power imbalances, the dominant hegemony and global hierarchy still shape the degree to which this is feasible.

Market Mechanisms

The shift in development and climate finance from traditional concessional loans and grants to more market-based mechanisms, often referred to as the 'New Washington Consensus', has reshaped how finance is provided to the Global South. Under this model, public financial institutions have become increasingly market-oriented, with the World Bank promoting the role of public banks in socialising financial risks to support private finance (Bracking and Leffel, 2021).

The type of capital used for development and climate finance – whether grants, concessional loans or market-rate loans – has profound implications for the economic sustainability of Global South countries. While Africa, for instance, must attract private investment to drive climate-friendly growth, the region's deteriorating sovereign debt situation has created significant barriers to investment. By 2021, African countries were dedicating 14% of their income from exports, remittances and services to servicing external debt, highlighting the challenge of balancing financial needs with existing debt burdens (McKinsey Sustainability, 2023). Relying solely on sovereign borrowing for climate investments can increase debt levels, potentially reducing the future willingness of international investors to engage in these markets (Arezki, 2022).

Different sources of finance have different impacts on the sustainability and financial stability of developing nations. While MDBs offer concessional finance in the form of loans and grants, even low-interest loans contribute to increasing debt levels, which many vulnerable countries cannot afford. The use of loans by MDBs is controversial from a justice perspective, as developing countries, despite being the least responsible for global environmental degradation, are often required to bear the financial burden of addressing it (Lee *et al.*, 2023).

Even the GCF (see Box 13.5), which is mandated to mobilise and deliver climate finance to countries lacking other sources of funding, has been criticised for its underinvestment in high-risk, high-need projects, especially those targeting the most vulnerable communities who often face complex and systemic risks. According to some studies, this 'banker's logic' undermines GCF's mission and exacerbates debt unsustainability, with vulnerable nations facing pressure to take on more debt to fund essential climate projects (Cholibois, 2020).

Loan and equity-based climate finance often exacerbate the existing debt burdens of countries in the Global South, potentially destabilising their financial markets and reinforcing economic dependency (Kalinowski, 2024). China's development banks, which often offer loans at higher rates than institutions like the World Bank, have been criticised for contributing to unsustainable debt levels in Africa. While there are advantages to obtaining finance from these banks (approvals are often quicker, and there are often fewer conditions), the involvement of these banks also complicates international efforts to manage debt crises by adding layers of complexity alongside the growing number of private sovereign debt borrowers (Kopinski and Sun, 2014).

It is important to acknowledge that the global development and investment communities do need ways to mitigate sovereign debt crisis risks and to restructure debts when necessary. Initiatives such as the Bridgetown Initiative have highlighted ways in which funders can improve upon the current approach. For example, the initiative calls for debt relief for climate-vulnerable countries and pushes MDBs to offer a more balanced mix of funding (see, for example, Box 13.6 regarding blended finance) that ensures climate-vulnerable countries can access resources without exacerbating debt situations. Other actors have noted that innovative approaches like debt-for-climate swaps, alongside sovereign debt restructuring and relief, could alleviate some of the debt pressures on developing nations (Arezki, 2022; McKinsey Sustainability, 2023). Without these reforms, financial risks will reinforce, rather than alleviate, the structural inequalities that the Global South faces in responding to climate change, while also needing to pursue other national development priorities.

Box 13.6 Blended Finance: Mobilising Finance for the Global South

Blended finance is 'the use of catalytic capital from public or philanthropic sources to increase private sector investment in sustainable development' (Convergence, 2025). Blended finance has gained significant attention in recent years, given its potential to fill the SDG and climate finance gap, especially as overseas development assistance declines (Christiansen, 2021). By providing a buffer against technology, climate and macroeconomic risks, for example, it can make investments in developing countries more commercially viable. Partnerships between local and foreign investors can provide benefits through the exchange of expertise, networks and knowledge, helping to achieve goals related to development impact and investment returns (Davis *et al.*, 2022).

Despite its promise, blended finance has not yet met expectations in enhancing the scale and speed of capital flows to the Global South. Blended finance remains a small part of the total capital being mobilised; for example, blended finance represents just 0.2% of the US$26 trillion managed for impact globally (Attridge, 2022).

The reality is that blended finance can only tip the balance of risk-adjusted returns, not change the fundamentals such as challenging local investment climates, dysfunctional markets and uncompetitive returns (Attridge, 2022). As such, its value will ultimately depend on the development stage of the country and sector.

Moreover, critics argue that blended finance often serves to de-risk investments for Global North capital without challenging the broader structures of financial power (Gabor, 2021), potentially socialising risks while privatising rewards. Others point out that green finance mechanisms, like municipal green bonds, can deepen existing inequalities by shifting financial and environmental risks onto poorer, racialised communities (Bigger and Millington, 2020).

Another issue that needs to be considered when looking at market mechanisms is that developing countries often face high interest rates due to the higher risk premiums associated with investing. Several challenges drive these higher risk-adjusted premiums. There are real additional risks that are built into rate calculations, such as those associated with macroeconomic policy, currency stability, unclear legal mechanisms and complex administrative procedures. In addition, Global North investors are often reluctant to invest in the Global South, recognising political instability or unstable market conditions as risks deterring investment or as risks that they need to be compensated for.

Transparency and Accountability

Standards and certifications provide structured frameworks for accountability, impact assessment and financial integrity. For example, the voluntary Green Bond Principles (GBP), managed by the International Capital Market Association (ICMA), provide guidelines for the issuance of bonds specifically intended to finance environmentally sustainable projects (International Capital Market Association (ICMA), 2021). In addition, the International Sustainability Standards Board (ISSB) provides guidelines to help companies report sustainability-related information that could significantly impact a company's financial performance or investors' decisions, notably through its IFRS S1 (General Requirements for Disclosure of Sustainability-related Financial Information) and IFRS S2 (Climate-related Disclosures) standards. IFRS S1 lays out the overarching requirements for companies to report on all financially material sustainability-related risks and opportunities, while IFRS S2 focuses on climate-related disclosures, encompassing both physical and transition risks, as well as opportunities. The development of these global sustainability standards is a crucial step towards harmonising disclosure practices and ensuring the comparability and reliability of sustainability information for investors (Zaid and Issa, 2023). If widely adopted, such standards could reduce the risk of fragmentation and ensure information and reporting are globally comparable (Zhan and Santos-Paulino, 2021).

It has been argued that the use of standards and certifications can help ensure that financial flows align with the needs of recipient economies, particularly in the Global South (Zhan and Santos-Paulino, 2021). The logic is that clearly defined accountability mechanisms ensure that investments contribute to genuine, measurable progress towards the SDGs; some authors have argued that a lack of clear and rigorous accountability mechanisms has been a core reason for shortcomings in development finance (McIntyre and Nanwani, 2019). It has also been argued that such alignment mechanisms help ensure that investments lead to positive outcomes (Wiegant *et al.*, 2024). Without these mechanisms, the allocation of funds becomes opaque, making it difficult to track their effectiveness, mitigate risks such as greenwashing and compare financial initiatives across different contexts.

While the arguments for standards and certifications are clear, it is important to acknowledge that they suffer from many of the same limitations that have been identified through this chapter: they are often developed by actors and institutions in the Global North, and they – because they are often interpreted as rules rather than guidance – may not allow for local conditions and considerations to be taken into account, perpetuating a top-down approach where the Global South is seen merely as a recipient of Northern expertise and capital (Stiglitz, 2002).

There is an interesting paradox at the heart of discussions around transparency and accountability (and the role of standards and certifications in these discussions). In the climate finance space, recipient countries are expected to adopt international measurement, reporting and verification frameworks to promote the appropriate allocation and utilisation of climate finance. At the same time, donor country reporting on climate finance is notoriously opaque, making it hard to ascertain the extent to which these countries are meeting their own climate commitments. To illustrate, in 2014, the OECD and Climate Policy Initiative reported US$62 billion in new or additional climate funding, while India argued that the correct number was just US$2.2 billion, as much of what was counted would have been provided for development anyway (Garschegan and Doshi, 2022).

Capacity and Inter- and Intra-State Inequalities

Capacity development and technology transfer are longstanding demands of the Global South in international finance and climate negotiations (Pauw *et al.*, 2019). The proliferation of sustainable finance instruments – including green bonds, blended finance and debt-for-climate swaps – has created an increasingly complex system that means that Global South countries require deep technical expertise to engage effectively with this system (Bracking and Leffel, 2021). Countries with strong public financial management systems are better positioned to benefit, while others struggle with bureaucratic bottlenecks and administrative burdens (Public Expenditure and Financial Accountability (PEFA), 2020).

Despite commitments from global finance actors, both public and private, to enhance capacity, inequalities in financial and governance capacity exist both between Global South countries and within them, shaping the accessibility and effectiveness of sustainable finance (Piketty, 2014). These disparities raise critical justice considerations, in particular in ensuring that the economically marginalised are not excluded from decisions that affect their lives (Cattaneo, 2022).

There are different issues at play when we look at capacity. Many donor-led capacity building programmes have been criticised for failing to deliver real, sustained institutional strengthening due to misalignment with local contexts, short-term project cycles and a lack of sustained engagement (Khan *et al.*, 2021; Stender *et al.*, 2020). This is important because countries with lower institutional capacity miss out on access to capital because they struggle to meet administrative and financial requirements; this includes access to instruments like the GCF, which are designed to reach the most vulnerable (Garschagen and Doshi, 2022; Kalinowski, 2024). Finance actors, including MDBs, bilateral donors and private investors, all have important roles to play in helping Global South countries to better navigate complex financial systems and exert greater ownership over their development trajectories. For example, they could fund technical assistance programmes, they could allow project co-investment (and thereby enable 'learning by doing'), and they could provide training and skills development.

The digital divide and the lack of access to modern technology in developing countries remain significant barriers to sustainable development and a low-carbon economy (UNCTAD, 2021). Investment in clean technology is essential to enable the transition to a low-carbon economy, to improve resource efficiency and to reduce pollution (Perez, 2010). Yet intellectual property restrictions and financial gaps prevent Global South countries from accessing clean technology at scale. Increased financial support, including green investment funds, technology transfer subsidies and impact-driven financing, is all crucial to overcoming these barriers and enabling developing countries to adopt clean technologies at the pace and scale required.

Within Global South countries, access to finance is also unevenly distributed. Capacity constraints at the subnational level mean that certain groups – particularly marginalised communities, women and informal sector workers – are often excluded from the benefits of sustainable finance. This has profound implications for equity and development outcomes. Large-scale infrastructure and climate finance projects are often directed towards urban centres or industrial sectors, while rural areas and marginalised communities remain underserved (Mawdsley, 2018). Political and economic elites frequently shape financial priorities, reinforcing existing hierarchies. For example, local actors, including municipalities and civil society groups, often encounter significant barriers in accessing adaptation finance due to complex application processes, lack of technical expertise and limited direct funding mechanisms (Colenbrander *et al.*, 2018). When sustainable finance mechanisms fail to include marginalised groups, the broader potential developmental co-benefits (e.g. job creation, gender inclusion, economic empowerment) are not fully realised (Anantharajah and Setyowati, 2022).

The principle of common but differentiated responsibilities (CBDR) has been widely recognised in climate negotiations. The principle emphasises that, while all countries share responsibility for global challenges, they do so in proportion to their historical contributions and capacities. Some have argued that this principle should be applied not only between nations but also within them. In this context, national policies are critical for addressing intra-state inequalities by ensuring that financial flows reach marginalised communities, local governments and small enterprises, rather than being concentrated among economic elites. International financial intermediaries can contribute to addressing these inequalities by providing direct access to finance, by providing technical support and advice and by creating incentives for state and citizen collaboration (Colenbrander *et al.*, 2018). They can also intentionally factor in the inclusion of vulnerable and marginalised groups, while integrating social outcomes into the design of finance mechanisms (Anantharajah and Setyowati, 2022). There is evidence of this happening (see, for example, Box 13.7). There has been significant progress on gender mainstreaming and women's empowerment in sustainable finance, but less progress has been made in other areas of marginalisation, such as conflict and fragile regions (Wong, 2023). Informal economies have proven particularly difficult to reach with sustainable finance, although finance models such as microfinance have been established to reach this significant market in the Global South (Box 13.8).

Box 13.7 Case-study: Green and Sustainable Bonds

Green and SDG bonds are designed to finance projects that deliver social and environmental benefits, with the wider aims of aligning financial returns with the SDGs and of fostering markets for sustainable finance. These bonds function as fixed-income debt instruments, similar to traditional bonds, but with the added purpose of supporting environmentally and socially responsible initiatives.

Despite their positive intentions, green and SDG bonds can inadvertently exacerbate inequality and poverty. Yunita *et al.* (2023) caution that such bonds may obscure conflicts between social, environmental and financial goals, leading to unresolved root causes of inequality. They also suggest that a focus on aligning financial returns with SDGs can result in the deeper structural issues that perpetuate inequality being overlooked. A study by Bigger and Millington (2020) on municipal green bonds issued by the New York Metropolitan Transit Authority and the City of Cape Town highlighted this challenge. They argued that these bonds, which were intended to fund climate change adaptation, often ended up increasing risks for poorer and marginalised communities by focusing on incremental adaptations rather than more transformative solutions that could better promote equity and climate justice.

The transfer of power and decision-making to market actors such as fund managers poses another risk as reduced accountability and transparency lead to a potential widening of inequalities (Bracking and Leffel, 2021). The lack of oversight means that any negative impacts caused by market-driven decisions may go unaddressed.

In conclusion, while green and SDG bonds represent a significant innovation in financing sustainable development, their implementation can sometimes reinforce existing inequalities and limit opportunities for more equitable solutions. Ensuring that these financial instruments contribute to genuine progress towards equity and climate justice requires careful consideration of their broader social impacts and enhanced accountability for market actors involved.

Box 13.8 In Focus: Microfinance

Microfinance and impact investing, particularly when directed at micro, small and medium enterprises (MSMEs), are frequently promoted as strategies for alleviating poverty and stimulating development in the Global South. One of their key benefits is their ability to promote local entrepreneurship, fostering innovation and job creation in sectors such as sustainable agriculture and renewable energy (Jackson, 2013). These instruments – designed to ensure that the poor get access to appropriate, welfare-enhancing financial products – can help to diversify economies and to build resilience against global market fluctuations. Microfinance helped promote financial inclusion by providing access to credit for populations traditionally excluded from formal banking systems and, in turn, enabling small-scale entrepreneurs to grow their businesses (Schoenmaker and Schramade, 2019).

Some researchers have argued that the popular discourse around microfinance benefits has been overblown (Consultative Group to Assist the Poor (CGAP), 2011). While microfinance can have positive impacts, these tend to be modest rather than revolutionary, to work in some populations and not others and do not transform informal markets. There is also evidence that microfinance instruments can do harm, as well as good, to the livelihoods of the poor (van Rooyen *et al.*, 2012). For example, the 2010 Andhra Pradesh microfinance crisis – when aggressive lending practices by microfinance institutions led to widespread over-indebtedness among borrowers, resulting in high levels of default and social unrest – highlighted how unregulated microfinance can result in profit-driven motives overshadowing the well-being of borrowers (Srinivasan, 2011).

Beyond the challenges of measuring and demonstrating outcomes, the underlying theory of change driving the growth of microfinance as a poverty alleviation tool has also been challenged (Karnani, 2007). The concept relies on a market-driven approach (i.e. that supporting the informal economy can get people out of poverty), but concern has been raised that microfinance may undermine other efforts focusing on systemic change to create more jobs and to increase productivity in the formal economy (see, for example, Bateman, 2010; Roy, 2010). In fact, some scholars have argued that inclusion infrastructures such as microfinance are turning precarious populations into sources of capital accumulation under the disguise of empowerment or support, an attempt to 'mine the fortune at the bottom of the pyramid' (Roy, 2010), something that was previously 'ethically off-limits' as a source of profit (Aitken, 2017). They also argue that the celebration of 'inclusion' in financial inclusion depoliticises inclusive infrastructures, ignoring any resistance and ideological struggles taking place at local levels. In fact, given the central role of international actors and the state, some academics have questioned the capacity of inclusion infrastructures to foster equitable outcomes, arguing that it is instead a tool for centralised control and resource extraction (Aitken, 2017; Roy, 2010).

Concluding Comments

Sustainable finance holds great potential to support the Global South in addressing critical development and environmental challenges. However, as this chapter has illustrated, the extent to which it can meet the needs of the Global South is deeply shaped by the governance, structure and priorities of financial actors, meaning that these actors and the decisions they make are crucial. This is clearly a complex area, where the interests of investment providers shape the demands and expectations placed on investment recipients, in a context where there are significant asymmetries of power and of expertise.

Meaningful improvements can be achieved if practitioners (a) are aware of these issues and of how they affect the interactions and behaviours of those involved, both the providers of capital and the recipients, (b) actively engage with complexities around the impacts and implications – positive and negative – of sustainable finance, (c) advocate for more equitable financial mechanisms and instruments and (d) make local agency central to investment decisions.

Such measures could go some way towards addressing the ongoing effects of colonialism on financial systems and policies, particularly in the Global South. As such, they are a partial but not a complete response. A more comprehensive approach to decolonising sustainable finance would require changing existing structures and power dynamics within international financial institutions, ensuring greater autonomy and equitable distribution of resources, and equitable, democratic and inclusive financial systems. This would, of course, require sustained effort, collaboration and a willingness to rethink traditional investment paradigms. However, if successful, it would allow sustainable finance to move beyond being a mechanism for capital allocation to becoming an instrument for global equity, resilience and sustainability.

To realise this potential, practitioners must challenge the assumption that financing renewable energy or climate-aligned infrastructure in the Global South is inherently 'sustainable'. Sustainable finance, in the form we often see it today, is not inherently just, equitable or inclusive. It requires conscious redesign and critical reflection if it is to have those features. Those working in the sustainable finance field should interrogate not only whether investments deliver environmental benefits, but also whether these investments reinforce existing inequalities, marginalise local voices or sideline the social and economic rights of recipient countries and communities. This requires embedding justice considerations throughout financial decision-making. Practitioners should consider who sets the terms of investment, who defines impact, who benefits and who bears the risk. Prioritising social equity within environmental and sustainable finance frameworks means moving beyond risk mitigation and compliance to actively promoting social inclusion, enhancing country ownership and empowering local stakeholders based on an equitable governance structure. This can be propelled by a perspective shift that recognises that finance in the Global South is not simply about mobilising more capital, but about transforming how and for whom finance works. This is essential for projects to serve as a pathway to climate justice rather than veering towards a new form of green extractivism.

Implications for Practitioners

1. Investors (public and private sector) should build their understanding of how their decisions and decision-making processes affect Global South countries.
2. Investors (public and private sector) should adopt context-sensitive investment approaches. Within this they should:
   - Apply frameworks and criteria that ensure that their investments minimise harm and safeguard human rights in contexts lacking stringent standards to uphold international law.
   - Move beyond one-size-fits-all frameworks by tailoring investment strategies to the specific needs of different regions, countries and communities.
   - Engage with local stakeholders, including the private sector, governments, civil society and affected communities, to ensure investments align with actual development priorities.
3. Investors (public and private sector) should work with governments and other stakeholders to improve the quality and governance of sustainable finance. Specifically, they should
   - Strengthen transparency and accountability mechanisms to ensure that financial flows benefit targeted communities.
   - Adopt and promote governance structures that prioritise local decision-making and ownership of sustainable finance initiatives.
   - Support policy measures at national and international levels that increase sustainable finance flows to the Global South.
   - Diversify financial flows to reach critical but underfunded sectors such as agriculture, water infrastructure, education and healthcare.
   - Strengthen financing mechanisms that support small and medium enterprises (SMEs), women-led businesses and informal economies

to foster inclusive economic growth while being cognisant of the risks.

4. Investors, policymakers and other stakeholders should address systemic financial barriers to investment in the Global South. They should:
   - Develop financial mechanisms that reduce high-risk premiums and provide affordable financing options for Global South economies.
   - Design financial mechanisms that are demand-driven to address funding gaps of enterprises and projects in the Global South.
   - Provide access to data and information to contextualise investment decisions.
   - Partner with local financial institutions to mitigate 'perceived' risks and manage real risks.
   - Advocate for international financial institutions to incorporate debt sustainability and risk-sharing mechanisms into their funding models.
   - Use available platforms to challenge and reform existing financial structures that perpetuate historical inequalities and prioritise the interests of the Global North.
   - Initiate and encourage partnerships between Global North and Global South financing institutions that respect local agency.
5. Investors, policymakers and other stakeholders should foster capacity-building and knowledge transfer. They should:
   - Invest in institutional capacity and technical expertise through partnerships and technical assistance within recipient countries to enhance their ability to manage and deploy sustainable finance effectively.
   - Support capacity and technology transfer initiatives that enable the Global South to adopt and scale up sustainable solutions without being dependent on external actors.

References

Aitken, R. (2017), 'All Data is Credit Data: Constituting the Unbanked', *Competition & Change*, Vol. 21, No. 4, pp. 274–300, https://doi.org/10.1177/1024529417712830

Alstone, P., Gershenson, D. and Kammen, D. (2015), 'Decentralized Energy Systems for Clean Electricity Access', *Nature Climate Change*, Vol. 5, No. 4, pp. 305–314, https://doi.org/10.1038/nclimate2512

Altieri, M. and Nicholls, C. (2017), 'The Adaptation and Mitigation Potential of Traditional Agriculture in a Changing Climate', *Climatic Change*, Vol. 140, pp. 33–45, https://doi.org/10.1007/s10584-013-0909-y

Anantharajah, K. and Setyowati, A. (2022), 'Beyond Promises: Realities of Climate Finance Justice and Energy Transitions in Asia and the Pacific', *Energy Research & Social Science*, Vol. 89, p. 102550, https://doi.org/10.1016/j.erss.2022.102550

Arezki, R. (2022), 'Unleashing Climate Investment in Africa', in Schoenmaker, D. and Volz, U. (eds.), *Scaling Up Sustainable Finance and Investment in the Global South* (CEPR Press), pp. 35–44, https://cepr.org/publications/books-and-reports/scaling-sustainable-finance-and-investment-global-south

Arora-Jonsson, S. (2023), 'The Sustainable Development Goals: A Universalist Promise for the Future', *Futures*, Vol. 146, pp. 1–14, https://doi.org/10.1016/j.futures.2022.103087

Atapattu, S. and Gonzalez, C. (2015), 'The North-South Divide in International Environmental Law: Framing the Issues', in Alam, S., Atapattu, S., Gonzalez, C. and Razzaque, J. (eds.), *International Environmental Law and the Global South* (Cambridge University Press), pp. 1–20, www.cambridge.org/core/books/abs/international-environmental-law-and-the-global-south/northsouth-divide-in-international-environmental-law-framing-the-issues/63B93BD7388E5413B7888F56A5F64909

Attridge, S. (2022), 'The Potentials and Limitations of Blended Finance', in Schoenmaker, D. and Volz, U. (eds.), *Scaling Up Sustainable Finance and Investment in the Global South* (CEPR Press), pp. 81–92, https://cepr.org/publications/books-and-reports/scaling-sustainable-finance-and-investment-global-south

Bateman, M. (2010), *Why Doesn't Microfinance Work? The Destructive Rise of Local Neoliberalism* (Bloomsbury Publishing), www.bloomsbury.com/uk/why-doesnt-microfinance-work-9781848133327/

Bigger, P. and Millington, N. (2020), 'Getting Soaked? Climate Crisis, Adaptation Finance, and Racialized Austerity', *Environment and Planning E: Nature and Space*, Vol. 3, No. 3, pp. 601–623, https://doi.org/10.1177/2514848619876539

Boston University (2024), 'Chinese Loans to Africa Database – Data Download', www.bu.edu/gdp/chinese-loans-to-africa-database-data-download/ (last viewed 21 June 2025).

Bracking, S. (2015), 'The Anti-Politics of Climate Finance: The Creation and Performativity of the Green Climate Fund', *Antipode*, Vol. 47, No. 2, pp. 281–302, https://doi.org/10.1080/01436597.2015.1086263

Bracking, S. and Leffel, B. (2021), 'Climate Finance Governance: Fit for Purpose?', *Wiley Interdisciplinary Reviews: Climate Change*, Vol. 12, No. 4, p. 709, https://doi.org/10.1002/wcc.709

Brautigam, D. and Xiaoyang, T. (2011), 'African Shenzhen: China's Special Economic Zones in Africa', *The Journal of Modern African Studies*, Vol. 49, No. 1, pp. 27–54, https://doi.org/10.1017/S0022278X10000649

Carmody, P. and Wainwright, J. (2022), 'Contradictions and Restructuring in the Belt and Road Initiative: Reflections on China's Pause in the 'Go World'', *Third World Quarterly*, Vol. 43, No. 12, pp. 2830–2851, https://doi.org/10.1080/01436597.2022.2110058

Cattaneo, O. (2022, May 19), '7 Sustainable Finance Challenges to Fix Global Inequality', *World Economic Forum*, www.weforum.org/stories/2022/05/sustainable-finance-challenges-global-inequality/

Cheru, F. and Oqubay, A. (2019), 'Catalysing China–Africa Ties for Africa's Structural Transformation: Lessons from Ethiopia', in Oqubay, A. and Lin, J. (eds.), *China-Africa and an Economic Transformation* (Oxford University Press), https://doi.org/10.1093/oso/9780198830504.003.0014

Cholibois, T. (2020), 'Electrifying the "Eighth Continent": Exploring the Role of Climate Finance and Its Impact on Energy Justice and Equality in Madagascar's Planned Energy Transition', *Climatic Change*, Vol. 161, No. 2, pp. 345–364, https://doi.org/10.1007/s10584-019-02644-x

Christiansen, J. (2021), 'Fixing Fictions through Blended Finance: The Entrepreneurial Ensemble and Risk Interpretation in the Blue Economy', *Geoforum*, Vol. 120, pp. 93–102, https://doi.org/10.1016/j.geoforum.2021.01.013

Ciplet, D. (2015), 'Rethinking Cooperation: Inequality and Consent in International Climate Change Politics', *Global Governance*, Vol. 21, pp. 247–274, https://heinonline.org/HOL/LandingPage?handle=hein.journals/glogo21&div=28&id=&page=

Climate Policy Initiative (CPI) (2024), 'Tracking and Mobilizing Private Sector Climate Adaptation Finance (Climate Policy Initiative)', www.climatepolicyinitiative.org/wp-content/uploads/2024/09/Tracking-and-Mobilizing-Private-Sector-Climate-Adaptation-Finance-2024.pdf

Colenbrander, S., Dodman, D. and Mitlin, D. (2018), 'Using Climate Finance to Advance Climate Justice: The Politics and Practice of Channelling Resources to the Local Level', *Climate Policy*, Vol. 18, No. 7, pp. 902–915, https://doi.org/10.1080/14693062.2017.1388212

Consultative Group to Assist the Poor (CGAP) (2011), *CGAP Annual Report. Fiscal Year Ending June 30, 2011*, www.cgap.org/sites/default/files/organizational-documents/CGAP-Annual-Report-Dec-2011.pdf

Convergence (2025), 'Blended Finance', www.convergence.finance/blended-finance (last viewed, 21 June 2025).

Davis, R., Levine, A., Rusconi, R. and Stewart, F. (2022), 'Mobilising Long-Term Finance in the Global South: Lessons from the 'South' and 'North'', in Schoenmaker, D. and Volz, U. (eds.), *Scaling Up Sustainable Finance and Investment in the Global South* (CEPR Press), pp. 21–24, https://cepr.org/publications/books-and-reports/scaling-sustainable-finance-and-investment-global-south

Di Nicola, V. (2020), 'The Global South: An Emergent Epistemology for Social Psychiatry', *World Social Psychiatry*, Vol. 2, No. 1, pp. 20–26, https://doi.org/10.4103/WSP.WSP_1_20

Doi, K. (2024, October 10), 'Forum on China-Africa Cooperation (FOCAC) amid US-China Strategic Competition: The Global South's Agency in Era of Geoeconomics', *Institute of Geoeconomics*, https://instituteofgeoeconomics.org/en/research/2024102201/

Duttagupta, R. and Pazarbasioglu, C. (2021, June), 'Miles to Go: Emerging Market Must Balance Overcoming the Pandemic, Returning to More Normal Policies, and Rebuilding their Economies', *Finance and Development*, pp. 4–9, www.elibrary.imf.org/downloadpdf/view/journals/022/0058/002/article-A002-en.pdf

Elias, R. J., & Victor, D. G. (2005). Energy transitions in developing countries: a review of concepts and literature. Program on Energy and Sustainable Development, Working Paper. Stanford: Stanford University.

Escobar, A. (2015), 'Degrowth, Postdevelopment, and Transitions: A Preliminary Conversation', *Sustainability Science*, Vol. 10, pp. 451–462, https://doi.org/10.1007/s11625-015-0297-5

Farias, D. (2024), 'Unpacking the 'Developing' Country Classification: Origins and Hierarchies', *Review of International Political Economy*, Vol. 31, No. 2, pp. 651–673, https://doi.org/10.1080/09692290.2023.2246975

Fichtner, J., Jaspert, R. and Petry, J. (2024), 'Mind the ESG Capital Allocation Gap: The Role of Index Providers, Standard-Setting, and "Green" Indices for the Creation of Sustainability Impact', *Regulation & Governance*, Vol. 18, No. 2, pp. 479–498, https://doi.org/10.1111/rego.12530

Fletcher, R. (2021), 'Review of Partha Dasgupta. 2021. The Economics of Biodiversity: The Dasgupta Review', *Journal of Political Ecology*, Vol. 28, No. 1, https://doi.org/10.2458/jpe.2289

Focus 2030 (2025, January 16), 'Slight Increase in Official Development Assistance in 2023', *Focus 2030*, https://focus2030.org/Slight-increase-in-Official-Development-Assistance-in-2023

Food and Agriculture Organization (FAO) (2022), *The State of Food Security and Nutrition in the World (SOFI) 2022*, https://openknowledge.fao.org/server/api/core/bitstreams/67b1e9c7-1a7f-4dc6-a19e-f6472a4ea83a/content

Fukuyama, F. (2004), 'The Imperative of State-Building', *Journal of Democracy*, Vol. 15, No. 2, pp. 17–31, https://doi.org/10.1353/jod.2004.0026

Gabor, D. (2021), "The Wall Street Consensus', *Development and Change*, Vol. 52, No. 3, pp. 429–459, https://doi.org/10.1111/dech.12645

Garschagen, M. and Doshi, D. (2022), 'Does Funds-Based Adaptation Finance Reach the Most Vulnerable Countries?', *Global Environmental Change*, Vol. 73, p. 102450, https://doi.org/10.1016/j.gloenvcha.2021.102450

Gelpern, A, Horn, S., Morris, S., Parks, B. and Trebesch, C. (2023), 'How China Lends: A Rare Look into 100 Debt Contracts with Foreign Governments', *Economic Policy*, Vol. 38, No. 114, pp. 345–416, https://doi.org/10.1093/epolic/eiac054

Ghosh, E., Shawoo, Z. and Nazareth, A. (2025), *Decolonial Climate Finance in Practice: Assessing Proposed Reforms* (Stockholm Environment Institute), https://doi.org/10.51414/sei2025.003

Global Commission on the Economy and Climate (2016), *The Sustainable Infrastructure Imperative: Financing for Better Growth and Development*, https://newclimateeconomy.net/Downloaded_Pdf/Global_report/2016/The-Sustainable-Infrastructure-Imperative/Global-Report-and-Sections/NCE_2016Report.pdf

Gordon, L. (2019), 'Problematic People and Epistemic Decolonization: Towards the Postcolonial in African Political Thought', in De Sousa Santos, B. and Meneses, M. (eds.), *Knowledges Born in the Struggle: Constructing the Epistemologies of the Global South* (Routledge), p. 18, https://doi.org/10.4324/9780429344596

Group of 77 (G77) (2005), 'About the Group of 77', www.g77.org/doc/ (last viewed 21 June 2025).

Gutierrez, J. (2023), 'Real Estate Oligarchs: Elites and the Urbanization of the Land Question in El Salvador', *The Journal of Peasant Studies*, Vol. 51, No. 2, pp. 489–511, https://doi.org/10.1080/03066150.2023.2252758

Hallding, K., Olsson, M., Atteridge, A., Vihma, A., Carson, M. and Roman, M. (2011), *Together Alone: BASIC Countries and the Climate Change Conundrum* (Stockholm Environment Institute), www.sei.org/publications/together-alone-basic-countries-and-the-climate-change-conundrum/

Hickel, J. (2019), 'The Contradiction of the Sustainable Development Goals: Growth versus Ecology on a Finite Planet', *Sustainable Development*, Vol. 27, No. 5, pp. 873–884, https://doi.org/10.1002/sd.1947

Hickel, J. and Kallis, G. (2020), 'Is Green Growth Possible?', *New Political Economy*, Vol. 25, No. 4, pp. 469–486, https://doi.org/10.1080/13563467.2019.1598964

Hoelscher, K., Dorward, N., Fox, S., Lawanson, T., Paller, J. and Phillips, M. (2023), 'Urbanization and Political Change in Africa', *African Affairs*, Vol. 122, No. 488, pp. 353–376, https://doi.org/10.1093/afraf/adad021

Hogan, E. and Patrick, S. (2024), *A Closer Look at the Global South* (Carnegie Endowment for International Peace), https://carnegieendowment.org/research/2024/05/global-south-colonialism-imperialism?lang=en

International Capital Market Association (ICMA) (2021), *Green Bond Principles Voluntary Process Guidelines for Issuing Green Bonds*, www.icmagroup.org/assets/documents/Sustainable-finance/2021-updates/Green-Bond-Principles-June-2021-140621.pdf

International Energy Agency (IEA) (2023a, September 15), 'Access to Electricity Improves Slightly in 2023, But Still Far from the Pace Needed to Meet SDG7', *IEA*, www.iea.org/commentaries/access-to-electricity-improves-slightly-in-2023-but-still-far-from-the-pace-needed-to-meet-sdg7

International Energy Agency (IEA) (2023b), *World Energy Outlook 2023* (IEA), www.iea.org/reports/world-energy-outlook-2023

International Renewable Energy Agency (IRENA) (2024), *Renewable Power Generation Costs in 2023* (IRENA), www.irena.org/-/media/Files/IRENA/Agency/Publication/2024/Sep/IRENA_Renewable_power_generation_costs_in_2023.pdf

Jackson, E. (2013), 'Interrogating the Theory of Change: Evaluating Impact Investing Where it Matters Most', *Journal of Sustainable Finance & Investment*, Vol. 3, No. 2, pp. 95–110, https://doi.org/10.1080/20430795.2013.776257

Jäger, J. and Schmidt, L. (2020, September 8–25), 'The EU's Green Deal Proposal and Finance in a Global Perspective: Conclusions for Progressive Policies'. Presentation to *26th Annual Conference on Alternative Economic Policy in Europe*, https://euromemo.eu/wp-content/uploads/pdfs/uploads/critical_international_political_economy_and_global_natural_resources_jaeger_schmidt_final.pdf

Kalinowski, T. (2024), 'The Green Climate Fund and Private Sector Climate Finance in the Global South', *Climate Policy*, Vol. 24, No. 3, pp. 281–296, https://doi.org/10.1080/14693062.2023.2276857

Karnani, A. (2007), 'Microfinance Misses Its Mark', *Stanford Social Innovation Review*, Vol. 5, No. 3, pp. 34–40, https://doi.org/10.48558/YS7P-NP89

Kasa, S., Gullberg, A. and Heggelund, G. (2008), 'The Group of 77 in the International Climate Negotiations: Recent Developments and Future Directions', *International Environmental Agreements: Politics, Law, and Economics*, Vol. 8, pp. 113–127, https://doi.org/10.1007/s10784-007-9060-4

Kenya Institute for Public Policy Research and Analysis (2024, January 5), 'Delivering Affordable Housing in Kenya', https://kippra.or.ke/delivering-affordable-housing-in-kenya/#:~:text=The%20government%20in%20the%20period,units%20being%20delivered%20by%202022

Khan, M., Mfitumukiza, D. and Huq, S. (2021), 'Capacity Building for Implementation of Nationally Determined Contributions under the Paris Agreement', in Pauw, W. and Klein, R. (eds.), *Making Climate Action More Effective* (Routledge), pp. 95–106, www.taylorfrancis.com/chapters/edit/10.4324/9781003162407-8/capacity-building-implementation-nationally-determined-contributions-paris-agreement-mizan-khan-david-mfitumukiza-saleemul-huq

Kohli, A. (2004), *State-Directed Development: Political Power and Industrialization in the Global Periphery* (Cambridge University Press), https://doi.org/10.1017/CBO9780511754371

Konadu-Agyemang, K. (2004), 'The Best of Times and the Worst of Times: Structural Adjustment Programs and Uneven Development in Africa: The Case of Ghana', *The Professional Geographer*, Vol. 52, No. 3, pp. 469–483, https://doi.org/10.1111/0033-0124.00239

Kopiński, D. and Sun, Q. (2014), 'New Friends, Old Friends? The World Bank and Africa When the Chinese Are Coming', *Global Governance*, Vol. 20, No. 4, pp. 601–623, www.jstor.org/stable/24526327

Kothari, U. (2006), 'Critiquing 'Race' and Racism in Development Discourse and Practice', *Progress in Development Studies*, Vol. 6, No. 1, pp. 1–7, https://doi.org/10.1191/1464993406ps123ed

Kuhl, L., Shinn, J. E., Arango-Quiroga, J., Ahmed, I. and Rahman, M. (2024), 'The Liberal Limits to Transformation in the Green Climate Fund', *Climate and Development*, Vol. 16, No. 9, pp. 826–837, https://doi.org/10.1080/17565529.2023.2235318

Lees, N. (2020), 'The Brant Line After Forty Years: The More North-South Relations Change, the More They Stay the Same?', *Review of International Studies*, Vol. 47, No. 1, pp. 85–106, https://doi.org/10.1017/S026021052000039X

Lee, N., Laxton, V. and Matthews, S. (2023), *What Would the Ideal Development and Climate MDB Look Like? CGD Policy Paper No. 299* (Center for Global Development), www.cgdev.org/publication/what-would-ideal-development-and-climate-mdb-look

Levander, C. and Mignolo, W. (2011), 'Introduction: The Global South and World Dis/Order', *The Global South*, Vol. 5, No. 1, pp. 1–11, https://doi.org/10.2979/globalsouth.5.1.1

Lopez, A. and Quintana-Vallejo, R. (2024), *The Routledge Companion to Literature and the Global South* (Routledge), www.routledge.com/The-Routledge-Companion-to-Literature-and-the-Global-South/Lopez-Quintana-Vallejo/p/book/9781032075471?srsltid=AfmBOoqzZDvLsc8ORLPbjjVcjpP-yqesY6fj1jQ8j7pAuq3K2xqi3ekS

Mawdsley, E. (2018), 'From Billions to Trillions: Financing the SDGs in a World Beyond Aid', *Dialogues in Human Geography*, Vol. 8, No. 2, pp. 191–195, https://doi.org/10.1177/2043820618780789

McIntyre, O. and Nanwani, S. (eds.) (2019), *The Practice of Independent Accountability Mechanisms (IAMs): Towards Good Governance in Development Finance* (Brill Nijhoff), https://brill.com/edcollbook/title/34264?rskey=85au9Q&result=15

McKinsey Sustainability (2023), 'Solving the Climate Finance Equation for Developing Countries', www.mckinsey.com/capabilities/sustainability/our-insights/solving-the-climate-finance-equation-for-developing-countries

Mendez, A. and Houghton, D. (2020), 'Sustainable Banking: The Role of Multilateral Development Banks as Norm Entrepreneurs', *Sustainability*, Vol. 12, No. 3, p. 972, https://doi.org/10.3390/su12030972

Mkandawire, T. (1998), 'Crisis Management and the Making of "Choiceless Democracies"', in Richard, J. (ed.), *State, Conflict, and Democracy in Africa* (Lynne Rienner Publishers), pp. 119–136, https://doi.org/10.1515/9781685851828

Mlambo, C. (2022), 'China in Africa: An Examination of the Impact of China's Loans on Growth in Selected African States', *Economies 2022*, Vol. 10, No. 7, p. 154, https://doi.org/10.3390/economies10070154

Nasiritousi, N., Hjerpe, M. and Linnér, B. (2016), 'The Roles of Non-state Actors in Climate Change Governance: Understanding Agency through Governance Profiles', *International Environmental Agreements*, Vol. 16, pp. 109–126, https://doi.org/10.1007/s10784-014-9243-8

Organisation for Economic Co-operation and Development (OECD) (2023), *Scaling Up the Mobilisation of Private Finance for Climate Action in Developing Countries: Challenges and Opportunities for International Providers* (OECD), www.oecd.org/en/publications/scaling-up-the-mobilisation-of-private-finance-for-climate-action-in-developing-countries_17a88681-en.html

Organisation for Economic Co-operation and Development (OECD) (2025), 'Official Development Assistance (ODA)', www.oecd.org/en/topics/policy-issues/official-development-assistance-oda.html (last viewed 21 June 2025).

Patrick, S. and Huggins, A. (2023, August 15), 'The Term "Global South" Is Surging. It Should Be Retired', *Carnegie Endowment for International Peace*, https://carnegieendowment.org/posts/2023/08/the-term-global-south-is-surging-it-should-be-retired?lang=en

Pauw, P., Mbeva, K. and Van Asselt, H. (2019), 'Subtle Differentiation of Countries' Responsibilities under the Paris Agreement', *Palgrave Communications*, Vol. 5, p. 86, https://doi.org/10.1057/s41599-019-0298-6

Peinhardt, C., Kim, A. and Pavon-Harr, V. (2019), 'Deforestation and the United States–Peru Trade Promotion Agreement', *Global Environmental Politics*, Vol. 19, No. 1, pp. 53–76, https://doi.org/10.1162/glep_a_00498

Perez, C. (2010), 'Technological Revolutions and Techno-Economic Paradigms', *Cambridge Journal of Economics*, Vol. 34, No. 1, pp. 185–202, https://doi.org/10.1093/cje/bep051

Piketty, T. (2014), *Capital for the Twenty-First Century* (Belknap Press).

Pretty, J., Benton, T., Bharucha, Z., *et al.* (2018), 'Global Assessment of Agricultural System Redesign for Sustainable Intensification', *Nature Sustainability*, Vol. 1, pp. 441–446, https://doi.org/10.1038/s41893-018-0114-0

Public Expenditure and Financial Accountability (PEFA) (2020), *2020 Global Report on Public Financial Management*, www.pefa.org/global-report-2020/

Randall, V. (2004), 'Using and Abusing the Concept of the Third World: Geopolitics and the Comparative Political Study of Development and Underdevelopment', *Third World Quarterly*, Vol. 25, No. 1, pp. 41–53, www.jstor.org/stable/3993776

Rangelova, K. (2024, May 30), '2023's Record Solar Surge Explained in Six Charts', *Ember*, https://ember-energy.org/latest-insights/2023s-record-solar-surge-explained-in-six-charts/

Raynolds, L. (2016), 'Food Security Governance: Empowering Communities, Regulating Corporations', *Journal of World-Systems Research*, Vol. 22, No. 1, pp. 279–281, https://doi.org/10.5195/jwsr.2016.644

Rogerson, C. (2016), 'Responding to Informality in Urban Africa: Street Trading in Harare, Zimbabwe', *Urban Forum*, Vol. 27, pp. 229–251, https://doi.org/10.1007/s12132-016-9273-0

Roy, A. (2010), *Poverty Capital: Microfinance and the Making of Development* (Routledge), https://doi.org/10.4324/9780203854716

Sachs, J. (2015), *The Age of Sustainable Development* (Columbia University Press), https://doi.org/10.7312/sach17314-014

Schmidt-Traub, G. (2015), 'Investment Needs to Achieve the Sustainable Development Goals: Understanding the Billions and Trillions', *Sustainable Development Solutions Network*, www.jstor.org/stable/pdf/resrep15864.pdf

Schoenmaker, D. and Schramade, W. (2019), 'Investing for Long-Term Value Creation', *Journal of Sustainable Finance & Investment*, Vol. 9, No. 4, pp. 356–377, https://doi.org/10.1080/20430795.2019.1625012

Schwebel, M. (2018), 'Gathering at the AOSIS: Perceived Cooperation among Pacific Small Island States', *International Environmental Agreements: Politics, Law and Economics*, Vol. 18, pp. 215–228, https://doi.org/10.1007/s10784-017-9379-4

Spangenberg, J. (2016), 'Hot Air or Comprehensive Progress? A Critical Assessment of the SDGs', *Sustainable Development*, Vol. 25, No. 4, pp. 311–321, https://doi.org/10.1002/sd.1657

Srinivasan, N. (2011), *State of the Sector Microfinance India 2011* (SAGE Publications).

Stender, F., Moslener, U. and Pauw, W. (2020), 'More than Money: Does Climate Finance Support Capacity Building?', *Applied Economics Letters*, Vol. 27, No. 15, pp. 1247–1251, https://doi.org/10.1080/13504851.2019.1676384

Stiglitz, J. (2002), 'Information and the Change in the Paradigm in Economics', *American Economic Review*, Vol. 92, No. 3, pp. 460–501, www.aeaweb.org/articles?id=10.1257/00028280260136363

Swain, A., Bruch, C., Ide, T., Lujala, P., Matthew, R., Weinthal, E. and Deligiannis, T. (2025), 'The U.S. Withdrawal from the Paris Agreement – Implications for Global Climate Governance and Security', *Environment and Security*, Vol. 3, No. 1, pp. 3–7, https://doi.org/10.1177/27538796251322680

UN Environment Programme (UNEP) (2024), *Adaptation Gap Report 2024*, www.unep.org/resources/adaptation-gap-report-2024

UN General Assembly (2015), 'Resolution Adopted by the General Assembly on 25 September 2015. Transforming our World: The 2030 Agenda for Sustainable Development', https://docs.un.org/en/A/RES/70/1

United Nations (UN) (2005), 'Least Developed Countries (LDCs)', www.un.org/development/desa/dpad/least-developed-country-category.html (last viewed 21 June 2025).

United Nations (UN) (2024), *Financing for Sustainable Development Report 2024* (United Nations), https://unctad.org/publication/financing-sustainable-development-report-2024

United Nations Conference on Trade and Development (UNCTAD) (2021), *Technology and Innovation Report 2021: Catching Technological Waves—Innovation with Equity. UNCTAD/TIR/2020*, https://unctad.org/system/files/official-document/tir2020_en.pdf

United Nations Conference on Trade and Development (UNCTAD) (2022), *World Investment Report 2022*, https://unctad.org/system/files/official-document/wir2022_overview_en.pdf

United Nations Conference on Trade and Development (UNCTAD) (2024), *World Investment Report 2024*, https://unctad.org/publication/world-investment-report-2024

Van Rooyen, C., Stewart, R. and De Wet, T. (2012), 'The Impact of Microfinance in Sub-Saharan Africa: A Systematic Review of the Evidence', *World Development*, Vol. 40, No. 11, pp. 2249–2262, https://doi.org/10.1016/j.worlddev.2012.03.012

Vihma, A., Mulugetta, Y. and Karlsson-Vinkhuyzen, S. (2011), 'Negotiating Solidarity? The G77 through the Prism of Climate Change Negotiations', *Global Change, Peace & Security*, Vol. 23, No. 3, pp. 315–334, https://doi.org/10.1080/14781158.2011.601853

Wale-Oshinowo, B., Omobowale, A., Adeyeye, M. and Lebura, S. (2022), 'Least Developed Countries in Africa', *The Palgrave Encyclopedia of Global Security Studies*, pp. 1–16, https://doi.org/10.1007/978-3-319-74336-3_346-1

Wiegant, D., Dewulf, A. and Van Zeben, J. (2024), 'Alignment Mechanisms to Effectively Govern the Sustainable Development Goals', *World Development*, Vol. 182, https://doi.org/10.1016/j.worlddev.2024.106721

Wong, C. (2023), 'Climate Finance, Conflict and Gender—Benchmarking Women's Empowerment and Sustaining Peace', *Environment and Security*, Vol. 1, No. (1–2), pp. 62–83, https://doi.org/10.1177/27538796231184933

World Bank Group (2018), *Learning to Realize Education's Promise*, www.worldbank.org/en/publication/wdr2018

World Bank Group (2023), 'Affordable Housing Program: AHP Delivery Framework Overview', https://thedocs.worldbank.org/en/doc/fff83f483c76eef814d7488b25689a10-0430012023/related/20230523-WBG-Affordable-Housing-Program-Rent-to-Own-2-0-Draft-v01-1.pdf

World Bank Group (2025), 'Urban Development', www.worldbank.org/en/topic/urbandevelopment/overview#:~:text=Today%2C%20some%2056%25%20of%20the,billion%20inhabitants%20%E2%80%93%20live%20in%20cities (last viewed 21 June 2025).

World Health Organisation (2023), *Tracking SDG7: The Energy Progress Report 2023*, www.who.int/publications/m/item/tracking-sdg7--the-energy-progress-report-2023

Yunita, A., Biermann, F., Kim, R. and Vijge, M. (2023), 'Making Development Legible to Capital: The Promise and Limits of 'Innovative' Debt Financing for the Sustainable Development Goals in Indonesia', *Environment and Planning E: Nature and Space*, Vol. 6, No. 4, pp. 2271–2294, https://doi.org/10.1177/25148486231159301

Zaid, M. and Issa, A. (2023), 'A Roadmap for Triggering the Convergence of Global ESG Disclosure Standards: Lessons from the IFRS Foundation and Stakeholder Engagement', *Corporate Governance*, Vol. 23, No. 7, pp. 1648–1669, https://doi.org/10.1108/CG-09-2022-0399

Zhan, J. and Santos-Paulino, A (2021), 'Investing in the Sustainable Development Goals: Mobilization, Channeling, and Impact', *Journal of International Business Policy*, Vol. 4, pp. 166–183, https://doi.org/10.1057/s42214-020-00093-3

Zhang, Y., Chao, Q., Zheng, Q. and Huang, L. (2017), 'The Withdrawal of the U.S. from the Paris Agreement and its Impact on Global Climate Change Governance', *Advances in Climate Change Research*, Vol. 8, No. 4, pp. 213–219, https://doi.org/10.1016/j.accre.2017.08.005

Chapter 14

Building a More Sustainable Investment System

Rory Sullivan and Richard Perkins

In Chapter 1, we stated that our aim was to understand the conditions under which sustainable investment might advance wider societal goals relating to sustainability, to systemic risk, to corporate governance, and to market stability and resilience. Chapters 2–13 explored various themes relevant to this question, analysing issues such as whether and how sustainable investment influences investment performance and sustainability outcomes, and how the legal and policy landscape shapes sustainable investment.

Before canvassing the impacts and implications of sustainable finance, we want to start with two wider observations, one relating to capital flows and one relating to social and environmental outcomes. In relation to capital flows, while there has been impressive progress in areas such as renewable energy and transport electrification, major gaps remain in relation to agriculture, land management, the built environment and infrastructure, and climate adaptation. Overall, despite significant increases in recent years, current investments for environmental protection and sustainable development continue to fall drastically short of what is required (see, further, Chapter 8). Furthermore, many of the investments that have been made, in particular in developing countries, do not always address the root causes of underdevelopment and inequality (as discussed in Chapter 13).

DOI: 10.4324/9781003467632-14

We have a similar observation about social and environmental outcomes (see Chapters 7–10). Global greenhouse gas emissions (and, in turn, global temperatures) continue to rise year-on-year. Furthermore, despite successes in areas – e.g. declines in extreme poverty, some progress towards ending hunger, progress in maternal mortality and education – we remain a long way from achieving the Sustainable Development Goals (SDGs). In fact, the United Nations' own *Sustainable Development Report 2024* states:

> The progress assessment carried out in 2024 reveals that the world is severely off track to realise the 2030 Agenda. Of the 169 targets, 135 can be assessed using available global trend data from the 2015 baseline to the most recent year, along with custodian agency analyses; 34 targets lack sufficient trend data or additional analysis. Among the assessable targets, only 17 per cent display progress sufficient for achievement by 2030. Nearly half (48 per cent) exhibit moderate to severe deviations from the desired trajectory, with 30 per cent showing marginal progress and 18 per cent moderate progress. Alarmingly, 18 per cent indicate stagnation and 17 per cent regression below the 2015 baseline levels (United Nations, 2024: 4).

What do these observations about capital flows and outcomes tell us about sustainable finance? Ultimately, they suggest that sustainable investment as currently designed, configured and implemented is nowhere near sufficient to meet the investment, the environmental or the social challenges faced by the world today. The question, therefore, is whether, and under what conditions, sustainable investment could make a meaningful contribution at scale to public social and environmental goals such as those set out in the SDGs.

Market Failure and Policy Advocacy

To answer this question, we need to start with incentives. Ultimately, financial incentives drive investment decisions. The areas where we have seen the most progress (e.g. investments in renewable energy) have been those where companies and investors have been incentivised to act in ways that align with sustainability-related goals and outcomes. Conversely, the areas where we have seen less progress are generally those where market failures have blunted economic incentives. Market failures arise when markets fail to efficiently allocate goods and services according to society's preferences. In the environmental domain, three sources of market failures are of particular significance. The first are *externalities* which arise when the costs (negative externalities) or benefits (positive externalities) of an activity spill over onto third parties. Because these costs and benefits are not fully reflected in market prices, actors tend to over-produce negative externalities and under-produce positive externalities. For example, in the case of climate change, the external social and environmental damages associated with greenhouse gas emissions are not fully internalised in market prices, reducing the incentive for economic agents to take actions which contribute to lower emissions. Second, market failures arise within the context of *common pool resources*, such as open access fisheries and groundwater. In the absence of property rights or appropriate governance arrangements, users have perverse economic incentives to over-use common pool resources, resulting in their degradation over time. Third, market failures arise in the case of *public goods*, such as clean air, climate system stabilisation and biodiversity. The provision of public goods is in everyone's interests. Yet, because one person's consumption does not reduce the availability for others, and because it is difficult to exclude people from the benefits of public goods, it is practically impossible to charge individuals for their use. Furthermore, individuals have no incentive to pay what the public goods are worth to them. The result is free-riding and the under-supply of public goods.

There can still be a business case for sustainable investment in the presence of market failures (as detailed in Chapter 6), although this may be limited in scope and oriented more towards managing financially material sustainability-related risks. If investors are to go further, particularly in making substantive contributions to advancing social and environmental goals, then action needs to be taken to correct market failures. Nowhere is this more apparent than in the climate change domain. Here, despite many investors publicly supporting climate mitigation efforts, their ability to act is frequently constrained by concerns over fiduciary duty (see Chapter 5). In practice, low carbon prices and uncertainties over the future development of these prices mean that moving too fast towards net zero risks impairing financial returns (Buentjen *et al.*, 2025).

This analysis points to the need for action to 'correct' market failures. One actor uniquely placed to do so is the state. For instance, governments and public regulators can introduce pricing of negative externalities and can offer subsidies for the provision of public goods. By doing so, states can shift the incentives for companies in the real economy and for the financial actors who supply capital to them, increasing the payoffs from sustainable versus unsustainable investments. The role of the state goes beyond influencing relative prices. For example, states can prohibit certain actions, can convene partnerships and networks, can mobilise and crowd-in significant resources, and can regulate definitions of sustainable investment. In short, by shaping the 'boundary conditions' within which investors operate (see, for example, Net-Zero Asset Owner Alliance, 2022), states can have a significant influence on both the volume, ambition and outcomes of sustainable finance.

While the potential contribution of the state is clear, a central challenge is how to encourage governments to intervene in ways (e.g. through the pricing of externalities) which align with the requirements of sustainability. Civil society has an important role here – not least in providing a democratic mandate for more ambitious public sustainability policies. Financial actors, given their influence, also have an important role to play. Indeed, it is our belief that one of the most significant actions that investors can take is to engage in policy advocacy. That is, they can actively support – i.e. lobby – for more ambitious public policies in support of sustainability goals, and they can encourage governments to fully implement these policies in good faith and in a timely manner. Against a backdrop where sustainability issues such as climate change are being weaponised by the political right, and where public support for sustainability policies is being challenged by economic headwinds, active support from the financial sector for ambitious public policy on sustainability is more important than ever.

We are not blind to some of the pitfalls of inviting profit-seeking financial actors to act as policy advocates (Sullivan *et al.*, 2022). It is possible that policy advocacy can be used as a strategic vehicle for greenwashing (Chapter 11). For example, financial actors may publicly support policies which do not threaten their interests (in turn, allowing them to enhance their reputations and brand value), while simultaneously working more covertly to undermine others. It is also possible that policy advocacy by investors risks undermining local democracy; for example, 'cosmopolitan' concerns (e.g. over global biodiversity) could override the concerns of affected communities over issues such as livelihood security. These potential pitfalls highlight the need for effective guardrails around policy advocacy to ensure that it is fully aligned with public sustainability goals and that it supports rather than undermines democratic politics.

Building On Existing Foundations

The idea that, in the continued presence of market failures and inadequate public policy support, the potential contribution of sustainable investment to social and environmental outcomes remains limited may come as a somewhat disappointing conclusion. However, it usefully serves as a corrective to the idea that voluntarism, enlightened self-interest and the collective energies of well-intentioned professionals are sufficient to drive finance-led transitions to sustainability. This is not to say that financial and related market actors, including private ones, have not made a significant contribution to the development of the market norms, devices and system architecture required to deliver positive social and environmental outcomes. We highlight three here.

First, financial and corporate actors have contributed to the development of new financial products. Examples include green and sustainability-linked bonds, low carbon indices and green mutual funds (Monk and Perkins, 2020; see, more generally, Kendall and Sullivan (eds.) (2023)). Such products form part of the essential infrastructure which allow companies and financial market participants to enact sustainable investment strategies. Second, market actors have developed capacities and resources, internally and across the financial system (Marti *et al.*,

2024). Many large investors now have dedicated teams covering environmental, social and governance (ESG) issues; ratings and other service providers offer sustainability-related ratings of companies, projects and assets; and various networks and coalitions support the work of sustainable finance through guidance, standards and information-sharing (see further Chapters 9, 10 and 12). A third contribution of financial actors has been better company disclosures. Investors have put pressures on real economy corporates to improve their sustainability-related reporting and have supported governments and regulators in their efforts to introduce mandatory requirements.

In aggregate, these developments mean that financial actors are now better placed to respond to the signals created by public policy. For example, many institutional investors have access to data on corporate sustainability performance, have developed capabilities to evaluate sustainability-related risks and opportunities, and have investment strategies which allow them to respond to the incentives provided by public policymakers. The challenge is to ensure that these incentives align with sustainability-related goals, and for policymakers to ensure that incentives are seen as dependable, clear and reliable (or 'long, loud and legal' to adopt a phrase that has been widely used in sustainable investment). The time and effort that has been devoted to system-building efforts (e.g. building a community of practice, constructing data, tools and evaluation methodologies, developing and testing sustainable investment strategies) mean that sustainable investment now has, under the right conditions, the potential to deliver better financial outcomes, positive social and environmental outcomes, and to enable and catalyse action by others.

The Role (and the Responsibility) of the Sustainable Investment Professional

We want to conclude by stressing the critical role of individuals working within the investment industry. These individuals include, but are not limited to, those involved in investment research and decision-making, in data analysis, in engagement and in policy dialogue, and those working for asset owners, asset managers, research and data agencies, academic institutions, regulators and industry associations.

Our view is that sustainable investment, for all its potential, has suffered from a lack of ambition and from a lack of critical thinking about its own limitations. Investment practitioners have relied heavily on building a business case for action where these business cases have been defined by current norms and conventions, by investment 'best practices', and by the spaces provided by their organisations. Such caution was understandable during the period when sustainable investment needed to transition from being an ethical niche to becoming an increasingly mainstream part of finance. However, we are now at the point where the analysis of sustainability-related issues is a standard part of investment analysis, investors routinely engage with companies and other actors on sustainability-related issues, and investors and companies report on their sustainability-related practices and processes. We therefore believe that investment professionals need to proactively and assertively shape their roles and their activities to ensure that they make a meaningful, at-scale contribution to positive social and environmental outcomes. In our opinion, all sustainable investment professionals need to:

1. **Critically reflect on their personal and professional goals.** Practitioners need to be clear about why they are working in sustainable finance, and what they are trying to achieve. This involves defining what 'success' looks like. It also involves asking questions about whether and how their personal sustainability goals are aligned with public sustainability goals (e.g. as enshrined in frameworks such as the SDGs or the Paris Agreement on Climate Change) and with stakeholder expectations.
2. **Challenge the means.** Practitioners need to ask whether what they are doing – in terms of, for example, their investment research and decision-making, their product offerings, their engagement, voting and governance activities – could plausibly contribute to substantive improvements in sustainability outcomes (e.g. reductions in greenhouse gas emissions, nature positive outcomes). Practitioners need to be honest with themselves and be prepared to subject their theories of change and their assumptions to critical scrutiny.
3. **Be honest with themselves – and others – about what is working, about what isn't working and about what is working but has marginal value, influence or impact.** As well as celebrating successes, practitioners need to acknowledge challenges, shortcomings and even failures. Sustainable finance can be understood as a series of experiments. Some of these (e.g. a new financing instrument or governance initiative) will be successful in making a significant contribution to sustainability goals, some will be partially successful and some will be unsuccessful. What is important is for practitioners to face up to shortcomings and failings in order to understand why interventions did not work as intended, to understand what would need to change if they were to work effectively and to understand whether there is any plausible prospect of success.
4. **Take appropriate and effective action when things aren't working.** Appropriate implies measures which are proportional. This may involve minor changes ('tweaks') which do not fundamentally change, say, the basic design of a financing instrument. However, proportional action may require more fundamental change, e.g. pursuing very different sustainable investment instruments, initiatives and approaches when current ones consistently fail to deliver.

5. **Define what they – and their organisation – can do to affect substantive change.** Different individuals and organisations (e.g. asset managers, financial regulators) have different resources, capabilities, responsibilities and mandates. Practitioners need to think about how they can strategically deploy their specific strengths (e.g. their convening power, their knowledge of decarbonisation strategies) to achieve the greatest sustainability impact. For example, which sustainability issues are they, or their organisation, best positioned to effectively address? Which sustainability issues can they address alone, and which can they productively partner with others to affect positive outcomes? Which sustainability issues are already being effectively addressed by others?
6. **Engage with, and be accountable to, stakeholders.** Finance professionals and institutions have responsibilities toward their stakeholders. These include their beneficiaries and clients but also include other actors (e.g. communities, workers) affected by their decisions and actions. Understanding and responding to on the sustainability preferences of stakeholders is important if sustainable finance is to be inclusive and address the economic, the environmental and the social aspects of sustainability. Accountability implies a need for organisations to publicly communicate their sustainability goals and policies and to be transparent about their sustainability performance (the good, the bad and the ugly).
7. **Acknowledge that sustainable finance has justice and equity implications.** Practitioners should consider the distributional consequences of their activities. For example, do investments in renewable energy projects predominantly benefit wealthier groups while negatively impacting poorer ones? Within this, it is particularly important for practitioners to ensure that sustainable financing addresses the needs of different groups, including disadvantaged groups in the Global South and Global North. Raising the bar on the ambitions of sustainable finance means that justice considerations – including questions of fairness and differential responsibility – should take centre-stage in investment decision-making (Reynolds and Ciplet, 2023).

A Final Reflection

We are at a pivotal point in sustainable investment. Practitioners need to adopt a more critical perspective on what needs to happen. They need to be far more reflexive, self-critical and evidence-based in relation to their policies, practices and assessments. They need to ask questions, even uncomfortable ones, about whether what they are doing stacks up and whether some practices are not working or cannot work. Ultimately, practitioners need to ask themselves: Is what I am doing going to make a real, positive and significant difference to advancing sustainability for current and for future generations? The claims of sustainability professionals and of their organisations, should be judged against whether their efforts, individually and collectively, make a substantive contribution to improving the lives of people and the health of our planet.

References

Buentjen, C., Perkins, R. and Sullivan, R. (2025), 'Net-Zero Norms in Sustainable Finance: What Explains Asset Managers' Target-Setting?' *Journal of Sustainable Finance & Investment*, pp. 1–32, https://doi.org/10.1080/20430795.2025.2520524

Kendall, J. and Sullivan R. (eds.) (2023), *Responsible Investment in Fixed Income Markets* (Routledge, London).

Marti, E., Fuchs, M., DesJardine, M., Slager, R. and Gond, J. (2024), 'The Impact of Sustainable Investing: A Multidisciplinary Review', *Journal of Management Studies*, Vol. 61, pp. 2181–2211, https://doi.org/10.1111/joms.12957

Monk, A. and Perkins, R. (2020), 'What Explains the Emergence and Diffusion of Green Bonds?', *Energy Policy*, Vol. 145, pp. 111641, https://doi.org/10.1016/j.enpol.2020.111641

Net-Zero Asset Owner Alliance (NZAOA) (2022), *The Future of Investor Engagement: A Call for Systematic Stewardship to Address Systemic Climate Risk (April 2022)*, www.unepfi.org/wordpress/wp-content/uploads/2022/03/NZAOA_The-future-of-investor-engagement.pdf

Reynolds, D. and Ciplet, D. (2023), 'Transforming Socially Responsible Investment: Lessons from Environmental Justice', *Journal of Business Ethics*, Vol. 183, pp. 53–69, https://doi.org/10.1007/s10551-022-05070-9

Sullivan, R., Black, R., Perkins, R. and Richards, C. (2022), *Company Lobbying and Climate Change: Good Governance for Paris-Aligned Outcomes*. Policy Brief (February 2022) (Grantham Research Institute on Climate Change and the Environment, London School of Economics and Political Science), www.lse.ac.uk/granthaminstitute/wp-content/uploads/2022/02/Company-lobbying-and-climate-change_good-governance-for-Paris-aligned-outcomes.pdf

United Nations (2024), *The Sustainable Development Goals Report 2024*, https://unstats.un.org/sdgs/report/2024/The-Sustainable-Development-Goals-Report-2024.pdf

For Product Safety Concerns and Information please contact our EU representative GPSR@taylorandfrancis.com Taylor & Francis Verlag GmbH, Kaufingerstraße 24, 80331 München, Germany